This book aims to provide an interesting and readable introduction to the principles of book-keeping for the beginner in the business and professional world, and to help those embarking upon a career in accountancy by furnishing a sound basis for more advanced work. Each chapter contains worked examples and is followed by carefully graded exercises to test the reader's understanding of the subject. Students with examinations to pass will find the R.S.A. examination papers printed at the end particularly helpful.

TEACH YOURSELF BOOKS

The book is naturally intended for the beginner, and it does not make the fatal mistake of attempting too much. Nevertheless, the careful elimination of inessentials leaves room for extremely lucid chapters on depreciation, adjustments, partnership, bank reconciliation and petty cash. The question and answer method of instruction seems ideally suitable here, but that may be due solely to the searching nature of the questions—evidence of the author's wide teaching and examining experience.

The Times Educational Supplement

Introduction

I believe I am justified in offering this book in the 'Teach Your-self' series, if only in an effort to correct the view, so widely and so mistakenly held, that the subject of Book-keeping is dull, and that its teaching must needs be unimaginative.

My aim has been to offer a guide to the beginner in the Business and Professional world which shall:

(a) be readable and interesting;

(b) carefully avoid the error of treating the subject as though it were altogether unrelated to the ordinary routine of business life;

(c) adequately cover the usual examination syllabuses.

There are few walks of life wherein an understanding of the first principles of Book-keeping and Accounts can fail to be of some practical use.

To those beginning their studies in the Accountancy profession this volume will, I hope, give real inspiration and help, and pro-vide a sound basis for the more advanced work that comes later.

To the business executive who may have little taste for the counting-house and records generally I hope it will give an insight into an indispensable business function.

Very largely, the Accountant, as such, is concerned with inter-preting the Book-keeper's work and 'pointing the moral,' but it is from the Book-keeper's hands that he derives the necessary raw material.

In equal measure, the executive must be able to make full use of all the information which his book-keeping system provides, and it will be conceded that none can criticise who is totally un-familiar with the way in which that system operates.

Doubts may be resolved, unspoken questions answered and weak points in an existing system shown up when a fresh pair of eyes is brought to bear; the writer has on more than one occasion been asked by a business man: 'I wish you would tell me why both sides of a Balance Sheet add up to the same figure,' or, 'why does the stock in my Trading Account differ from the stock in the Balance Sheet?'

Many carefully graded exercises, for self-examination and the class-room alike, follow the individual chapters, and as an appendix there is a reprint of some Stage I papers of the Royal Society of Arts.

In conclusion, the writer has not been unmindful of the needs of the teacher, and has endeavoured to deal with each stage of the subject so as to facilitate class-room exposition.

DONALD COUSINS

Note to Seventh Edition

Continuing demand for this elementary introduction to book-keeping both in the U.K. and overseas and the proposed deci-malisation of the currency in the United Kingdom are the main reasons for this new edition and all amounts have been converted to the new forms. When exact pounds are tabulated they may be recorded as £7 or £7·00 and throughout this edition the former has been adopted in the text and the latter in tabular matter.

The questions after each chapter have also been amended with the permission of the following examining bodies whose co-operation is hereby acknowledged:

Birmingham Commercial College   Royal Society of Arts
College of Preceptors   Union of Educational Institutions
East Midland Educational Union   Union of Lancashire and Cheshire
Institute of Bankers   Institutes
Institute of Book-keepers   University of Birmingham
London Chamber of Commerce   University of Edinburgh
National Union of Teachers   University of Manchester

The Royal Society of Arts kindly agreed that its most recent papers on the subject BOOK-KEEPING (Principles of Accounts) Stage I (Elementary) should be substituted in place of the earlier ones.

A. G. PIPER
E. C. TURNER

Contents

I	What is Book-keeping?	1
II	The Business Transaction, Purchases and Sales	6
III	Purchase and Sales Transactions, and the Ledger Accounts	24
IV	Cash Transactions	52
V	The Bank Reconciliation	73
VI	Petty Cash, Etc.	84
VII	The Debit and Credit Journal	90
VIII	Writing Up the Books	100
IX	The Trial Balance	118
X	Four-Column Trial Balance	123
XI	What is Profit or Loss?	130
XII	The Revenue Account	133
	The Trading Account	
	The Profit and Loss Account	
	The Appropriation Account	
XIII	The Balance Sheet	144
XIV	Adjustments in the Final Accounts	160
XV	Depreciation	171
XVI	Partnership	181
XVII	The Criticism and Interpretation of Accounts	197
XVIII	Limited Companies, and the Companies Acts, 1948 and 1967	209
XIX	Value Added Tax	226
	Answers	231
	Appendix. Examination Papers—Royal Society of Arts	237
	Index	255

CHAPTER I

WHAT IS BOOK-KEEPING?

Question
What is Book-keeping?

Answer
The process of correctly recording in Books of Account transactions in money, or money's worth.

Question
What are Books of Account?

Answer
The Ledger is the only Book of Account, so called because all the transactions, after being first recorded in subsidiary books, are afterwards grouped or summarised in **Accounts** in the Ledger.

Question
What is the difference between 'money' and 'money's worth' transactions?

Answer
If £5 is paid in cash as wages to a workman, this is a transaction in *money*; if I buy goods on credit from Smith value £100, it is a transaction in *money's worth*.

Question
Why should goods be bought on 'credit'?

Answer
Almost all business dealings are conducted on a credit basis, that is, the supplier of goods, like Smith, is content to accept payment at some future date; the only exception is in the case of 'ready money' transactions in the retail trade, like those of a private individual, who buys goods over the counter.

Question
How does the necessity for recording these transactions arise?

Answer

Even in the smallest business the proprietor or manager will want to have accurate and up-to-date information about how much he has bought and sold, how much money he has received and paid away in respect of his purchases and sales, and so on. In respect of their cash receipts and payments, even private individuals often find it convenient to have the same information.

You can imagine that with a very large business, chaos would quickly result without this information.

Question

So Book-keeping really involves analysing in some way or another these various transactions?

Answer

You should rather say, recording these transactions so as to permit of analysis, but in a systematic fashion, in some way that can be applied to all businesses, of whatever kind, and which is intelligible not only now, but at any future time.

Question

Do you mean by this 'the Double Entry System of Book-keeping'?

Answer

Yes.

Question

What is its real meaning?

Answer

That just as every transaction involves at least two parties, so the record of the transaction should be made in the light of its two-fold aspect.

Question

So it does not mean recording the same transaction twice?

Answer

No, not at all. Let me put it in this way. If I have bought goods value £100 from Smith on credit, the first part of the twofold aspect is that my business has received goods for the disposal of which my storekeeper, or some other person, is accountable; the second part of the twofold aspect is that Smith, my supplier, has become my creditor, and has a claim on me for £100.

Question

Would it be the same if you had bought the goods and paid for them at once, instead of getting credit?

Answer

Yes, that would be in this case a cash purchase. But instead of Smith, my banker or cashier would be my creditor, having paid money away for me. They then would have the claim on me for £100.

Question

I do not quite see how your cashier or your banker could be your creditor. The cashier would be a servant, dependent on a weekly or monthly salary.

Answer

What you say about the position of the cashier is very true, but in the first place, when you began business, you would entrust a sufficient sum of money to these people for which you would at the outset consider them as accountable or indebted to you. They would be your debtors. So if later they paid money away for you, such payments reduce their indebtedness which after all is just the same thing as saying they are your creditors to that extent, the position of the creditor being the reverse of that of debtor.

Question

What is the real advantage of the Double Entry System?

Answer

For the reason that every transaction can be looked at from its twofold aspect, the record made is complete instead of being partial only.

The practical advantage is that you put the whole of the facts on record. These are:

(*a*) Your storekeeper is answerable for £100 worth of goods.

(*b*) Somebody, Smith or your banker, has a claim on you for £100.

Obviously, to know both these facts is of first importance in any business.

Question

Well, does this hold good with other than just buying transactions? Would the same state of affairs exist with the selling of goods?

Answer

In exactly the same way. The first aspect in the selling transaction is that your storekeeper has issued £100 worth of goods as an ordinary sale. The second is that the person who has received them has become your debtor, i.e. he is indebted to you, on the assumption that you, in this case, are giving him credit, because *you* are the supplier.

Question

Does the Double Entry System stop at this?

Answer

No. It goes much further. Because of this twofold aspect I have been talking about, it enables you to compare the proceeds of the sales you have made with the cost to you of the goods you have bought, and so obtain your profit or loss on trading.

Similarly, as it shows the claims other people have on you (your creditors), and the claims you have on other people (your debtors) you can tell very quickly what is the position of affairs of your business at any particular date so far as these people are concerned.

Question

Is the latter point important?

Answer

Yes. If the creditors of the business exceed in amount its debtors, any stock in its warehouse which it hopes to sell, and the ready money it has available, it may be insolvent, that is to say, it cannot pay its debts as they become due.

Question

When we began talking, you said the Ledger was the only Book of Account, and that all transactions were first recorded in what you called 'subsidiary books'.

What are these Subsidiary Books, and why are they kept in addition to the Ledger?

Answer

The Subsidiary Books are termed Journals or Day Books because, very much like a journal or diary, they are entered up daily.

They are designed to relieve the various accounts in the Ledger of a great amount of detail which, while indispensable to the business, can better be given in a subsidiary book than in the Ledger itself.

If you take, for example, the purchasing side of a business, a very great amount of detail may have to be recorded as to the supplier, the quantity, quality and price per unit of the goods, total amount payable and so on.

But, so far as the Double Entry or twofold aspect of all the buying transactions is concerned, they are all in the first place purchases or goods for which the storekeeper is responsible. In the second place, credit must be given to all the various suppliers from whom the purchases have been made. Thus there will be one account in the Ledger for incoming goods, or purchases, and other accounts, also in the Ledger, for the individual suppliers.

Question

So the Journals or Day Books do not form part of the Double Entry System at all?

Answer

That is so. These Subsidiary Books are outside the Double Entry System altogether. Their function is to provide, in the first instance, the material from which the Ledger Accounts are entered up subsequently.

That is why they are so often referred to as books of **prime or first entry.** With very few exceptions indeed, it is a well-recognised rule in Book-keeping that no transaction shall be recorded in a Ledger Account that has not first been made the subject of record in a subsidiary book, or Book of First Entry.

Question

Now that you have given me this introduction, can we proceed to take a typical business transaction, and record it first in the subsidiary books, and then in the Ledger?

Answer

Yes, that is what we are now going to do. But first of all we will consider the various kinds of business transactions.

CHAPTER II

THE BUSINESS TRANSACTION, PURCHASES AND SALES

THE BUSINESS TRANSACTION

We are familiar in our daily life with buying articles we want and paying cash for them. But unless we are in business the idea of selling goods is not so familiar, nor is the process of receiving payment for what we have sold. And yet every business is concerned with buying and selling goods as has been seen, usually on a credit basis, so that at some later date it pays for what it has bought and is in turn paid for what it has sold.

These are clearly recurrent transactions in particular goods which the business merchants or manufactures.

Merchanted Goods are those which it resells in the same condition as when purchased. **Manufactured Goods** are the finished article which, with the assistance of work-people, are worked up from the raw material.

Thus from the purely trading standpoint a kind of trade cycle can be recognised. Goods are bought first of all in sufficient quantity to meet customers' requirements, either as the finished article or as raw material. They are what is called the **Stock** or **Stock in Trade** of the business.

When the goods are sold in the finished state to customers at selling price, and on credit terms, these customers become the **debtors** of the business, i.e. they are indebted to it, and when they in turn make payment the **Cash in Hand** or **Cash at Bank** of the business is replenished.

From these increased cash resources moneys once again become available for the business to buy more goods, and so the cycle repeats itself.

We should remember that not only is this the case, but that at any given time a business will necessarily possess:

(a) Stock in Trade;
(b) claims on customers, which may shortly be described as Debtors, or Book Debts;
(c) Cash in Hand and/or Cash at Bank.

These forms of property, property of very different kinds, represent the trading resources of the business, and in total form part of its **Capital.**

It is very important for us to understand correctly the meaning of **Capital** in the book-keeping sense.

Supposing we bought goods from Jones, value £100, for payment a month after they had been delivered, Jones would be our creditor, and during that month we might sell the goods at a profit and so obtain the cash to pay him when the time came.

That would be an ideal case, because then the business apparently need have no cash resources **of its own**; it could rely on Jones, and other suppliers, to finance its operations. The capital invested in the business, represented by the stock of goods value £100 supplied by Jones, would be in effect **Jones's Capital**, and not the proprietor's Capital at all.

In practice we find, however, that such an ideal state of affairs can seldom, if ever, arise.

First of all, we may not be able to sell all the goods we purchased from Jones in the credit period of one month.

Secondly, we shall in all probability be obliged to extend credit to our customers, just as Jones did to us.

Thirdly, we shall be obliged to possess certain (cash) resources to pay our staff and workpeople week by week, and

Fourthly, if ours is a new business, Jones or any other supplier may be unwilling to supply us with goods on credit until they have experience of what may be called our 'credit-worthiness'.

There is also to be remembered that an important part of every business's resources will be a factory, or warehouse, or office, or the right to occupy these, for which a rent will be paid. Such property does not, and cannot form part of the trading resources, because it would clearly never occur to us to sell our business premises in which all the work was carried on.

Enough has been said for us to realise that a certain minimum amount of property, or of **Capital**, must be possessed by the business from the time it was commenced, and we can realise also how varied are the forms which this Capital may take.

Our task will always be rendered easier if we think of Capital as the resources or the property of a business. Indeed, the term 'Capital' has no meaning to the business man unless it is represented by property of some kind or another, property to which he refers as the business **Assets**. In future, therefore, we will use the term 'Assets' alone.

While we are going to examine Capital more fully at a later stage, let us now remember that there are such forms of property as **Fixed Assets**, i.e. the factory or warehouse mentioned above, and other forms which we call **Current Assets**, which correspond to our trading assets, such as stock in trade, claims on customers and money in the bank.

The distinction between these two kinds of property is of the utmost importance, because our **Fixed Assets** have been bought to be retained, while our **Current Assets**, as we have seen, are an essential result of the business's everyday transactions. Indeed, they enter into and form part of these transactions.

There are just two more points, and the first is for us to grasp the business man's definition of **Capital** as representing not merely the **Assets**, but

The Excess of the Assets over the Liabilities of a Business.

An example will help to make this clear:

Example

Brown begins business on January 1, 19x1, with £1 000 in cash. He buys for cash factory premises at a cost of £500, and goods on credit from Smith costing £200.

The total assets of his business are:

Factory, cost	£500·00	
Stock of goods, cost	200·00	
Cash in Bank	500·00	
		£1 200·00

but this is **not** the amount of **Brown's Capital** invested in the business because £200 of these assets have been supplied on credit by Smith, for which the business is liable to him. What is owing to Smith is, therefore, a liability of the business and because we define Capital above as corresponding to 'the excess of the Assets over the Liabilities of a business', Brown's Capital = **Total Assets** £1 200, less **Liabilities** £200 = £1 000, or put in another way, Brown's Capital of £1 000 is represented by

Fixed Assets		£500·00
Current Assets	£700·00	
Less Liabilities	200·00	
		500·00
		£1 000·00

We are justified in deducting the liability to Smith from the total of the **Current** Assets, since it is out of them that we intend to pay him.

The other point which we ought now to be in a position to appreciate is that

Capital is a Liability of the Business to its proprietor.

At first sight this appears to be rather different from what we should expect.

We have seen that from its commencement the business must be provided with a certain minimum amount of property, or Capital and for the sake of convenience we defined Capital in the first place as the equivalent of property, or Assets, and more fully in the second place as representing 'the excess of the Assets over the Liabilities of a business'.

Let us now see if we can reconcile what appears to be a contradiction in terms.

If the proprietor, instead of investing a part of his Capital in setting up the business, had lent £1 000 to a friend in consideration of the payment of interest at 6% per annum, the loan would clearly be an investment yielding an annual income of £60, and the amount of the loan, looked at from the standpoint of the borrower, would as clearly be a liability.

The borrower's financial position could be stated thus:

'**Liability** £1 000, represented by **Cash** £1 000.'

In exactly the same way, when the proprietor invests Capital in a business, he is just as truly entitled to regard it as an investment, answerable to him for interest, or in this case **Profit,** period by period.

From the standpoint of the business, looked at as distinct from its proprietorship, there is a **Liability** to account for the amount of the proprietor's Capital put at its disposal for the purpose of profit earning.

At any time, therefore, the business should be able to prepare a statement of its position, and of how it has dealt with such Capital, that is to say, by what kinds of property that Capital is represented.

The financial position of the business would similarly be:

Liability to proprietor £1 000, represented by, in the first instance, **Cash** £1 000.

The only difference between the two examples is that, in the first case, the borrower would sooner or later have to repay the loan, while in the second the repayment of the proprietor's Capital would involve shutting down the business.

For this reason, in the latter case, the Capital invested is usually regarded as a **permanent** or **fixed liability,** or indeed, as it is in law, a postponed or deferred liability.

THE PLACE OF THE PURCHASE AND SALES JOURNALS IN THE BOOK-KEEPING SYSTEM

Most of us are familiar with the practice of making a daily note of matters in which we are interested. For this purpose we use our diary, as a kind of daily record, entering in it brief but sufficient details of what has taken place.

Such entries may be made by the private individual, and they form very often a useful reference for the future.

In the early stages of business development it is not difficult for us to imagine the proprietor of the business making a similar record of his transactions with people who had become his suppliers and customers, narrating what he had bought, and from whom; what he had sold, and to whom. Just as a diary is a daily record, so also is a **Journal.** It is written up as soon as possible after the transaction has taken place. It is essentially a **primary** record, and hence we derive the meaning of the term 'Journal' in book-keeping as a book of **'first entry'**. No matter what subsequent use we make of the particulars recorded in it, the desirability of a primary record is obvious.

To the extent that the transactions of the business are recurrent, even in the smallest undertaking we should expect to see a record of:

(a) purchases;

(b) sales;

(c) payments to suppliers;

(d) receipts from customers.

As soon as the transactions entered into became more numerous, some kind of analysis of the Journal would be imperative if the proprietor at any time wished to know:

(a) how much he had purchased;

(b) how much he had sold;

(c) what was the total of his cash payments, and of

(d) his cash receipts.

With numerous daily transactions, putting on record the fact that £100 worth of goods had been purchased on credit from Jones, and £100 worth of goods had been sold on credit to Smith, the Journal entries might take the following form:

(a) Warehouseman chargeable with incoming goods **at cost** £100. Jones to be credited with £100.

(b) Smith chargeable with goods £100. Warehouseman to be credited with issue of goods at selling price £100.

If, however, we took matters a step further, and used the Symbols **Dr.** (debtor) instead of 'chargeable with' and **Cr.** (creditor) instead of 'to be credited', the entries could easily be stated in the following way:

(a) Warehouseman	Dr.	£100·00
Jones	Cr.	100·00
and		
(b) Smith	Dr.	£100·00
Warehouseman	Cr.	100·00

This would be a much simpler and more concise way of putting the transaction on record, but the repetition of the recurrent entries over a period of time would make detailed analysis always essential to arrive at, for example:

(a) our total purchases, and

(b) our total sales for that period, quite apart from the need for similar analysis as regards cash paid and cash received.

For that reason, the first form of Journal was modified to accord with these requirements of the proprietor, and in one section of it were recorded **purchases,** in another **sales** and in yet another **cash,** either in total, or as in many cases to-day:

(a) **Cash received,** and

(b) **Cash paid.**

To the first of these subsections of the Journal was given the title: **Purchase Journal,**

to the second: **Sales Journal,**

and to the third: **Cash Book** or **Cash Journal,**

with the result that in them we now find:

(a) our total purchases;

(b) our total sales; and

(c) our purely cash transactions, in as great a detail as we desire, or the requirements of the business demand.

If it be said that certain transactions take place which do not permit of entry in the above three subdivisions of the Journal, the answer is that the early form of Journal is still retained for such (comparatively infrequent) transactions, and is dealt with in Chapter VII.

Supposing we begin with the **Purchase Journal,** or **Day Book:**

Example

Enter the following purchases in the Purchase Day Book of H. Yates, a cycle dealer, total the Day Book, but do not post the entries to the Ledger.

PURCHASE DAY BOOK

Date	Supplier	Description	Details	Total	Gent's Models	Ladies' Models	Crates and Packing
			£	£	£	£	£
19x1 Feb. 2	Speedy Cycle Co., Ltd.	2 Gent's Roadsters, Model A625, at £25·00	50·00				
		2 Ladies' Roadsters, Model A725, at £26·00	52·00				
			102·00				
		Less 20% Trade Discount	20·40				
			81·60				
		2 Crates at £0·50	1·00	82·60	40·00	41·60	1·00
15	Drake Cycle Co., Ltd.	3 Gent's Special Club models, B21, at £21·00	63·00				
		3 Ladies' Special Club models, B20, at £22·00	66·00				
			129·00				
		Less 15% Trade Discount	19·35				
			109·65				
		2 Crates at £0·75	1·50	111·15	53·55	56·10	1·50
27	Victoria Manufacturing Co., Ltd.	2 Racing models, A16, at £27·00	54·00				
		Less 15% Trade Discount	8·10				
			45·90				
		1 Crate at £0·50	0·50	46·40	45·90	—	0·50
				£240·15	£139·45	£97·70	£3·00

19x8

Feb. 2 Received invoice from the Speedy Cycle Co., Ltd., for:
2 Gent's Roadsters, model A625 at £25, less 20% trade discount.
2 Ladies' Roadsters, model A725 at £26, less 20% trade discount.
2 crates at £0·50 each.

15 The Drake Cycle Co., Ltd., invoiced:
3 Gent's Special Club models B21 at £21, less 15% trade discount.
3 Ladies' Special Club models B20 at £22, less 15% trade discount.
2 crates at £0·75 each.

27 Received invoice from the Victoria Manufacturing Co., Ltd.:
2 Racing models A16 at £27, less 15% trade discount.
1 crate at £0·50.

In these three purchase transactions, we notice:

(*a*) That the goods purchased are exclusively for resale, i.e. they are goods in which Mr. Yates is dealing.

(*b*) That a deduction is made on account of **trade discount.**
This is a usual allowance made by a supplier to a retailer with whom he has regular dealings, and may represent:

1 A margin of profit for the retailer, who sells the goods at the advertised list price.

2 An inducement to the retailer to continue to trade with the supplier.

Prior to entry in the last four columns of the Day Book, it is seen that the trade discount has been deducted in the 'details' column, and we must always be careful to follow this procedure.

All that concerns Mr. Yates is the **net cost** to him of the cycles he has bought.

(*c*) That the suppliers have in each case included in their invoice price the cost of crates. These clearly do not refer to the cost of the goods dealt in, and are therefore entered in a separate column. Moreover, it is usual for the suppliers to issue **credit notes** as and when the crates are later returned to them in good condition. There may in consequence be a recovery of all or the greater part of the total purchase cost under this heading.

The solution to the example, as shown, enables Mr. Yates to see at a glance:

(a) From whom he has purchased.
(b) What has been purchased.
(c) The total cost of the purchases, suitably analysed, including
(d) The cost of crates, packing, etc.

Example

From the following particulars compile the Sales Day Book, Purchase Day Book and Returns Book of D. Morris.

Full details must be shown in the Day Books. No posting to the Ledger is required.

Mar. 10 Sold to W. Humphrey, Lincoln, 200 yards black cloth at £1 per yard; 100 yards of best brown cloth at £1·40 per yard. Whole invoice less 10% trade discount.

12 Received invoice from R. Ridgewell, Bolton, for 50 pairs of blankets at £3·50 per pair; 3 dozen woollen shawls £2·80 each.

15 Sent a debit note to W. Hunt for £12, being an overcharge on goods supplied on February 5.

18 Sent an invoice to S. Boham, Coventry, for 100 yards of velvet at £1·50 per yard, less 5% trade discount; 300 yards of black cloth at £1 per yard; trimmings £15.

20 Bought goods from B. Davis, Ely, 500 yards of black cloth at £0·50 per yard; 400 shawls at £2 each; sundry remnants £15.

22 W. Humphrey, Lincoln, returned 50 yards of the black cloth supplied on March 10, as being of inferior quality.

PURCHASE DAY BOOK

MARCH, 19x1

Date	Supplier	Description	Invoice No.	Details	Total	Cloth	Blankets	Shawls	Sundries	Special Items
				£	£	£	£	£	£	£
19x1 Mar. 12	R. Ridgwell	50 pairs Blankets at £3·50 pair	—	175·00	275·80		175·00			
		3 dozen Woollen Shawls at £2·80 each	1	100·80				100·80		
20	B. Davis, Ely	500 yards Black Cloth at £0·50 per yard		250·00	1065·00	250·00				
		400 Shawls at £2·00 each	2	800·00				800·00		
		Remnants		15·00					15·00	
29	General Supplies Ltd., London	Showcases and Fittings	3		100·00					100·00
					£1440·80	£250·00	£175·00	£900·80	£15·00	£100·00

D. MORRIS   Fo. 2

SALES DAY BOOK

MARCH, 19x1

Date	Customer	Description	Invoice No.	Details	Totals	Cloth	Velvet	Sundries
				£	£	£	£	£
19x1 Mar. 10	W. Humphrey, Lincoln	200 yards Black Cloth at £1·00 per yard		200·00				
		100 yards best Brown Cloth at £1·40 per yard		140·00				
				340·00				
		Less 10% Trade Discount	4	34·00	306·00	306·00		
18	S. Boham, Coventry	100 yards Velvet at £1·50 per yard		150·00				
		Less 5% Trade Discount		7·50				
				142·50				
		300 yards Black Cloth at £1·00 per yard	5	300·00				
		Trimmings		15·00	457·50	300·00	142·50	15·00
24	T. Butterworth, Norwich	300 yards Velvet at £1·75 per yard		525·00				
		Less 5% Trade Discount		26·25				
				498·75				
		150 yards best Brown Cloth at £1·40 per yard	6	210·00				
		Less 10% Trade Discount		21·00				
				189·00				
		Assorted Buttons		10·00	697·75	189·00	498·75	10·00
					£1 461·25	£795·00	£641·25	£25·00

Mar. 23 Received a debit note from A. Jenkinson, Wolverhampton, for 20 yards of velvet returned at £2 per yard less 20% trade discount.

24 Sent an invoice to T. Butterworth, Norwich, for 300 yards of velvet at £1·75 per yard less 5% trade discount; 150 yards of best brown cloth at £1·40 per yard less 10% trade discount; assorted buttons £10.

27 Received a credit note from V. Luxton, for 30 yards of white cloth returned at £0·50 per yard.

29 Bought from General Supplies, Ltd., London, showcases and fittings £100 net.

Note.—Great care must be exercised in setting out the Day Books.

Before beginning to record these transactions in the Purchase and Sales Journals, it is essential for us to realise that they are being stated from the point of view of the business of which D. Morris is the proprietor.

Indeed, we may first proceed to classify each of them as being:

(*a*) A purchase transaction.

(*b*) A sales transaction.

(*c*) The return of goods to a **supplier,** or the obtaining of an allowance *from* him.

(*d*) The return of goods by a **customer,** or the granting of an allowance *to* him.

In the two latter cases the result will be, as we shall expect, that the amount of the original purchases and sales will be reduced accordingly, but **instead of altering** the entries in the Purchase and Sales Journals, we shall make use of **Purchase Returns Journals** and **Sales Returns Journals.** (See page 19.)

Let us now summarise the points arising in this and the first example.

In the first place, the **analysis columns** which under each ruling follow the total column, enable us to dissect as fully as we may wish the details of our purchases and sales.

D. MORRIS

PURCHASES RETURNS AND ALLOWANCES BOOK

Date	Supplier	Description	Debit Note No.	Details	Total	Cloth	Blankets	Shawls	Sundries
				£	£	£	£	£	£
19x1 Mar. 15	W. Hunt	Overcharge goods supplied Feb. 5	7		12·00				12·00
27	V. Luxton	30 yards White Cloth returned at £0·50 per yard	Their credit note 8		15·00	15·00			
					£27·00	£15·00			£12·00

D. MORRIS

SALES RETURNS AND ALLOWANCES BOOK

Date	Customer	Description	Credit Note No.	Details	Total	Cloth	Velvet	Sundries
				£	£	£	£	£
19x1 Mar. 22	W. Humphrey, Lincoln	50 yards Black Cloth, invoice Mar. 10, inferior, at £1·00 per yard Less 10% Trade Discount	9	50·00 5·00	45·00	45·00		
23	A. Jenkinson, Wolverhampton	20 yards Velvet at £2·00 per yard Less 20% Trade Discount	Their debit note 10	40·00 8·00	32·00		32·00	
					£77·00	£45·00	£32·00	

Secondly, we see that an **Invoice No.** column is provided. In this is entered the No. **given by the business** to its suppliers' invoices, as well as to its own invoices to customers. If for any reason the original purchase invoice or copy sales invoice has to be consulted, it can quickly be referred to on the purchase or sales invoice files.

Thirdly, Returns and Allowances Books, whether for purchases or sales, are ruled in almost exactly the same way as the Purchase and Sales Journals themselves, the difference being that the heading 'Invoice No.' is replaced by 'Debit Note No.,' and 'Credit Note No.' respectively, thus facilitating reference to these documents.

Fourthly, it is apparent that a check can be placed on the arithmetical accuracy of the book-keeping work by agreeing periodically, say at the end of each month, the 'cross' cast or 'cross addition' of the **Analysis Columns** with the cast or addition of the **Total Column** in each of the subsidiary books.

Finally, in the second example we have an instance of the purchase by the business of capital goods, or **fixed assets,** in the shape of the showcases and fittings.

As these have been bought for retention and not for resale, it is essential to provide an additional analysis column, in this case headed 'Special Items'. Alternative headings might be 'Capital Items', or 'Capital Additions'.

The provision of this column enables us to see at a glance the total value of such special or capital purchases during the period.

TESTS AND QUESTIONS

1 Explain briefly the theory of 'Double Entry', and of 'Debit and Credit'.

2 What do you understand by the term Double Entry, as applied to a system of account keeping? Give examples to illustrate.

3 'Book-keeping by Double Entry means recording the same transaction twice.' Criticise this assertion briefly.

4 State the advantages to be derived from keeping a set of books on the Double Entry System and contrast this method with any other system you know of.

5 In arranging the work of the counting house of a manufacturing company, enumerate your recommendations for dealing with inward invoices and give the ruling of the book in which you suggest they should be entered.

6 Explain fully the functions of the Purchase Analysis Journal. Give a specimen ruling thereof and insert six entries therein, showing totals, and explain how these should be dealt with.

7 Goods purchased by a business may comprise either goods for resale at a profit, or goods for retention and use. Give two examples of each, and explain how such purchases are recorded in the books of account.

8 'The books of prime entry are developments from the ordinary Journal.' Comment on this statement, and give draft rulings for a Purchase Day-Book and a Sales Day-Book in a business having three main departments.

9 Explain clearly the nature of the following documents: invoice, debit note, statement.

10 What is the columnar method of recording credit purchases and sales? Illustrate your answer by examples.

11 P.Q. & Co., Merchants, have three departments, A, B and C. It is desired to keep separate trading accounts for each. With this end in view, give the ruling of the Sales Day Book, making therein six specimen entries, and explain how the book would function.

12 A trader wishes to ascertain separately the gross profit earned by each of the two departments which comprise his business.
   Show how the columnar system of book-keeping would allow him to do this without opening any additional books or accounts. Give any necessary rulings and explain how the system works.

13 What are Returns Inwards and Outwards? Where should these items be entered in the books of a trader? What effect has each upon the profits of a business?

14 On February 1 B. Grey owed A. White £6 for goods supplied.
   On February 13 he bought from White on credit three shirts at £2 each, six pairs of socks for £2 and a pair of flannel trousers for £4. The following day he sent a cheque for £10 on account, and on February 20 he bought a dressing gown for £4.
   Set out in full the invoice made out by White relating to the purchases on February 13, and the statement at the end of the month.

15 XY is a manufacturer of electrical appliances. Give the ruling for a Purchase Book which you would recommend he should keep, entering therein the undermentioned items, representing invoices

received, and explain how the book would function in the system of Double Entry book-keeping.

Feb. 2 AB, £25 for goods.
      4 PQ, £12 for repairs to machinery.
      5 CD, £10 for advertising.
      6 AB, £75 for goods.
      8 X Corporation, £40 for general rates.
         P.O. telephones, £14.
     12 GH, £100 for goods.
     14 Y Railway Company, £10 for carriage.
     15 AB, £250 for new plant.

16 On February 1, 19x1, you supplied to T. Thomas, 20 doz. grey pullovers at £2 each, less a trade discount of 7½%. Thomas returned 4 doz. pullovers as not up to sample and you agreed to credit him with their value.

   Enter the items in the Returns Book concerned and draw up the credit note to Thomas. How would you deal with this transaction in the Ledger?

17 On January 1, 19x1, R. Rich sold G. Jones goods to the amount of £50·25, on February 13, Jones paid Rich £25 on account; on February 27, Rich sold Jones £48·5 of goods; on March 3, Jones returned to Rich £7·75 goods (not being up to sample); on March 13, Jones paid Rich £24 and was allowed £1·25 discount to clear the January account. As on March 31, Rich sent a quarterly statement to Jones. Set out the statement so sent in proper form.

18 Enter the following transactions of Milner & Co., Ltd., in the appropriate books of prime entry; rule off at February 28, 19x1, and post as necessary to the Impersonal and Private Ledgers.

   Note.—Special care should be taken in drafting the form of the books of prime entry.

   19x1.
   Feb. 4 Bought of T. Lloyd, Lincoln, 500 yards of baize at £0·35 per yard, 2 000 yards of satin at £0·60 per yard, less 10% trade discount in each case.
        10 Sold to T. Williams, York, 400 yards curtain material at £0·50 per yard, and sundry fittings £8. Box charged £1.
        11 Bought showcase and counter for showroom from Universal Supplies, Ltd., London, £37·50.
        12 Returned to T. Lloyd, Lincoln, 200 yards of satin as invoiced on February 4.

Feb. 18 Bought of J. Grey, Taunton, 300 yards velvet at £1·25 per yard, less 5% trade discount and 250 yards baize at £0·35 per yard net.

   20 Received debit note from T. Williams, York, for box invoiced on February 10.

   24 Sold to D. Wilson, Coventry, 300 yards baize at £0·50 per yard net, and 600 yards satin at £0·75 per yard less 10% trade discount.

CHAPTER III

PURCHASE AND SALES TRANSACTIONS AND THE LEDGER ACCOUNTS

Question

As I see it, the Purchase and Sales Day Books are written up from the original purchase invoices, and the copies of the sales invoices to customers?

Answer

Yes, that is so, but it is of the utmost importance that every purchase invoice, whether for goods or services, shall be certified by the responsible officials of the business as to its correctness before being entered in the Purchase Journal. With regard to sales invoices, these may be issued on the basis of the warehouseman's record of deliveries.

Question

The final column in the first example's Purchase Journal was headed 'Crates and Packing', but there was no similar column in the second one. Why is this?

Answer

Suppliers may or may not charge for crates and packing material. If they do so, a record must clearly be made of the expense. Under this head, it is, however, a cost which we should record separately because it may be recoverable if and when such items as crates are returned to the suppliers; otherwise the cost must be borne by the business.

Question

With both the Purchase and the Sales Journals there is then no one particular form of ruling?

Answer

No. There cannot be. The system of book-keeping must be such as will give the information in each particular case in the form in which it is required, or can be of the greatest use. For this reason care must be exercised in the choice of the analysis columns. These may represent the principal materials dealt in, or the departments responsible for their production and sale, and so on.

Question

If goods are bought and sold on credit, I should have thought it was also very important to know:

(a) How much the business has purchased **from any one supplier**, and

(b) How much it has sold **to any one customer.**

But as there are numerous transactions with different suppliers and customers, how could this be done from the Journals alone ?

Answer

By means of the **Ledger,** or principal book of account, we are able to discover very quickly not only what has been purchased from or sold to any particular person, but **how that person stands in relation to the business at any particular time,** that is, whether he is its creditor or debtor. Put in another way, we want to know how much we have sold to each customer period by period because if possible we hope to increase our sales to him, and we also want to know how much that customer owes us for goods delivered, since his payments to us provide the monies out of which we have to pay our suppliers.

Question

So the Ledger Account records not only the trading aspect of our transactions, but also the cash aspect?

Answer

Yes. Both aspects must be recorded as affecting suppliers and customers, but at the moment we are only concerned with the **trading aspect.**

THE LEDGER

(a) Personal Accounts

We have spoken of Ledger Accounts as playing an essential part in summarising the transactions of the business so far as they concern those with whom it deals.

It is now necessary to describe the Ledger Account rather more precisely, and to consider its other functions.

Its usual **form** is as follows:

JONES

Dr.					Cr.
Date	Details	Amount	Date	Details	Amount
		£			£

In the form, we notice:

(*a*) **Name of Account.** This may be the name of the person, in this case Jones, who is either a supplier or a customer of the business. It may represent, on the other hand, the impersonal subject-matter with which the account deals. For the moment, we will take it to be the former only.

(*b*) The vertical double line in the centre divides the account into two equal parts. That on the left we term the **Debit** or debtor side, denoted by the symbol **Dr.**, and that on the right the **Credit**, or creditor side, with the symbol **Cr. On both sides** of the account, it will be observed, there are three columns, headed respectively:

Date,
Details, and
Amount.

In the ordinary way, a separate page, or folio of the Ledger, is used for each account opened, and the Ledger itself may be a bound book, a loose-leaf book, or in the form of cards, with a separate card for each account.

If we assume that Jones is a **supplier of goods** to the business, the structure of the account enables us to put to his credit, i.e. on the right-hand, or **credit** side, the value of the goods supplied by him. The right-hand side may also be regarded generally as that on which we enter benefits received **by the business.** The supply of goods on credit is clearly such a benefit and Jones may be said to have performed, to this extent, a 'credit-worthy' action.

· Furthermore, his account is said to be 'in credit', in that he is
a **creditor** of the business. Let us suppose Jones has supplied
goods to the value of £10. This being an ordinary purchase
transaction, the first record will be made in the Purchase Journal,
as we have seen. It will ultimately be put (or 'posted' as we must
accustom ourselves to saying) to the credit of **Jones's account,**
as follows:

JONES

Dr.							**Cr.**
Date	Details	P.R.J. Fo.	Amount	Date	Details	P.J. Fo.	Amount
				19x1 Jan. 1	Goods	2	£ 10·00

At this point we must remember:

(*a*) It is not necessary but in appropriate circumstances it might
be helpful to repeat here the full description of the goods. By
inserting a column for the Purchase Journal folio (P.J. Fo.)
we can readily turn back to the initial entry in the Purchase
Journal and, if we wish, to the original document, on which
it was based, i.e. the supplier's invoice.

(*b*) The purpose of our Ledger Account with Jones is to summarise or assemble within it **all our transactions** with him;
otherwise it would be impossible to determine the position
of the business in relation to him.

Because we are now thinking of Jones as a **supplier,** it is logical
to assume, in the first instance, that any items on the left-hand
or **debit** side will be in respect of payments made to him: offsetting the amounts standing to his credit.

If, however, the business has had occasion to return goods to
him owing to unsatisfactory quality, or error in price, and a
credit note is received signifying his acceptance of them, this also
is a matter which must be recorded on the **debit** side. The effect
of the return of the goods is **to reduce the liability of the business**
to Jones as its creditor. In this case, the initial entry will have
been made in the **Purchase Returns** or **Allowances Book,** and from

that we shall post to the **debit** of Jones's Ledger Account, as under:

JONES

DR.							CR.
Date	Details	P.R.J. Fo.	Amount	Date	Details	P.J. Fo.	Amount
19x1 Jan. 6	Returns or Allowances	3	£ 1·50	19x1 Jan. 1	Goods	2	£ 10·00

Should Jones, on the other hand, be a **customer of the business** a Ledger Account will be opened in identical **form,** but if goods to the value of £10 are **sold to him,** his account will be **debited,** that is the entry will be made on the **left-hand** side:

JONES

DR.							CR.
Date	Details	S.J. Fo.	Amount	Date	Details	S.R.J. Fo.	Amount
19x1 Jan. 1	Goods	2	£ 10·00				

He now appears as a **debtor** to the business, as indeed he is, the details of the original sale being found on Folio 2 of the **Sales Journal.**

The **business** in this case has performed the 'credit-worthy' action, and as such is entitled to regard Jones as **chargeable** with it. He is **indebted** to the business, and therefore the entry appears on the debit side.

Finally, should goods be returned by him, or the business make him any kind of allowance, the amount, as posted from the **Sales Returns and Allowances** Book, will be put to his credit.

The result will be, as we should expect:

(*a*) To offset to that extent his original indebtedness of £10.
(*b*) To indicate that the business, having delivered defective goods, or made an overcharge, now proceeds to give Jones **the necessary credit.**

The Ledger Account would then appear:

JONES

DR.							CR.
Date	Details	S.J. Fo.	Amount	Date	Details	S.R.J. Fo.	Amount
19x1 Jan. 1	Goods	2	£ 10·00	19x1 Jan. 6	Returns or Allowances	3	£ 1·50

When the **cash** as well as the **trading** aspect of these transactions has been dealt with, we shall be in a position to determine,
at any time and irrespective of the number of items, the **balance
of indebtedness** due either to or by the business.

So far as we have been dealing with **persons external to the
business,** the **personal** aspect of the sales and purchase transactions has now been recorded.

By that we mean **the effect upon the persons** with whom the
transactions have been entered into, resulting in their becoming,
until the question of **payment** arises, the creditors or debtors of
the business.

If we have carefully followed the construction of the Ledger
Account as shown, it is apparent that the entries are postings
from the various books of first entry—from the Journals. That is
to say, the Journals provide the basis for the writing up of all
Ledger Accounts.

We may even lay it down as a rule with very few exceptions
that:

'No entry shall be made in a Ledger Account, unless it has
first appeared in the Journal.'

We should remember that the Journal will not necessarily be a
bound book. It may consist of tabulation prepared by a computer of a file of invoices.

(b) Impersonal Accounts

It was stated on page 26 that the name of the account might be
that of the person with whom the business dealt, or of the
impersonal subject-matter referred to in it.

The former we may now term a **Personal Account,** and the latter an **Impersonal,** or **Nominal** Account.

Jones's account, whether he be a supplier or a customer, is a **Personal Account.** His position, as someone external to the business, has been looked at from the personal aspect.

There is, however, **another aspect** to be considered, and that is:

The effect upon the business as an impersonal unit, of the transactions with Jones and any other suppliers and customers.

When in the first place we regarded him as a **supplier** his account was credited with £10, but at the same time we must remember that the business then came into possession of £10 worth of goods. It is therefore natural to regard the stores or warehouse as **chargeable** in this amount. As a department of the business it may further be regarded **impersonally,** and the necessary charge made to it in an **impersonal account,** headed

Warehouse, or,
Goods purchased, or, more usually,
Purchases.

Thus the heading refers to the **subject-matter** of the account and not to the name of the warehouseman, or storekeeper, which is immaterial because he represents the **business.** If at first sight it seems strange that the charge to the warehouse for goods purchased should call for record in such an account we may find an explanation in the following:

(*a*) The essence of the double-entry system is to record the dual aspect of each transaction **within the Ledger,** or book of account.

In the event of no 'Warehouse' or 'Purchases' Account being opened we should have recorded in the Ledger **one aspect of the transaction only**—the personal aspect.

(*b*) The business, or its proprietor, desires to know, period by period, how much has been **purchased** of the various kinds of goods dealt in.

The opening of the Ledger Account for **'purchases'** permits the periodic totals of the Purchase Journal to be posted to it on the chargeable, or debit side.

Sometimes it is contended, and with truth, that the total cost of purchases, suitably analysed, can be seen at a glance in the Purchase Journal.

This, however, is no reason for eliminating the Ledger Account for 'purchases', because, as stated above, we desire to complete the double entry within the Ledger, and also obtain, in the summarised form which the Ledger Account gives, the total charge to the warehouse for goods received by it month by month during the trading year.

As in practice the various subdivisions of the Journal are ruled off at monthly intervals, a note of the monthly totals in summarised form is clearly very helpful.

The following illustrates in another way what has been described above:

PURCHASE JOURNAL

(Book of First Entry)

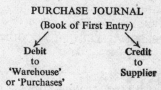

Debit   Credit
to   to
'Warehouse'   Supplier
or 'Purchases'

or, in account form:

IMPERSONAL LEDGER ACCOUNT

PURCHASES

DR.   CR.

Date	Details	P.J. Fo.	Amount	Date	Details	Fo.	Amount
19x1 Jan. 31	Total Purchases for Month	2	£ 10·00				

We may also add that, from the point of view of the business, the charge or debit to the 'Purchases' Account may be made by taking the total only of the appropriate column in the Purchase Journal.

This is in striking contrast to the necessity for giving credit to each separate supplier in his own personal account. We cannot avoid this latter step because we must know at any time how the business stands in relation to each supplier.

PURCHASE RETURNS AND ALLOWANCES

It was seen on page 28 that Jones, as a supplier, was charged or **debited** with the goods returned to him, or the allowance claimed from him. As the result in either case is to **reduce the initial debit** to 'Purchases' Account, the double entry will be completed by **crediting** that account, as follows:

PURCHASE RETURNS AND ALLOWANCES BOOK
(Book of First Entry)

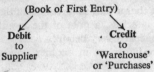

Debit   Credit
to   to
Supplier   'Warehouse'
                 or 'Purchases'

or, in account form:

IMPERSONAL LEDGER ACCOUNT
PURCHASES

Dr.   Cr.

Date	Details	P.J. Fo.	Amount	Date	Details	P.R.J. Fo.	Amount
19x1 Jan. 31	Total Purchases for Month	2	£ 10·00	19x1	Total Returns and Allowances for Month	3	£ 1·50

PURCHASES OF A CAPITAL NATURE

In the second example we saw that the purchase by D. Morris of showcases and fittings was recorded, together with his other purchases, in the Purchase Journal kept by him.

The personal aspect of this transaction is a credit to the suppliers in the Ledger Account opened in their name, i.e. a **personal account.**

But, as with the receipt of goods by the warehouse on behalf of the business, we have similarly to put on record somewhere the purchase of these capital goods, or **fixed assets.**

There can be no question of charging them to the warehouse, since they are not goods in which the business is dealing.

But, nevertheless, an account must be opened for them in the Ledger, having regard to the necessity for completing the double entry in the Ledger, and so we may decide to open an account under the general heading of:

'Fixtures and Fittings.'

In this case the business has acquired property for the use or value of which it is liable to account to its proprietor, even though such property is not intended for resale, and it is right that it should be charged or, as we say, **debited** with the purchase cost of £57·50.

The question now arises: 'In which section of Ledger shall the account be opened?'

What we have already done is to describe:

(*a*) **Personal Accounts,** as with Jones,

(*b*) **Impersonal Accounts,** e.g. Purchases,

the latter being the counterpart, in summarised form, of the former, so far as concerns the effect upon the business.

It is customary, in practice, having regard to the existence of these two types of account, to utilise **two entirely separate Ledgers,** known respectively as the **Personal Ledger** and the **Impersonal Ledger.**

As in the ordinary trading business of even quite moderate size the number of customers may be very large, we often find that the Personal Ledger is divided into two parts. The first part we call the **Sales Ledger,** as it is restricted to accounts with customers, and the latter the **Purchase Ledger,** as in it all the suppliers' accounts are opened.

By contrast, the accounts in the **Impersonal Ledger** will not be very numerous, and in the main they relate to those matters which affect the business in its **ordinary trading activities,** such as purchases, sales, wages, etc.

We could, of course, from the standpoint of the effect upon the business, open the 'Fixtures and Fittings' Account in the Impersonal Ledger, and in that account record all dealings in that particular class of property.

But because the fixtures and fittings have no direct relation to the day-to-day trading activities, a **further section of the Ledger** is provided for the accounts of this and similar types of **fixed asset.**

This further section is termed the **Private Ledger,** and represents the third and final division of the Ledger as a book of account.

Once again, we post the **total** of the 'special items' or 'capital items' column in the Purchase Journal, so that the Fixtures and Fittings Account appears as follows:

FIXTURES AND FITTINGS

DR.   CR.

Date	Details	P.J. Fo.	Amount	Date	Details	Fo.	Amount
19x1 Jan. 31	Showcases and Fittings	2	£ 57·50				

or in diagram form:

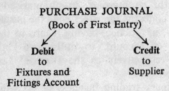

Sales

Much of what we have said in regard to the completion of the double entry under the heading of purchases will apply in the case of **Sales,** although in the **reverse direction.**

We are still dealing with the **impersonal aspect, or the effect upon the business** of the delivery of goods from the warehouse to the customer.

What we must realise is that if goods are sold to Brown, for example, in his capacity as a **customer,** the warehouse having delivered the goods, is entitled to take credit to itself, as representing the business, for the goods that have passed out of its possession.

From the **personal aspect,** the customer Brown must, of course, be charged or **debited** with what he has received at **selling price.**

Impersonally the business is thus entitled to **credit** in an impersonal account, which may be headed:

Warehouse, or
Goods sold, or more usually,
Sales.

Our reasons for so doing are:

(*a*) As in the case of purchases, the double entry must be completed **within the Ledgers.**
(*b*) The business, or its proprietor, desires to know, period by period, how much has been **sold** of the various kinds of goods dealt in.

Therefore, if we open an account in the Impersonal Ledger, headed 'Sales', the periodic totals of the Sales Journal will be posted to it on the **credit** side, and, as with purchases, the Sales Journal will usually be ruled off at monthly intervals.

At any time, therefore, we may obtain a comparison of the **cost of purchases,** with the **proceeds of sales,** by examining these two accounts in the **Impersonal Ledger.**

Stated in another way, we have:

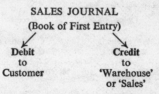

SALES JOURNAL
(Book of First Entry)

Debit   Credit
to   to
Customer   'Warehouse'
or 'Sales'

or, in account form, assuming the sales value for the period to be £20:

SALES

Dr.							Cr.
Date	Details	Fo.	Amount	Date	Details	S.J. Fo.	Amount
				19x1 Jan. 31	Total Sales for Month	4	£ 20·00

It will be noted from the 'Details' column in the account, that we need concern ourselves only with the **total sales** as shown in the Sales Journal.

This is because, irrespective of the **kind** of goods sold, they may all be regarded as **sales,** and dealt with in the Ledger as one item.

In recording the **personal aspect,** however, a separate **debit** to each customer **in his own personal account** is essential if we are to know precisely:

(a) How much has been sold to him.

(b) The amount of his indebtedness to the business at any particular time.

SALES RETURNS AND ALLOWANCES

Should Brown, to whom £20 worth of goods have been sold, return any part of the goods, or make a claim on the business for an allowance in respect of the invoice price to him, the effect upon the business will be to reduce the initial **credit** to 'Sales' Account. In other words, the latter account will be **debited**:

SALES RETURNS AND ALLOWANCES BOOK
(Book of First Entry)

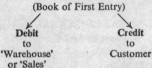

Debit   Credit
to   to
'Warehouse'   Customer
or 'Sales'

or, in account form, assuming the amount of the allowance to be £5:

IMPERSONAL LEDGER ACCOUNT
SALES

DR.   CR.

Date	Details	S.R.J. Fo.	Amount	Date	Details	S.J. Fo.	Amount
19x1 Jan. 31	Total Returns and Allowances for Month	5	£ 5·00	19x1 Jan. 31	Total Sales for Month	4	£ 20·00

SALES OF A CAPITAL NATURE

These are far less frequently encountered than purchases of this class of goods.

It is possible to record such sales by inserting a 'special items' column in the Sales Journal, but in practice use is almost always made of the earliest form of Journal, or the ordinary Debtor and Creditor Journal (without analysis columns) as illustrated in Chapter 7.

Examples that may be cited are the sale of a motor lorry, traveller's motor-car or machine tool.

The Journal entry in such a case provides the basic narrative of the transaction for entry in the Ledgers, these being the personal (Sales) Ledger so far as the person to whom they are sold is concerned, and the account of the particular asset in the Private Ledger so far as concerns the effect on the business.

For the sake of completeness we may take the following:

Example

On January 1, 19x1, D. Morris had in his factory machinery of a book value of £500. On January 15 a stitching machine was sold to a dealer, realising £15.

PRIVATE LEDGER ACCOUNT
MACHINERY

Dr.							Cr.
Date	Details	Fo.	Amount	Date	Details	Fo.	Amount
19x1 Jan. 1	Balance		£ 500·00	19x1 Jan. 15	A. Dealer, Stitching Machine		£ 15·00

An important point in connection with this transaction would be the loss or profit on sale, i.e. the proceeds of sale of £15 would have to be compared with that proportion of the commencing balance of £500 which represented the actual machine sold.

In this respect, no such difficulty would, of course, arise with **purchases** of capital goods. Here we are concerned with the purchase cost alone.

Once again, we may state the transaction in diagram form:

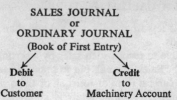

SALES JOURNAL
or
ORDINARY JOURNAL
(Book of First Entry)

Debit   Credit
to   to
Customer   Machinery Account

While the **Personal Ledger** is restricted to the accounts of suppliers and customers in its purchase and sales sections respectively, the following examples are typical of the accounts appearing in the **Impersonal Ledger** and the **Private Ledger**:

Impersonal Ledger (sometimes also called the Nominal Ledger)	Private Ledger
Purchases	Capital (of Proprietor)
Sales	Factory, Warehouse or Office Premises
Purchase Returns	Machinery
Sales Returns	Tools
Wages	Fixtures and Fittings
Carriage	Motor Vehicles
Salaries	Patents
Cash Discounts Allowed	Trade Marks
Cash Discounts Received	Stock
Bad Debts	Bills of Exchange (Payable and Receivable)
Travelling Expenses	Investments
Packing Expenses	Loans
Repairs	
Interest Paid	
Interest Received	and so on.
Rent	
Rates	
Commission	

It might be added that in a general way, of the items appearing above, those under the heading of the 'Impersonal Ledger' relate to accounts in which we find details of the **profit and loss,** or **revenue position of the business.**

Those, on the other hand, under the heading of the 'Private Ledger' relate to the **assets and liabilities of the business.**

Now that we have become acquainted with the general application of Double Entry principles to the recording of Purchases and Sales transactions **within the Ledgers,** let us carry the Example on page 15 a stage further, and imagine we have been instructed to **post to the Ledger Accounts** from the various books of Prime Entry which we have already written up.

(a) Purchases

In the Purchase Day Book of D. Morris we see it is necessary to give **credit** to each one of the three suppliers whose names appear therein. Such credit will clearly be given in the **Personal (Purchase) Ledger,** and the three accounts required will be opened as follows:

D. MORRIS

PURCHASE LEDGER

R. RIDGWELL, BOLTON

DR.   CR.

Date	Details	Fo.	Amount	Date	Details	P.J. Fo.	Amount
				19x1 Mar.12	Goods	1	£ 275·80

B. DAVIS, ELY

DR.   CR.

Date	Details	Fo.	Amount	Date	Details	P.J. Fo.	Amount
				19x1 Mar. 20	Goods	1	£ 1065·00

GENERAL SUPPLIES, LTD., LONDON

DR.   CR.

Date	Details	Fo.	Amount	Date	Details	P.J. Fo.	Amount
				19x1 Mar. 29	Goods	1	£ 100·00

In each case the entries appear on the **credit side** since, until payment is made to them, the suppliers are creditors of the business.

The use of the word 'Goods' in the 'Details' column is all that is necessary, as full particulars of the goods can quickly be found on Folio 1 of the Purchase Journal itself.

We must now consider the **impersonal aspect,** which is the
charge to the warehouse for 'Goods Purchased,' or **'Purchases'.**
It is necessary, too, for us to remember that by this is meant
'goods purchased for resale', so that we must in any event exclude
the item of Showcases and Fittings.

Our Impersonal Ledger Account for Purchases will then be:

PURCHASES

Dr.							Cr.
Date	Details	P.J. Fo.	Amount	Date	Details	Fo.	Amount
19x1 Mar. 31	Total for Month: Cloth Blankets Shawls Sundries		£ 250·00 175·00 900·80 15·00				
		1	£1340·80				

But it is scarcely likely that we shall rest content with the *form*
of this account, because month by month new totals will appear
in it, and the subsequent addition of the 'Amount' column will
be somewhat complicated.

For this reason, it may be preferred to open a separate Purchases Account **for each class of goods,** or to enter them in one
account, but in **columnar** form.

Let us assume the former method is selected. We shall then
have:

IMPERSONAL LEDGER

PURCHASES—CLOTH

Dr.							Cr.
Date	Details	P.J. Fo.	Amount	Date	Details	Fo.	Amount
19x1 Mar. 31	Total for Month	1	£ 250·00				

PURCHASES BLANKETS

Dr.							Cr.
Date	Details	P.J. Fo.	Amount	Date	Details	Fo.	Amount
19x1 Mar. 31	Total for Month	1	£ 175·00				

PURCHASES—SHAWLS

Dr.							Cr.
Date	Details	P.J. Fo.	Amount	Date	Details	Fo.	Amount
19x1 Mar. 31	Total for Month	1	£ 900·80				

PURCHASES—SUNDRIES

Dr.							Cr.
Date	Details	P.J. Fo.	Amount	Date	Details	Fo.	Amount
19x1 Mar. 31	Total for Month	1	£ 15·00				

In regard to the showcases and fittings purchased, an account in the **Private Ledger** will be opened, as under:

FIXTURES AND FITTINGS

Dr.							Cr.
Date	Details	P.J. Fo.	Amount	Date	Details	Fo.	Amount
19x1 Mar. 31	Total for Month	1	£ 100·00				

It must be noted that the charge to the business for **purchases** and **fixtures and fittings** is made on the **debit** side, the amount in each case being the **total** of the appropriate analysis column in the Purchase Journal.

We thus see that:

(*a*) The Purchase Journal as a Book of Prime Entry provides a basis for the Double Entry.

(b) The dual aspect of the transactions has been recorded **within the Ledgers.**

(c) Arithmetical agreement has been obtained, in that the sum of the **credit** entries or postings in the Purchase Ledger is equal to the sum of the **debit** postings in the **Impersonal** and **Private Ledgers.**

(d) While the postings to the Impersonal and Private Ledger Accounts are made on March 31 and in **total** only, those to the Personal Ledger are made as soon as possible after the initial record in the Journal. It is essential to have our Ledger Account with each supplier 'up to date'.

(b) Purchase Returns and Allowances

In the Purchase Returns Book we see there are two entries relating, in the first case, to an overcharge, and in the second, to the return of goods by the business to one of its suppliers.

In recording the **personal aspect** we must therefore remember that the suppliers' accounts in the Purchase Ledger will be **debited,** resulting in a reduction of any amounts hitherto standing to their **credit.**

This is a logical step to take because, had the overcharge not been detected, we should have **debited** Hunt with a payment **greater** than was actually due to him. The issue of a Debit Note now clearly reduces the amount of any subsequent payment to him by the business.

Further, the **receipt of a Credit Note** from Luxton enables the business to debit him with the cost of the goods returned for which, when purchased, it had originally given him credit.

The Purchase Ledger Accounts of the two suppliers will then appear as follows:

PURCHASE LEDGER

W. HUNT

Dr.							Cr.
Date	Details	P.R.J. Fo.	Amount	Date	Details	P.J. Fo.	Amount
19x1 Mar. 15	Overcharge	1	£ 12·00				

V. LUXTON

Dr.							Cr.
Date	Details	P.R.J. Fo.	Amount	Date	Details	P.J. Fo.	Amount
19x1 Mar. 27	Returns	2	£ 15·00				

As this is the only information we have concerning these suppliers the result is that they are shown as **debtors** to the business to this extent, it being assumed that they have received payment in full in some previous period.

In practice, however, it is almost certain that in the first case at least, payment would not be made until the overcharge in question had been corrected.

With regard to the **impersonal** aspect, we can now appreciate that the warehouse will be **credited.** The reason for giving it credit now, is that it was originally charged or **debited** with the goods purchased at the invoice or cost price to the business. The credit thus given to it puts on record the fact that its responsibility is lessened by the amount, in total, of £27·00.

The Purchase Returns, or Returns Outwards Accounts, will then be credited on March 31 with the **total of** the appropriate analysis columns in the Purchase Returns Journal as under:

PURCHASE RETURNS—CLOTH

Dr.							Cr.
Date	Details	Fo.	Amount	Date	Details	P.R.J. Fo.	Amount
				19x1 Mar. 31	Total for Month	1	£ 15·00

PURCHASE RETURNS—SUNDRIES

Dr.							Cr.
Date	Details	Fo.	Amount	Date	Details	P.R.J. Fo.	Amount
				19x1 Mar. 31	Total for Month	1	£ 12·00

Once more, it is seen that:

(*a*) The Double Entry is completed within the Ledgers, Personal and Impersonal.

(*b*) Arithmetical agreement is maintained, the sum of the **debit** items being equal to the sum of the **credits**, and

(*c*) While the postings to the accounts of Hunt and Luxton are made on the dates of the transactions with them, those to the Purchase Returns Accounts are made in total on March 31.

(*c*) Sales

The Sales Journal gives us full particulars of the sales to the three customers for whom we shall open separate accounts in the **Sales Ledger.**

To record the personal aspect, we must show that they are debtors to the business, and therefore their accounts will be in **debit,** taking the following form:

W. HUMPHREY, LINCOLN

Dr.							Cr.
Date	Details	S.J. Fo.	Amount	Date	Details	Fo.	Amount
19x1 Mar. 10	Goods	2	£ 306·00				

S. BOHAM, COVENTRY

Dr.							Cr.
Date	Details	S.J. Fo.	Amount	Date	Details	Fo.	Amount
19x1 Mar. 18	Goods	2	£ 457·50				

T. BUTTERWORTH, NORWICH

Dr.							Cr.
Date	Details	S.J. Fo.	Amount	Date	Details	Fo.	Amount
19x1 Mar. 24	Goods	2	£ 697·75				

We should now be able to understand the meaning of what has been done in our book-keeping work. If in the case of

personal accounts, like those set out above, the entries appear on the debit side, or there is an excess in value of debit entries over credit entries, the person whose name appears at the head of the account is always a debtor to the business. He is chargeable to the extent of paying the business for the goods it has sold to him.

If a similar state of affairs is found to exist in an **impersonal** account, such as 'Purchases', it indicates that the official of the business under whose control the goods have come is chargeable to account for them until the time of their ultimate sale.

But as we are here dealing with **sales,** it is necessary to give **credit** to the warehouse which has parted with goods on the instructions of the Sales Department, and has therefore reduced its responsibility to account in the proper way.

Thus, an account will be opened in the **Impersonal** Ledger for 'Goods Sold' or 'Sales', as follows:

SALES

Dr.							Cr.
Date	Details	Fo.	Amount	Date	Details	S.J. Fo.	Amount
				19x1 Mar. 31	Total for Month: Cloth Velvet Sundries	2	£ 795·00 641·25 25·00
							£1461·25

As explained on page 40, in connection with the analysis of purchases, we shall, however, almost certainly prefer to open separate Sales Accounts for the various kinds of goods to correspond with the columns in the Sales Journal.

The result will then be:

SALES—CLOTH

Dr.							Cr.
Date	Details	Fo.	Amount	Date	Details	S J. Fo.	Amount
				19x1 Mar. 31	Total for Month	2	£ 795·00

SALES—VELVET

Dr.							Cr.
Date	Details	Fo.	Amount	Date	Details	S.J. Fo.	Amount
				19x1 Mar. 31	Total for Month	2	£ 641·25

SALES—SUNDRIES

Dr.							Cr.
Date	Details	Fo.	Amount	Date	Details	S.J. Fo.	Amount
				19x1 Mar. 31	Total for Month	2	£ 25·00

By means of these analysed Impersonal Accounts it is now possible for the proprietor of the business to compare, month by month, the **purchase cost** with the **proceeds of sale** of the various articles in which he is dealing.

(d) Sales Returns and Allowances

As with Purchases, we find in this book two entries which must be posted to the Ledger, involving the completion of the **personal aspect** at once and as a separate posting to the account of each customer, and of the **impersonal aspect** at the end of the month, and in total only.

We find, however, this difference from Purchases: The goods returned by Humphrey are part of those sold to him during the month under review; while both items come under the head of 'Returns', there being no question of an overcharge.

Let us try to visualise what these two entries mean. If we are in any doubt, it may be simpler to deal first with the Impersonal aspect.

The warehouse has received the goods, increasing its stock, for which it is accountable. It is, therefore, logical that we should charge or **debit** it with the **total** value of the returned goods.

At the same time, the customers have performed a 'credit-worthy' action, to this extent offsetting the original charge or debit made to them individually. It is equally reasonable, there-fore, to **credit** them with the returned goods. This credit, in the case of Humphrey, will cause his account to appear as follows:

W. HUMPHREY, LINCOLN

DR.							CR.
Date	Details	S.J. Fo.	Amount	Date	Details	S.R.J. Fo.	Amount
19x1 Mar. 10	Goods	2	£ 306·00	19x1 Mar. 22	Returns	2	£ 45·00

and from it we can see that his original indebtedness is now reduced, which is in line with the facts.

As regards Jenkinson, he too will receive credit, as follows:

A. JENKINSON, WOLVERHAMPTON

DR.							CR.
Date	Details	Fo.	Amount	Date	Details	S.R.J. Fo.	Amount
				19x1 Mar. 23	Returns		£ 32·00

But, since we know nothing of his original indebtedness to the business, the position is that he appears as a creditor for the amount shown above. Payment may either be made to him in settlement, or more probably, the credit will be taken into account by him when he next pays for any further goods supplied.

Finally, to complete the double entry, we shall post the totals of the appropriate columns in the Sales Returns Journals to the Debit of the Impersonal Ledger Accounts for 'Sales Returns—Cloth' and 'Sales Returns—Velvet', just as we did with Purchases.

In both cases, the warehouse has received goods, either from a supplier, or from a customer.

SALES RETURNS—CLOTH

DR.							CR.
Date	Details	S.R.J. Fo.	Amount	Date	Details	Fo.	Amount
19x1 Mar. 31	Total for Month	2	£ 45·00				

SALES RETURNS—VELVET

DR.							CR.
Date	Details	S.R.J. Fo.	Amount	Date	Details	Fo.	Amount
19x1 Mar. 31	Total for Month	2	£ 32·00				

SUMMARY

With each of the Journals we have been careful to regard them
as providing the basis for the completion of the double entry
within the Ledgers. They have, therefore, served their purpose in
enabling us to look at each one of the **purchasing** and **selling
transactions** from their **dual aspect,** or the Personal and Impersonal aspect.

Irrespective of the **Number** of these transactions during any
particular period, we are now in a position to tabulate the
information contained in the Ledger Accounts in the form of the
balances thereon. These balances will be obtained by a scrutiny
of each account, so that the amount of one item or of the total
items on the debit side will be termed a **debit balance,** or if on the
credit side, a **credit balance.** Where entries appear on both debit
and credit sides, the excess of the one side over the other will
also be termed the balance, according to its nature, but this we
shall appreciate more readily after dealing with Cash Receipts
and Cash Payments.

In the meantime, we will extract and state the balances as they
now appear in the various Ledger Accounts:

Page	Ledger	Name of Account	Dr.	Cr.
			£	£
39	Purchase	R. Ridgwell		275·80
		B. Davis		1065·00
		General Supplies Ltd.		100·00
42		W. Hunt	12·00	
43		V. Luxton	15·00	
47	Sales	W. Humphrey	261·00	
44		S. Boham	457·50	
		T. Butterworth	697·75	
47		A. Jenkinson		32·00
40	Impersonal	Purchases—Cloth	250·00	
41		Blankets	175·00	
		Shawls	900·80	
		Sundries	15·00	
43		Purchase Returns—Cloth		15·00
		Sundries		12·00
45		Sales—Cloth		795·00
46		Velvet		641·25
		Sundries		25·00
47		Sales Returns—Cloth	45·00	
		Velvet	32·00	
41	Private	Fixtures and Fittings	100·00	
			£2961·05	£2961·05

It should be mentioned that in the average business by far the greater number of accounts will be found in the **Personal Ledgers,** and especially in that section of those Ledgers containing the accounts of customers, or **Sales** Ledger. So large may this become as a result of the business enlarging its sales connection that its division on an alphabetical or territorial basis may be essential if the Accounting Department is to do its work with speed and efficiency.

TESTS AND QUESTIONS

1 Name the different Ledgers employed in the ordinary trading concern, and mention the classes of account you would expect to find in each.

2 Explain carefully:

   (a) Nominal Accounts.

   (b) Real Accounts.

   (c) Personal Accounts.

3 On which side of the following Ledger Accounts would you expect to find the balance? Give reasons for your answer in each case:

   Bad Debts Account.

   Plant and Machinery Account.

   Sales Account.

   Discount Account.

   Returns Outwards Account.

4 W. Green has the following transactions with J. Black:

19x1		£
July 10	Goods sold to W. Green	420·00
15	Goods returned by W. Green	20·00
Sept. 30	Interest charged	2·00
Oct. 10	Cheque received from W. Green	392·00
10	Discount deducted	10·00
11	W. Green charged with discount deducted in error	10·00

You are required to show how each of the foregoing items would be recorded in the books of J. Black.

5 Brown and Smith are two merchants. At January 1, 19x2, Smith
   owes Brown £146·40 and during the month of January the following
   transactions took place between them:

19x2		£
Jan.	5 Brown purchased goods of Smith	126·21
	12 Smith sends goods to Brown	50·09
	15 Brown pays cash to Smith	95·00
	Smith allows discount	5·00
	20 Smith allows Brown's claim for damaged goods	10·00
	24 Smith sells to Brown goods	131·33
	30 Brown borrows from Smith for temporary accommodation	50·00

   You are required:

   (a) To give the account of Brown in the Ledger of Smith, and

   (b) To bring down the balance at the end of January, 19x2, and

   (c) To state which party is indebted to the other.

6 From the following particulars, draw up the Capital Account of
   J. Owen as it would appear in his books for the year 19x3. Balance
   it off as on December 31, 19x3, and bring down the balance:

	£
Capital as January 1, 19x3	416·25
Profit for the year 19x3 was	314·27
On October 15 J. Owen paid in additional capital	500·00
During the year J. Owen drew out of the business for private expenses	250·00
On December 31, 19x3, interest on capital was allowed	22·00

7 (a) Make entries to record the following:

       19x5
       Jan. 5 Purchase of goods from B. & Co., £300.
       Feb. 5 Payment by cheque to B. & Co., *less* 5% cash discount.

   (b) On February 20, 19x5, it was discovered that bank charges
       under date of December 31, 19x4, amounting to £5·25, had not
       been recorded. Adjust.

   (c) On December 31, 19x4, the balance on Motor Vans Account
       was £100, representing an Élite lorry. A new Élite lorry was
       purchased for cash on March 31, 19x5, for £1 775, and £75
       was allowed in part exchange for the old lorry, the cash passing
       being £1 700. Make the appropriate entries to record and dispose
       of the matter.

8 In what Ledger or other accounts, and upon which side of such
accounts, would you expect to find the following:

(a) £500 paid for new machinery.

(b) £170 received from J. Robinson in full settlement of his account
of £172·60.

(c) £600 received from an Insurance Company in settlement of a
claim for damages to premises by fire.

(d) £75 received for the sale of old motor van.

(e) £250 paid to J. Fitter in full settlement of an account due to him
three months hence of £260·75.

CHAPTER IV

CASH TRANSACTIONS

Question

From what you have been saying about the accounts in the various Ledgers, am I correct in thinking that all they show at the moment are balances in respect of Trading Transactions?

Answer

Yes, in respect of Purchases and Sales on Credit Terms. What we now have to do is to consider the Receipt and Payment of **Cash** by the business, usually at the end of the period of credit allowed to or by it.

Question

You said at an earlier stage that some portion of the Capital with which the business was begun must necessarily be in the form of Cash. That would be in order to pay its running expenses?

Answer

Not only such expenses as Wages and Salaries, but also to pay suppliers who might at the outset be unwilling to give credit to a new business.

Question

Would it be right to describe such Cash as the **Working Capital** employed?

Answer

It forms a part, but by no means the whole, of the Working Capital, as we shall see later. A better definition would be that it is a **Liquid Asset,** and its subsequent use for the purposes of the business may result in its becoming a **Current Asset,** as when goods are bought for stock, or a **Fixed Asset,** when Plant, Fittings, etc., are purchased.

Question

In the case of goods in which the business dealt, you said these were entrusted to the warehouse manager, who was responsible for their receipt and issue. Is the cashier similarly responsible for the Cash Assets?

Answer

No, only for what is termed **Cash in Hand**; this, however, is negligible in amount as compared with the moneys lying in the Bank Account of the business, or **Cash at Bank.** Between the two, there is this difference: the **Cashier,** as a servant of the business, will always be, on balance, accountable to it for cash held by him. The **Bank,** on the other hand, may sometimes be the creditor of the business, as where moneys are advanced on loan or by way of overdraft.

PROCEDURE IN OFFICE ON RECEIPT OF CASH

On the opening of each day's incoming mail, all remittances from customers will be passed on to the cashier. They will usually be accompanied by the statements of account which the business has issued at monthly intervals to its customers.

The cashier will:

(a) Compare the amount remitted with the total of the statement and, at the same time, check the **Cash Discount** which the customer may have deducted.

(b) **Cash Discount** is the inducement offered by the business to its customers to pay within the recognised period of credit. As such it is an expense to the business, which must always be taken into account with the accompanying remittance. If the terms upon which business is done are '$2\frac{1}{2}\%$ monthly account', and the customer's debt is £100, then **if he pays on or before the end of the month following delivery of the goods to him,** he need remit £97·50 only. On the other hand, if he pays after the expiry of the credit period, the discount will not ordinarily be allowed.

To the extent that Cash Discount refers to the customers of the business, it is termed **Discount Allowed,** and it differs from **Trade Discount,** which we discussed on page 14, in that it always relates to the cash or financial aspect of each transaction. Looked at in another way, it assists the business in collecting what is due to it from its customers, and in maintaining a minimum of **Cash** or **Liquid Assets.**

The cashier will also:

(c) So far as **cheques** are received, cross these, if they are un-crossed, or if already crossed, insert the name of the bankers of the business who are, of course, the collecting bankers.

(d) Enter the remittances in detail in either a rough cash diary or Journal, as a preliminary to entry in the Cash Book proper, or enter them at once in the Cash Book. Whichever alternative is adopted, such initial entry is a **Prime** or **First** entry, and therefore corresponds to the record of Purchases or Sales in the Purchase and Sales Journals.

(e) List the remittances on the counterfoil of the bank paying-in book, so that the total thereof is in agreement with the total of the entries for the particular business day appearing in the Cash Book of the business. Thus, the amount actually banked will agree with the business records.

(f) Make out, in the name of each customer, formal receipts, which may be attached to the statements of account and then issued to the customers for retention by them.

The Cash Book or Cash Journal will then be available for the ledger clerks, whose duty it will be to post the amount of each remittance **to the credit of the Ledger Account of the customer from whom it was received.**

BOOK-KEEPING ENTRIES

We can best approach these by considering the cashier as being very much in the same position as the warehouseman, with the difference that he is responsible for **cash** instead of **goods.**

If, therefore, we apply the same reasoning to his responsibility as a servant of the business we shall charge him with **all incoming cash.** It is logical to do this, so that he may at any time be accountable for its safe custody and disposal.

Using a term with which we have now become familiar, the cashier will be **debited** with all moneys received and, as was indicated above, each of the customers will be **credited,** the latter having performed a 'credit-worthy' action in paying to the business what is due by them.

We may, therefore, if we so desire, as is often done in practice, commence our records by opening a **Cash Received Journal** in which all moneys received from customers, whether in the form of cheques, notes, coin, etc., will be entered. Bearing in mind the fact that in many cases Cash Discount has been allowed to the customers, it will be helpful to show the amount of the discount **by the side of** the item to which it relates, as follows:

CASH RECEIVED JOURNAL

Date	Customer	Total	Discount	Cash
19x1 Feb. 20	G. Green	£ 100·00	£ 2·50	£ 97·50

From this it is apparent that G. Green has now settled his debt of £100, and in collecting its due from him, the business has been obliged to incur an **expense** of £2·50 which, clearly, must reduce the figure of **profit** it expects to make.

Like the Purchase and Sales Journals, the Cash Book will probably be ruled off and totalled at the end of each month, with the result that, as with our Purchase and Sales transactions, we shall find it desirable:

(*a*) To give **credit** to **each customer** immediately on receipt of his separate remittance.

(*b*) To **debit** or charge the **cashier** in total with the cash receipts, irrespective of the individual details making up the total.

The Cash Received Journal enables us to do this, and at the same time to comply with **double entry principles,** as the following diagram shows:

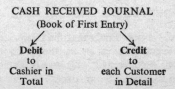

CASH RECEIVED JOURNAL
(Book of First Entry)

Debit	Credit
to	to
Cashier in	each Customer
Total	in Detail

or in account form:

CASH RECEIVED JOURNAL

Date	Customer	Total	Discount	Cash
19x1		£	£	£
Feb. 20	G. Green	100·00	2·50	97·50
22	B. Brown	50·00	—	50·00
		£150·00	£2·50	£147·50

SALES LEDGER
G. GREEN

DR.   CR.

Date	Details	Fo.	Amount	Date	Details	C.R.J. Fo.	Amount
				19x1			£
				Feb. 20	Cash	1	97·50
					Discount	1	2·50
							£100·00

B. RROWN

DR.   CR.

Date	Details	Fo.	Amount	Date	Details	C.R.J. Fo.	Amount
				19x1			£
				Feb. 22	Cash	1	50·00

PRIVATE LEDGER
CASH

DR.   CR.

Date	Details	C.R.J. Fo.	Amount	Date	Details	Fo.	Amount
19x1			£				
Feb. 28	Total cash	1	147·50				

In the above, we note **firstly** that the **Cash Account** appears in the **Private Ledger.** This is as we should expect because the Private Ledger is concerned with **Assets** and **Liabilities,** and Cash Received is manifestly an **Asset.**

Secondly, we note that, while our aim is to complete the Double Entry **within the Ledgers,** the sum of the two credit balances on the accounts of Green and Brown is £150, whereas we have a debit balance on Cash Account of £147·50 only.

That is to say, so far as **discount allowed** is concerned, we have given credit to G. Green personally **in the Ledger** for that amount, but we have not impersonally noted its effect upon the business. The business must be charged with that amount as an expense or loss resulting from its dealings with Green, and it is therefore necessary to open in the Impersonal Ledger an account for **Discounts Allowed.**

DISCOUNT ALLOWED

DR.							CR.
Date	Details	C.R.J. Fo.	Amount	Date	Details	Fo.	Amount
19x1 Feb. 28	Total Discount	1	£ 2·50				

Arising from this we see that:

(a) The double entry is completed **within the Ledgers.**

(b) A Debit Balance in an **Impersonal** Ledger Account, e.g. Discount, is a business **expense,** and a debit balance on a **Private** Ledger Account is for our present purpose an **Asset** of the business.

(c) Any Debit Balances formerly appearing on the accounts of Green and Brown in the **Sales Ledger** will have been extinguished by the posting to their credit of the cash now received.

PROCEDURE IN OFFICE ON PAYMENT OF CASH

Periodically, say at monthly intervals, the business will pay its **suppliers** for what has been purchased from them. At the end of each month a statement of account may have been received from them setting out the balance in their favour. This will be compared with the total standing to their credit in the various **Purchase Ledger** Accounts. Care will be taken to deduct, if omitted in the statement, the value of any goods returned to them by the business, and similarly a deduction will be made for

Cash Discount, discount which in this instance we may rightly term **discount received,** or **receivable,** considering it, that is, from the standpoint of the business.

Thus on or before the end of the month following delivery of the goods a list will be prepared of all **accounts payable,** setting out:

(*a*) The folio of the supplier's account in the Purchase Ledger,

(*b*) The name of the supplier,

(*c*) The total amount due,

(*d*) The amount of the discount, and

(*e*) The sum now payable.

This list, together with the Statement of Account received from the suppliers, will be submitted to the proprietor, or to some responsible official of the business, by whom the cheques issued in settlement will be signed.

BOOK-KEEPING ENTRIES

When the warehouseman issued goods to customers, it was seen at an earlier stage that he would be given credit for their value at **selling price,** the credit being given in 'Goods Sold' or **Sales** Account.

With the **payment** of cash, we have likewise to give **credit** to the cashier, which is only logical, having charged or **debited** him with cash **received.**

We shall, at the same time, **debit** the cash payment to each of the suppliers, thus offsetting the amounts for which they appear as **creditors,** and indicating that the liability of the business to them is now discharged.

For this purpose, **a Cash Paid Journal,** or Cash Paid Book, may be opened, as a Book of First Entry, ruled with columns for discount and the actual cash paid.

CASH PAID JOURNAL

Date	Supplier	Total	Discount	Cash
19x1 Feb. 23	L. Lindsay	£ 30·00	£ 0·75	£ 29·25

The record shown above indicates that a liability to L. Lindsay of £30 has been satisfied by a cash payment of £29·25 and that a profit of £0·75 has been earned.

The Cash Paid Journal enables us to:

(a) Charge or **debit each supplier** immediately on payment of money to him.

(b) **Credit** the **cashier** in total with the total cash payments, irrespective of the individual details.

This may be put in another way:

CASH PAID JOURNAL

(Book of First Entry)

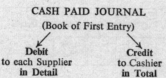

Debit   Credit
to each Supplier   to Cashier
in Detail   in Total

or in account form:

Fo. 2

CASH PAID JOURNAL

Date	Supplier	Total	Discount	Cash
19x1		£	£	£
Feb. 23	L. Lindsay	30·00	0·75	29·25
26	M. Morris	60·00	1·50	58·50
		£90·00	£2·25	£87·75

PURCHASE LEDGER

L. LINDSAY

DR.   CR.

Date	Details	C.P.J. Fo.	Amount	Date	Details	Fo:	Amount
19x1			£				
Feb. 23	Cash	2	29·25				
	Discount	2	0·75				
			£30·00				

M. MORRIS

Dʀ.							Cʀ.
Date	Details	C.P.J. Fo.	Amount	Date	Details	Fo.	Amount
19x1 Feb. 26	Cash Discount	2 2	£ 58·50 1·50				
			£60·00				

PRIVATE LEDGER
CASH

Dʀ.							Cʀ.
Date	Details	Fo.	Amount	Date	Details	C.P.J. Fo	Amount
				19x1 Feb. 28	Total Cash	2	£ 87·75

As the counterpart of cash received, but in the reverse direction, the Cash Account in the Private Ledger has a credit balance, which here denotes a **liability.** This will be clearer to us if we think of the banker of the business instead of its cashier. If he has paid money away on behalf of the business to its suppliers, the banker will have a claim upon it to that extent, and this claim is, of course, a liability of the business.

So far as the balances on the Ledger Accounts are concerned, the sum of the **debits** in the Purchase Ledger is seen to be £90, while the **credit** on Cash Account is £87·75.

The impersonal aspect of discount received, or discount earned, is that a profit of £2·25 has been made for which credit may be taken. We may therefore open, again in the Impersonal Ledger, the following account:

DISCOUNT RECEIVED

Dʀ.							Cʀ.
Date	Details	Fo.	Amount	Date	Details	C.P.J. Fo.	Amount
				19x1 Feb. 28	Total Discount	2	£ 2·25

Once more, the double entry is completed **within the Ledgers,**
and we see that a credit balance on an Impersonal Ledger Account is a business **profit,** a similar balance on a Private Ledger
Account being a **liability** of the business.

GOODS AND CASH COMPARED

(a) When **goods** are bought, **Purchases** Account is debited and
the individual suppliers credited; when **goods** are sold, the
individual customers are debited, and **Sales** Account is
credited.

In the Impersonal Ledger there are thus two accounts in
respect of the trading transactions, purchases and sales.

But in our **cash** dealings, recorded in total in the Private
Ledger, **we have only one cash account,** debited as regards
cash received and credited with cash paid.

(b) Goods purchased will be valued at **cost price** per unit, but
goods sold at **selling price.** Moreover, in a manufacturing
business at least, goods purchased may largely consist of raw
materials, while goods sold will be the finished product—an
essentially different article. With cash, however, whether it
be cash received or cash paid, the value per unit is the same
in a country having a stable currency.

For these reasons, we are able to **merge** our cash received
and our cash paid **in one account** only, or by using the figures
given above:

CASH

DR.							CR.
Date	Details	C.R.J. Fo.	Amount	Date	Details	C.P.J. Fo.	Amount
19x1 Feb. 28	Total Cash	1	£ 147·50	19x1 Feb. 28	Total Cash	2	£ 87·25

It is clear that the excess of the debit side, or £60·25, represents an **asset** of the business, while if the larger amount appeared
on the credit side, it would be a **liability.**

From this we may draw three conclusions:

(a) That instead of having two Books of First Entry, a Cash
Received Journal and a Cash Paid Journal, **one book will**

suffice, and we may call it the Cash Journal, or as is more usual the **Cash Book.**

(b) That if such is the case the Ledger Account for cash can be dispensed with, and because it contains all our cash receipts and payments, **the Cash Book is not only a Book of Prime Entry, but is also a Ledger Account,** in that,

(c) Whether the cashier or the banker is entrusted with the cash resources, **the position of the business in relation to either** can quickly be seen from a perusal of the Cash Book.

Proceeding on the basis that incoming cash remittances are banked intact on the day of receipt, and all payments are made by cheque, writing up the Cash Book daily as a Book of First Entry is equivalent to writing up the Ledger Account with the bank.

If, however, a minimum amount of cash must be retained by the business in order to pay petty expenses, and if, also, wages and salaries have to be paid in cash and not by cheque, it is necessary to provide **additional columns** in the Cash Book to record purely cash, as distinct from banking transactions.

We may now take an example to make this clear:

Example

From the following particulars, draw up the three-column Cash Book of V. Treat. No posting to the Ledger is required and no money is to be paid into the bank unless and until instructions are given.

19x1

Jan. 1 Commenced business with cash in hand £21 and cash at bank £175.

2 Paid into bank out of office cash £17.

3 Cash sales £36.

4 Drew cheque £10 for private use; paid Wages by cash £6.

5 Paid Rent by cheque £22.

6 Paid into bank additional capital £110.

8 Received a cheque from Light Bros. £22 in settlement of their account of £22·75

9 Paid Brown & Sons cheque for £48, receiving discount £2·55.

CASH BOOK

V. TREAT

Dr.

Date		Fo.	Discount	Cash	Bank
19x1					
Jan. 1	Capital A/c			21·00	175·00
2	Cash				17·00
3	Cash Sales			36·00	
6	Capital A/c				110·00
8	Light Bros.		0·75	22·00	
10	Bilton, Ltd.		0·50	14·00	
11	Bank			28·00	
12	Cash, cheques per contra,				36·00
16	Light Bros. discount charged		[0·75]*		
			£0·50	£121·00	£338·00
19x1					
Feb. 1	Balances b/d			62·00	111·50

Cr.

Date		Fo.	Discount	Cash	Bank
19x1					
Jan. 2	Bank			17·00	
4	Drawings				10·00
4	Wages			6·00	
5	Rent				22·00
9	Brown & Sons		2·55		48·00
11	Cash				28·00
12	Bank, cheques from Light Bros. and Bilton, Ltd.			36·00	
13	Jennens, Ltd.		5·00		95·00
16	Light Bros. cheque returned.				22·00
31	Interest and Bank charges				1·50
31	Balances c/d			62·00	111·50
			£7·55	£121·00	£338·00

* When Light Bros.' cheque is returned the discount previously allowed to him must be *deducted* from discounts allowed and *debited* to his account.

Jan. 10 Received a cheque from Bilton, Ltd., value £14, in settlement of their account £14·50.

 11 Drew cheque £28 for office use.

 12 Paid into bank the two cheques received from Light Bros. and Bilton, Ltd., respectively.

 13 Paid Jennens, Ltd., cheque £95, having deducted discount 5% from their account.

 16 Light Bros. cheque was returned by the bank marked R/D.

 31 Interest and bank charges for the month £1·50.

Balance off the Cash Book and bring down the balances as on January 31, 19x1.

If we look more closely at this example, we shall see that provision is made in the columns headed 'Cash' and 'Bank' respectively for a statement at any time of the position of the business as regards:

(a) its cashier, and

(b) its banker.

At the beginning of the month the proprietor introduced as Cash Capital £196, divided as shown, and the description of the item 'Capital A/c' indicates that that is the Account in the Ledger which is to be credited.

In addition, during the month, as we should expect, cheques are drawn on the Bank Account in order to replenish the moneys in the hands of the cashier. It should not be difficult for us to realise what happens in this case. Firstly, the bank pays out money, and thereby reduces its accountability to the proprietor of the business. For this it must be **credited**, but, simultaneously, the accountability of the **cashier** is increased, and so, on the left hand, or debit side of the Cash Book we enter the amount of £28 in the **cash** column.

Secondly, in our wording of the items in the Cash Book, we must be careful to choose words which will indicate at once **where the corresponding (debit or credit) entry is to be found.** For example, on January 2, when money is paid **from cash** into the bank, we say on the **credit side,** 'Bank,' indicating that the bank column is to be charged with the amount.

Thirdly, when a cheque received from a customer is returned by the bank marked R/D (refer to drawer, or Light Bros.) we must bring the Cash Book into line with the bank's own view of the position, and having **charged** the bank with £22 on January 12 now give them credit on January 16. We thus cancel the original charge to the bank and, **to complete the double entry within the Ledgers,** post the amount to the **debit** of Light Bros.' Account, thereby reviving the original debt due from them. Their position is thus what it was before the worthless cheque was received.

Fourthly, we see that columns are provided in which to record cash discount **allowed** and **received.** When the cheque from Light Bros. was first received on January 8, £0·75 was allowed to them as discount, the **total** due by them being £22·75. But as their cheque is returned on January 16 it is not enough merely to credit the bank with the amount of the **cheque;** we must in addition write back to Light Bros. the discount which was, of course, only allowed by the business in the belief that the cheque was good.

And lastly, credit is given to the bank for interest and charges made by them for the month. They will, **in their own books,** have debited the business with this sum, and in order that the two sets of records shall be in agreement, this entry must be made.

In the result, and on January 31, balances can be inserted on the **credit side** of the Cash Book (representing the amount by which the debit side exceeds the credit side) and **brought down** on February 1, as the **opening balances** for the new period. The balances, it will be noted, are in both cases **debit balances,** indicating the existence of an Asset in the form of:

(a) Cash in hand £62, and

(b) Cash at bank £111·50.

Before we pass from this example let us look at the **Discount Allowed** and **Discount Received** Accounts in the Impersonal Ledger.

DISCOUNT ALLOWED

Dr.							Cr.
Date	Details	Fo.	Amount	Date	Details	Fo.	Amount
19x1 Jan. 31	Total for Month		£ 0·50				

DISCOUNT RECEIVED

DR.   CR.

Date	Details	Fo.	Amount	Date	Details	Fo.	Amount
				19x1 Jan. 31	Total for Month		£ 7·55

To deal with the former, we notice that while both the cheques
received from, **and** the discount allowed to Light Bros. and
Bilton, Ltd., appear on the **debit** side of the Cash Book these
customers will each receive **credit** for the **total** in their respective
Ledger Accounts. But only the amount of the **actual money** they
pay is debited in the cash and bank columns. Accordingly, to
complete the double entry, we must have in the Impersonal
Ledger an account for **discounts allowed,** in which the further
debit required will be shown.

Let us take one other

Example

John Smith, a merchant, does not pay all cash received into his
bank. He desires to record all cash received and paid and all his
bank transactions in one Cash Book. His transactions during the
first few days of January, 19x2, were as under:

		£
19x2		
Jan. 1	Cash in hand	150
	Bank overdraft	72
	Received cash from A.B. (after allowing him discount £1)	15
2	Paid into bank	145
3	Drew cheque for C.D. (after deducting discount £3)	27
4	Received cheque from E.F. (after allowing him discount £30) and paid it into bank	270
5	Drew from bank in cash	20
	Paid wages (on presentation of an open cheque at bank)	30
7	E.F.'s cheque returned by bank, dishonoured.	
8	Received cash from G.H. (after allowing discount £2)	48
9	Paid into bank	25
10	Paid cash to J.K. (after deducting discount £4)	36
11	Cheque book received from bank	1

JAMES SMITH

CASH BOOK

Dr.   JANUARY, 19x2 Cr.

Date	Receipts	Discount	Cash	Bank	Date	Payments	Discount	Cash	Bank
19x2		£	£	£	19x2		£	£	£
Jan. 1	Balance b/d		150·00		Jan. 1	Balance b/d			72·00
1	A.B.	1·00	15·00		2	Bank		145·00	
2	Cash			145·00	3	C.D.	3·00		27·00
4	E.F.	30·00		270·00	5	Cash			20·00
5	Bank		20·00		5	Wages			30·00
7	E.F. discount not allowed	[30·00]*			7	E.F. cheque returned			270·00
8	G.H.	2·00	48·00		9	Bank	4·00	25·00	
9	Cash			25·00	10	J.K.		36·00	
					11	Bank charges, Cheque Book			1·00
					11	Balances c/d		27·00	20·00
		£3·00	£233·00	£440·00			£7·00	£233·00	£440·00
19x2 Jan. 12	Balances b/d		27·00	20·00					

Debited to   Credited to
'Discount Allowed' Account   'Discount Received' Account

* When E.F.'s cheque is returned the discount previously allowed to him, £30, must be recharged to him. It is therefore *deducted* in the discounts allowed column and *debited* to E.F.'s account.

You are required (a) to record these transactions in a suitable form of Cash Book; (b) to rule off and balance the book; (c) to state clearly how the discounts are dealt with in the Ledger.

CASH BOOK POSTINGS TO LEDGER ACCOUNTS

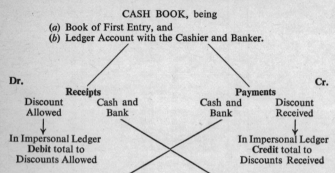

CASH BOOK, being
(a) Book of First Entry, and
(b) Ledger Account with the Cashier and Banker.

Dr.   Cr.

Receipts   **Payments**
Discount   Cash and   Cash and   Discount
Allowed   Bank   Bank   Received

In Impersonal Ledger   In Impersonal Ledger
Debit total to   **Credit** total to
Discounts Allowed   Discounts Received

(a) In Purchase Ledger **debit** to individual suppliers.

(b) In Impersonal Ledger **debit** to Wages, Cash Purchases or other Expense Accounts.

(c) In Private Ledger **debit** to Asset Accounts (if purchased) or Liability Accounts if paid off or reduced.

(a) In Sales Ledger **credit** to individual customers.

(b) In Impersonal Ledger **credit** to Bank Interest Received, Cash Sales, or other Income Accounts.

(c) In Private Ledger **credit** to Asset Accounts (if sold) or Liability Accounts if, e.g. money borrowed, or new capital introduced.

TESTS AND QUESTIONS

1 Say what benefits a trader will derive from his having an account at a bank, and explain how he would open the account.

2 Define trade discount and cash discount. State clearly how these are treated in books of account.

3 What is a cheque? What is the effect of crossing it? How many parties are there to a cheque?

4 A trader receives an account from X.Y., his landlord, for £75 in respect of one quarter's rent, which he pays on the date of receipt.
   Explain the different ways which might be adopted to record this item in books kept on the Double Entry System.

5 From the following particulars write up A. Bondman's Cash Book
   for the week commencing July 5, 19x1, and balance the Cash Book
   as at July 10, 19x1:

July 5 Cash in hand £15·50, and in bank £176.
      5 Paid by cheque to F. Abbot his account of £47, less 5%
         cash discount
      6 Paid in cash, postage stamps £2, new typewriter ribbon
         £0·75.
      7 Purchased goods for cheque £10·50.
         Received cheque from R. Beal in payment of his account
         of £40, less 2½% cash discount, and paid the cheque into
         bank.
      8 Purchased for cheque new office desk £30.
     10 Paid wages in cash £120.
         Cash sales for week £150·75.
         Withdrew from bank for office purposes £20.
         Withdrew from bank for self £15.
   Post the items in your Cash Book to the Ledger.

6 Leslie Morris commences business on January 1, 19x1. Record in
   a suitable ruled Cash Book the following transactions for the first
   week of January, 19x1, and bring down the balances on January 7:

19x1		£
Jan. 1	L. Morris paid into bank on account of Capital	700·00
2	Received and paid into bank direct the following:	
	Jones (after allowing discount £5)	45·00
	Wilson (after allowing discount £0·50)	12·50
	Graham (after allowing discount £0·75)	15·00
2	Draw cheque for office cash	40·00
4	Wilson's cheque returned by bank unpaid.	
5	Drew cheque for	330·00

		£	
	Covering Wages	£300·00	
	Salaries	30·00	

5	Bought goods for cash	25·00
6	Received the following (in notes):	
	Peters, covering goods	£250·00	
	Rent receivable	10·00	
	Sanders (after allowing discount £1)	60·00	
			320·00
6	Paid cash into bank	300·00
7	Paid by cheque:	
	Lister (after deducting discount £0·50)	19·50
	White (after deducting discount £1·50)	58·50

How would you deal with the totals of the columns Discounts Allowed, and Discounts Received, when the Cash Book is ruled off on January 7, 19x1.

7 On June 20, 19x1, H. Rivers received from S. Wells an invoice for £514. Of this amount £510 represented the cost of goods purchased and £4 the carriage thereon.

On June 30, 19x1, H. Rivers returned to S. Wells goods to the value of £60.

After the invoice had been entered in the books, it was discovered that a trade discount of 20% had not been deducted from the cost or from the item relating to goods returned and an adjusting entry was made to correct these mistakes.

The account was paid by cheque on July 31, 19x1, less 2½% discount.

You are required to show the entries in the respective books of account of H. Rivers to record the foregoing transactions.

8 From the following particulars write up the Cash Book of Thomas Mixture for the month of January, 19x2, and bring down the balances at the end of the month. It is not Mr. Mixture's rule to bank all cash and make all payments by cheque.

19x2		£
Jan.	1 Cash in hand	18·00
	1 Balance overdrawn at bank	36·75
	2 Received cash sales	42·50
	4 Banked cash	15·00
	4 Paid Jackson & Co. by cheque	14·25
	5 Received Jones' cheque (direct to bank)	14·50
	6 Paid salaries in cash	34·75
	7 Bought goods for cash (paid from office cash)	11·00
	8 Drew office cash from bank	16·00
	9 Received cash sales	25·50
	13 Paid salaries in cash	33·50
	16 Received Smith's cheque at bank	56·75
	20 Paid Brown by cheque	16·00
	20 Received from Jones in coin	55·50
	20 Paid salaries in cash	34·75
	23 Draw office cash from bank	35·00
	26 Received Jones' cheque (direct to bank)	17·50
	27 Paid salaries in cash	34·75
	27 Paid office cash into bank	20·00
	28 Jones' cheque returned by bank unpaid	17·50

9 The Cash Book of Thomas Jones for the first week of January, 19x1, is as follows:

19x1		Discount £	Bank £	19x1		Discount £	Bank £
Jan. 1	Balance		752·00	Jan. 3	Wages		59·00
2	Sundry Customers:			5	Sundry Suppliers:		
	L. Smith	1·00	39·00		G. Green	3 00	57·00
	V. Latham	4·00	76·00		T. Robson	2·00	78·00
4	Rents Receivable		17·00	5	V. Latham cheque		
6	Plant A/c (machine				returned		76·00
	tool sold)		26·00	6	Cash Purchases		18·00
		£5·00	£910·00			£5·00	£288·00

You are required:

(a) To indicate to which Ledger each entry in the above Cash Book would be posted.

(b) To make the Cash postings in such Ledger Accounts, including the Discount Account.

10 From the following particulars you are required to write up the three-column Cash Book of K. Walker. No posting to the Ledger is required:

19x1

Mar. 1 Cash in hand £46·50.

1 Overdrawn at bank £93·60.

2 Paid into bank £30·00.

3 Paid wages by cash £41·50.

4 Received cheque from R. Francis value £35·75 in settlement of an amount owing £37·00.

4 Cash sales £153·60.

4 Received a cheque from M. Scott £23·75, and allowed him discount £0·75.

5 Paid S. Marsh by cheque the balance of his account £34·00, less 5% discount.

5 Cash purchases £33·00.

6 Paid cheques from R. Francis and M. Scott into the bank.

8 K. Walker paid into the bank additional capital £240·00.

9 Drew cheque £36·00 for office use.

10 Paid L. Hopecraft cheque £18·80, being allowed discount £0·80.

Mar. 10 M. Scott's cheque was returned by the bank marked R/D.
      11 Drew cheque £15·00 for private use.
      11 Bought plant and machinery £370·00 and paid the amount
          by cheque.
      12 Paid sundry small expenses by cash £16·40.
      31 Bank charges £7·20.

Balance the Cash Book as on March 31 and bring down the
balances.

CHAPTER V

THE BANK RECONCILIATION

It is the practice of banks to render periodically to their customers, whether they are business houses or private individuals, a statement of their position in relation to the bank. This statement is a copy of the customer's account in the bank's Ledger, and usually will be rendered from the bank's standpoint. That is to say, moneys paid in, or **lodgments** by the customer will be put to his credit, and moneys withdrawn by cheque will be debited to him. Thus, at any time, there will be a balance either in favour of or against the customer.

Before the use of book-keeping machines became general, **Bank Pass Books** were issued to all new customers, the items in which were written up by the bank for the customer to compare with the bank columns in his own Cash Book. He could thus satisfy himself that:

(a) The bank had given him credit for all moneys which he had debited to it in his Cash Book.

(b) Similarly, when the bank **debited him** with paid cheques, he could see that the name of the payee and the amount for which the cheque had been drawn were also in agreement with the **credit** side of his Cash Book.

At intervals it was, of course, necessary for the Pass Book to be returned to the bank in order to be written up to date.

In many cases today, however, the bank's statement is rendered in the form of **loose sheets,** which the customer can insert in a suitable cover or binder, so that he has a continuous record of the bank's version of the position between them.

We have seen elsewhere that it is the custom for suppliers of goods to the business to render statements of account which are valuable corroborative evidence of the accuracy of the Purchase Ledger Accounts.

This being the case, the importance of a similar statement as regards cash itself—the most liquid asset of the business—can readily be appreciated, more particularly if the bank is the **creditor** of the business, as on loan or overdraft account to which a limit has been set.

The occasions on which a bank makes a mistake in writing up the Pass Book or loose sheets are rare indeed, but we do not infrequently find that at times mistakes are made by the cashier in the **Cash Book,** and also in **omitting to record** some particular receipt or payment.

Many banks, to prevent lack of agreement between their own records and the Cash Books of their customers, print at the bottom of each Pass Book sheet:

'The items and balance shown on this statement should be verified and the bank notified promptly of any discrepancy.'

In ordinary business practice, it is the custom to rule off and balance the Cash Book at monthly intervals, bringing down the ascertained balance to the beginning of the new period. To the extent that it refers to the bank columns in the Cash Book, this balance represents:

either   (*a*) Cash at bank   (Dr.)
or   (*b*) Bank overdraft   (Cr.)

and as such will certainly be required for the information of the proprietor of the business, or of the Board of Directors in a Limited Company.

It will, therefore, be the cashier's duty to prepare at the end of each month what is termed a **bank reconciliation,** or **bank agreement,** attesting the accuracy and completeness of his Cash Book records.

In the affairs of a private individual, this reconciliation may be easily and quickly prepared; it may be the work of a few minutes only, but with a business house, where lodgments are being made daily throughout the month, and the number of cheques drawn by the business is very large, the labour involved may be much greater.

We must now consider the nature of the work to be done,

bearing in mind that the **Pass Book** shows the position of the business **in the light of the information in the bank's possession.**

Supposing the reconciliation is to be prepared on January 31, we may commence with the **Pass Book balance** at that date, using a sheet of cash-ruled paper which we can later file away for future reference. Our task is then to **reconcile** or **agree** this balance with the balance appearing in the **Cash Book.**

If, as is usually the case, there is a difference between the two balances, it may be due to:

(*a*) **Cheques drawn and issued by the business to its suppliers** and entered in the proper way on the credit side of the Cash Book, **but not yet presented** by the collecting banker for payment.

As the cheques so drawn have to be sent to suppliers, banked by them, and subsequently passed through the clearing, several days may elapse before they reach the paying bank. We must thus **deduct** from the Pass Book balance if favourable to the business, the amount of the unpresented cheques, or **add** if an overdraft exists. On the other hand, if we have begun by taking the **Cash Book figure,** we should add the amount to a debit balance, or deduct it from a credit balance.

(*b*) **Cheques paid in by the business** which on presentation to the paying bank are refused because of, e.g.:

1 Lack of funds to meet them.
2 Countermand of instructions to pay by the Drawer.
3 Death of the Drawer.
4 Some irregularity on the face of the cheque, such as absence of Drawer's signature, inacceptable endorsement, etc.

In these cases, the collecting banker, having given credit when the cheque was lodged, will now **debit the account,** returning the unpaid cheque to the business. The latter will at once take up the matter with its own customer, and endeavour to obtain satisfaction.

In any event, as we saw on page 65, the cashier should credit the bank with the amount involved, i.e. enter it as though it were a payment on the credit side of the Cash Book. Should he have omitted to do this, for purposes of the reconciliation he must, if beginning with a favourable **Pass Book** balance, add the amount, or deduct it if unfavourable.

In beginning with the **Cash Book,** the reverse steps would of course be taken.

(*c*) 1 **Bank interest allowed.**

2 **Bank interest and commission charged.**

We have already explained these items as representing, so far as the business is concerned, either a **profit** or an **expense.**

The bank will enter them in its own account with the customer at half-yearly intervals, as on June 30 and December 31, but does not usually give the customer a separate advice that it has done so. Accordingly, the latter may be altogether unaware of the items until he receives his Pass Book. The proper course is then to **debit** the Bank Column in the Cash Book with the interest allowed by the bank, or **credit** it with the interest and commission charged.

If this has not been done, we shall proceed as follows in preparing the Bank Reconciliation:

Interest Allowed

(*a*) **Commencing with the Pass Book balance.**

If 'in favour', deduct.

If overdrawn, add.

(*b*) **Commencing with Cash Book balance.**

If a debit balance, add.

If overdrawn, deduct.

The reverse, of course, applies with interest and commission charged, i.e.:

(*a*) **Commencing with Pass Book balance.**

If 'in favour', add.

If overdrawn, deduct.

(*b*) **Commencing with Cash Book balance.**

If a debit balance, deduct.

If overdrawn, add.

In making these adjustments, we must always remember **the aim in view, which is to link the Pass Book balance with the Cash**

Book balance, or vice-versa. Whether we begin with the Pass Book or the Cash Book does not affect the result, but the former may give the more reliable commencing figure, as it is so much less subject to the risk of error.

Example

The balance shown by the Bank Statement on March 31, 19x7, indicates an overdraft of £20·98, while, on the same date, the Bank Column in the Cash Book shows a credit balance of £41·90.

Comparing the two records, you find that two cheques drawn on March 31, one for £20·40 and the other for £7·72, had not been presented for payment, while one of £7·20 paid into the bank on the same date had not yet been credited.

Prepare a Reconciliation Statement.

	£	£
Overdrawn per Pass Book		20·98
Add cheques drawn but unpresented:		
March 31	20·40	
„ 31	7·72	
		28·12
		49·10
Less cheque paid in but not yet credited		7·20
Credit balance as per Cash Book		£41·90

In this second illustration, we will begin instead with the balance according to the **Cash Book.**

Example

On March 30, 19x5, your Cash Book shows that you have in the bank the sum of £817·24.

On checking your Cash Book with the Bank Pass Book you find that cheques drawn by you amounting to £214·17 have not passed through the bank, that a cheque for £84·12 has not yet been credited to you, and that the bank has credited you with interest £22·07, and debited you with discount and other charges

£14·36. Draw up a reconciliation statement, showing adjustments between your Cash Book and Bank Pass Book.

	£
Balance in hand per Cash Book	817·24
Add cheques drawn but unpresented	214·17
	1031·41
Less cheque paid in but not credited	84·12
	947·29
Add interest credited by bank	22·07
	969·36
Less discount and other charges made by bank	14·36
Balance per Pass Book	£955·00

Here we see that only the balance per Cash Book is given, and that we have to calculate the Pass Book figure.

Our third illustration introduces other kinds of error in the Cash Book:

Example

From the following particulars, prepare a reconciliation of the Bank Pass Book balance with the Cash Book balance.

	£
Balance per Pass Book in favour	60·00
Balance per Cash Book overdrawn	80·00
Unpresented cheques	144·00
Uncleared cheques inwards	26·00

Further,

(a) A cheque for £20 paid to J. Jones has been entered in error in the Cash Column of the Cash Book.

(b) The debit side of the Cash Book (Bank Column) has been undercast by £50.

(c) The cashier has omitted to record bank commission of £8.

If we decide to begin with the **Pass Book** figure:

	£
Balance per Pass Book (in favour)	60·00
Adjust unpresented cheques	144·00
i.e. when presented there will be an **overdraft** of	84·00
Less uncleared cheques	26·00
(Paid in but not credited by bank)	
	58·00
Less cheque to J. Jones	20·00
(As this has been paid by the bank and will appear	
in the Pass Book)	38·00
Less Commission	8·00
(Charged by the bank and appearing in the Pass	
Book)	30·00
Add undercast in Bank Column of Cash Book	50·00
Overdrawn per Cash Book	£80·00

If we preferred, we could begin instead with the **Cash Book**:

	£
Overdrawn per Cash Book	80·00
Adjust unpresented cheques	144·00
(Drawn and entered in Cash Book but not in	
Pass Book)	
Favourable balance of	64·00
Less uncleared cheques	26·00
(Paid in but not credited in Pass Book)	
	38·00
Less cheque to J. Jones	20·00
(Paid by bank and therefore appearing in	
Pass Book)	18·00
Less commission charged by bank	8·00
	10·00
Add undercast in Bank Column of Cash Book	50·00
Balance per Pass Book (in favour)	£60·00

TESTS AND QUESTIONS

1   Upon a cashier obtaining the Pass Book from the bank, he finds
    that the amount of the overdraft appearing therein differs from that
    shown by his Cash Book.
       Give the possible explanations of this difference and, using your
    own figures, prepare a statement showing how the two amounts
    would be reconciled.

2   On January 1, 19x4, a trader obtained his Pass Book and on com-
    paring it with his Cash Book discovered that all items agreed
    except the following:

    (a) Cheques drawn and entered in the Cash Book, totalling £317·28,
        had not been presented at the bank.

    (b) A country cheque for £17·50, lodged the previous day, did not
        appear in the Pass Book.

    (c) The Pass Book showed an item of interest on overdraft amount-
        ing to £7·16 not entered in the Cash Book.

    (d) The trader had, in December, discounted with the bank bills of
        exchange for £1 200 and entered this amount in his Cash
        Book. The proceeds credited, as shown by the Pass Book,
        amounted to £1 193·07.

    The trader's Cash Book showed a balance, on December 31, 19x3,
    of £219·87 overdrawn.
       State (a) what balance the Pass Book showed on the same day,
    and (b) what would be the balance of the trader's Cash Book after
    making the necessary additional entries.

3   On June 30, 19x6, a trader's Cash Book showed his bank balance
    to be £71·18 overdrawn.
       On procuring his Pass Book from the bank he found that a country
    cheque for £19·50, lodged by him on June 29 had not yet been
    credited by the bank, four cheques drawn on June 30, amount-
    ing in total to £181·34, had not yet been presented for payment,
    and the bank on June 30 had entered a charge of £10·27 for com-
    mission and interest.
       Draw up a statement showing the balance as shown by the Pass
    Book.

4   From the following particulars prepare a statement showing how
    the differences between the Cash Book balance and the Pass Book
    balance is reconciled:

	£
Pass Book balance—June 30, 19x1	1 401·62
Cash Book balance—June 30, 19x1	557·51

Cheques drawn prior to June 30, 19x1, but not presented until after that date:

	£
P.	29·20
Q.	801·17
R.	5·73
S.	132·32

	£
Country cheques paid into the bank on June 30, 19x1, not collected until July 2, 19x1	116·20
Bank charges and interest to June 30, 19x1, not entered in the Cash Book	8·12

5 On November 30, 19x2, the Cash Book of E. Simpson disclosed a debit balance of £212, and his Bank Pass Book at the same date a balance in his favour of £261.

Prepare a bank reconciliation at November 30, taking into account that a cheque payable to E. Simpson in respect of a 4% dividend (less tax at 25%) on his holding of 1 000 ordinary shares of £1 each in Greystones Foundry, Ltd., was entered in the Cash Book on November 30, but not credited in the Pass Book until December 1, and that cheques drawn by E. Simpson on November 28, as follows, were not presented at the bank by the payees until December 3.

	£
H. Simpson, salary	8·33
Corporation electric supply	35·68
Trade Supplies, Ltd. (a creditor)	35·00

6 On December 31, 19x9, John Smith found that his Bank Pass Book showed a balance in the bank of £88·62, whereas according to his Ledger his Bank Account was overdrawn by £57·69. On checking over the figures he discovered that the following cheques had not been presented:

	£
Wilkins & Co.	96·17
Turnbull & Snow	63·00
Samuel & Son	85·50

while a payment in of £90 on December 31 had not yet been credited by the bank, and the bank's charges for the half-year amounting to £8·36 had not been entered in his Ledger.

How would John Smith reconcile his Ledger with the Pass Book, and how would this affect his accounts?

7 A. Shiner's Cash Book for July, 19x6, is as follows:

DR.					CR.
19x6		£	19x6		£
June 30	Balance	817·22	July 3	Lomas & Co.	151·23
July 4	J. Bell	15·75	8	Smith, Ltd.	32·00
9	Salt & Son	92·53	10	C. Jervis	1·84
18	Williams, Ltd.	1·22	20	Evans & Co.	10·91
29	E. Harris	81·17	27	P.M.G. Telephones	5·32
31	James & Co.	14·81	29	D. Greene	1·80
			30	J. Johnson	84·89
			31	Kenrick, Ltd.	25·72

His Bank Pass Book shows for August, 19x6, the following:

19x6		£	19x6		£
July 31	Balance	806·59	Aug. 3	Kenrick Ltd.	25·72
Aug. 2	James & Co.	14·81	6	F. David	10·53
3	Saul & Co.	100·78	7	D. Greene	1·80
			7	J. Johnson	84·89

Prepare a Bank Agreement as at July 31, 19x6.

8 At January 31, 19x8, the Cash Book of Hugh Gibson showed a
balance overdrawn of £117, while according to his Bank Pass Book
at that date there was a balance in his favour of £72. A comparison
of the two records revealed the following:

(a) A cheque for £25 sent to B. Murray had been entered in the
cash column of the Cash Book.

(b) Bank charges of £17 at December 31, 19x7, were not entered
at all in the Cash Book.

(c) The Bank had debited Gibson's Account with a cheque for £11
received from D. Carter, which had been returned dishonoured.
The fact of dishonour was not shown in the Cash Book.

(d) The Bank Column on the Receipts side of the Cash Book was
found to be undercast £10.

(e) Unpresented cheques amounted to £232.

You are required to prepare the Bank Reconciliation at January
31, 19x8, in proper form, setting out your adjustments clearly.

9 A cash book which you are examining shows a balance at the bank
on May 31, 19x4, of £1 531·11. The Bank Pass Book at the same
date shows a different balance. Your investigations reveal: —

A cheque drawn for £12·31 was entered in the Cash Book as
£13·21.

An item for goods sold £125·48 which had been settled on April
30 had been entered in full whereas the customer had deducted
£5·10 discount.

On page 70 of the Cash Book the receipts side was short cast £100.

A lodgement amounting to £7·44 in respect of cash sales was not
entered in the Cash Book.

A cheque amounting to £159·27 received from a customer, who

subsequently went bankrupt, had been returned by the bank but no entry of the return had been made in the Cash Book.

Cheques amounting in all to £394·60 issued to creditors and entered in the Cash Book had not been presented for payment at May 31, 19x4.

Cheques paid into the bank on June 2 amounting to £954·81 were entered in the Cash Book on May 31.

Make the appropriate adjustments to the Cash Book balance and prepare a statement reconciling it with the balance in the Pass Book.

CHAPTER VI

PETTY CASH, ETC.

We have seen that the general rule in cash transactions is to pay all cash received into bank on the day of receipt, and to make all payments by cheque.

We have also seen that as regards wages and salaries payable by the business to its workpeople and staff, some departure from this rule is inevitable, although in the first instance a cheque is issued to the Cashier in order that he may obtain the necessary notes and coin from the bank.

It is, however, necessary in all businesses, irrespective of their type or size, to make provision for the payment in notes or coin of a great variety of *small amounts* which may be regarded as sundry or incidental expenses. They are usually termed **Petty Cash payments,** and must receive our attention because:

(a) They recur at regular intervals.

(b) It is usually impracticable to issue a cheque in payment of any one of them.

(c) The person receiving payment may be an employee of the business.

(d) In total they may amount, period by period, to a not inconsiderable sum.

From the standpoint of the business it is most desirable to separate the records of Petty Cash payments from the main Cash Book records. It would clearly be inconvenient to have the latter cumbered with a large number of miscellaneous small payments and for this reason, **as a separate book of prime entry,** it is usual to keep a Petty Cash Book, the responsibility for the entries in which, and for the **Petty Cash balance,** may be entrusted to the Cashier or, in the case of a large business, to one of his assistants.

Weekly or monthly, the latter may be handed a sum in cash thought sufficient to meet all demands for the selected period. He will then submit a list of his payments to the Cashier and receive a sum to replenish his reduced cash balance.

It is often made a rule that the Petty Cashier shall take a receipt for each payment, and frequently specially printed forms bearing the name of the business are provided for this to be done. These receipt forms, when completed with the name of the recipient, and details of the amount and nature of the expense, are preserved by the Petty Cashier as independent evidence of payment.

To permit of a suitable classification of expense items, the Petty Cash Book may be ruled with **analysis columns** into which the total paid can be extended. This facilitates the subsequent posting of the analysis columns to the Impersonal and other Ledger Accounts.

Example

On March 1, £20 cash was handed to the Petty Cashier to pay Petty Cash expenses for the month, which were as follows:

		£
Mar. 1	Postage stamps	2·00
3	Carriage	0·23
4	Bus fare	0·03
5	Shorthand note books	0·52
6	Postage stamps	1·00
8	Fare to London	1·25
9	Sundry trade expenses	0·51
11	Pencils	0·14
14	Telephone call	0·05
16	Envelopes	0·25
18	Stationery	0·87
31	Carriage	0·72

Rule a Petty Cash Book in analysis form, with five analysis columns, headed Postages and Telephone, Carriage, Travelling Expenses, Stationery and Sundry Trade Expenses respectively. Enter the foregoing items and close the books as on March 31, showing clearly the balance of cash in hand.

PETTY CASH BOOK

Dr. Cash Received	Date	Details	Receipt No.	Total	Postages and Telephone	Carriage	Travelling Expenses	Stationery	Cr. Sundry Trade Expenses
£ 20·00	19x3 Mar. 1	Per Cashier		£	£	£	£	£	£ £
	Mar. 1	Brown, Stamps	1	2·00	2·00				
	3	Collins, Carriage	2	0·23		0·23			
	4	Hunt, Fares	3	0·03			0·03		
	5	White, Notebooks	4	0·52				0·52	
	6	Brown, Stamps	5	1·00	1·00				
	8	Lyle, Rail fare, London	6	1·25			1·25		
	9	Sundry expenses	7	0·51					0·51
	11	White, Pencils	8	0·14				0·14	
	14	Hunt, Trunk Call	9	0·05	0·05				
	16	White, Envelopes	10	0·25				0·25	
	18	White, Stationery	11	0·87				0·87	
	31	British Rail, Carriage	12	0·72		0·72			
				7·57	3·05	0·95	1·28	1·78	0·51
	31	Balance	c/d	12·43					
£20·00				£20·00					
12·43	Apr. 1	Balance	b/d						

As regards the above, it should be noted that in certain cases, e.g. Rail Fares, the nature of the payment does not permit of a receipt being obtained from an outside source. For this reason, the employee receiving the money should be required to fill up a Voucher Form giving the required details, but wherever possible an independent receipt should always be procured and filed with the firm's voucher.

Further, **like the main Cash Book,** the Petty Cash Book is not only a book of First Entry; it is also a Ledger Account with the **Petty Cashier.** In other words, he is debited with what he receives, and given credit for what he pays away on behalf of the business. The balance of £12·43 is therefore the sum for which he is accountable at the end of the month. Since credit is given to him personally for his payments, it remains to consider **their effect upon the business.** Impersonally, the business must be debited with the **totals** of the expenses set out in the analysis columns, for each one of which an account will be opened in the **Impersonal Ledger.** With Postages and Telephones we should have, for example:

POSTAGES AND TELEPHONES

DR.							CR.
Date	Details	P.C.B. Fo.	Amount	Date	Details	Fo.	Amount
19x3 Mar. 31	Petty Cash Total	1	£ 3·05				

IMPREST SYSTEM

As applied to Petty Cash, this means that a definite sum of money, say £20, is handed to the Petty Cashier and at the end of the week or month he is reimbursed the **amount expended,** e.g. £7·57 in the above example. His Petty Cash balance is thus restored to its original figure.

The merits of the system are that:

(a) At any time actual cash, or vouchers and receipts should be available for the imprest of £20.

(*b*) As the periodic reimbursements are the actual expenses paid,
and not mere advances on account only, they are as such
brought prominently to the notice of the Chief Cashier or
other responsible official of the business.

POSTAGE BOOK

It will be observed that in the last example an analysis column
headed 'Postages' was provided in the Petty Cash Book.

This is a typical Petty Cash payment, recurring at regular
intervals. The employee of the business having the custody of the
stamp money may or may not be the Petty Cashier, but in any
case it is desirable to have a record of the outgoing mail.

For this purpose it is customary to use a **Stamp Book** or
Postage Book, of which the following is a suitable ruling:

Date	Cash Received	Name of Addressee	Town	Stamps used
	£			£

The Postage Book may be properly described as a **Memorandum Book** whose purpose is to amplify and serve as a check upon
the payments appearing in the 'Stamps' column. It does not
form a part of the Double Entry System.

The Petty Cashier, when making each payment, should himself enter the **date** and **amount** in the first two columns, and it
should be expected that the difference between the **'Cash Received'** column and the **'Stamps Used'** column represents either
the value of stamps in hand and unused or, alternatively, the
balance of cash in hand available for their purchase.

It is desirable that when further advances are made for buying
stamps, the Postage Book should be produced to the Petty
Cashier and initialled by him after seeing that it is written up to
date and verifying the balance shown.

TESTS AND QUESTIONS

1 Assuming that you are handing over to a junior your duties as Petty Cashier, write short and concise instructions as to his duties, and how they are to be performed.

2 Give a ruling for a Petty Cash Book with separate analysis columns for wages, national insurance, postage and stationery, and office expenses.

  Insert sufficient entries to illustrate fully the method of using a book of this description and briefly explain its advantages.

3 Give a ruling for an analysed form of Petty Cash Book; insert specimen entries for a short period and show what postings are made.

  How would you deal with any exceptional payments not falling under one of the columnar headings provided for?

4 What is the Imprest System of dealing with Petty Cash?

  Rule a columnar Petty Cash Book illustrating the principle, and insert *three* entries therein.

CHAPTER VII

THE DEBIT AND CREDIT JOURNAL

Question

You said on page 12 that the Journal in its earliest form was still used for certain purposes, and that it would be referred to at a later stage?

Answer

Yes, and for the reason that while the majority of the transactions carried out relate to purchasing, selling and the receipt and payment of cash, there are nevertheless others which do not fall under these headings.

Question

So that in the absence of a Book of Prime Entry, like this earliest form of the Journal, you cannot set out the dual aspect of these particular transactions prior to entry in the Ledger?

Answer

As was stated earlier, **it is desirable that no entry shall be made in a Ledger Account unless it has first been recorded in a Book of Prime Entry.** Thus in certain cases the use of the Journal, or Debit and Credit Journal as it is sometimes termed, is essential. Moreover, while the information that can be given in the ordinary form of Ledger Account is limited, as much information as may be required including reference to documents, correspondence, etc., may be shown in the Journal proper. This we describe as the **'Narration'.**

Question

Can you give me examples of such entries?

Answer

It will help you to consider them as representing business transactions which are not capable of entry in the ordinary Purchase, Sales and Cash Journals. For example, if Brown, a customer, owes the business £20 which he cannot pay, a Bad Debt of £20 has been made. Brown will be **credited** with £20 in his Personal Account in the Sales Ledger, and **Bad Debts** Account (an expense to the business) will be **debited** with that amount in the Impersonal Ledger. Supposing also that Smith both buys goods from and sells goods to the business, in the Purchase Ledger there will be an account with him as a supplier, and in the Sales Ledger as a customer. If on balance he is indebted to the business he will only remit the difference in full settlement, therefore the balance on his Purchase Ledger Account must be transferred or posted to the credit of his Sales Ledger Account.

Question

In effect then, for these and other similar transactions the Debit and Credit Journal is the only book in which the prime or first entry can be made?

Answer

Yes, but it is also appropriate, as we shall see shortly, for recording what are termed **opening** and **closing** entries. The former relate to the introduction into the business of **Capital** in one form or another; the latter refer either to the construction of the periodic **Profit and Loss Account** and the **Balance Sheet,** or to the realisation of the business property by sale or otherwise, and so on.

Question

And in all these cases it is important to give adequate **narration**?

Answer

If this were not done, the exact meaning of each Journal entry might be difficult to explain at some later date. Further, the making of the entry enables us conveniently to summarise the position for subsequent posting to the **Ledger Accounts.** Let us now proceed to work through some definite examples.

Example

Give the necessary Journal entries to record the following:

(*a*) Having deducted 5% cash discount when paying the account of Lakeside, Ltd., a letter is received from them notifying us that only $2\frac{1}{2}\%$ can be allowed.

The difference (£2·77) is being carried forward in their books.

(b) Goods to the value of £51·50 have been purchased from C. Ridley and goods value £30 sold to him. Both accounts are subject to a cash discount of 5%, and a cheque for the net balance is forwarded to him. Close the account.

			Dr. £	Cr. £
(A) 19x8 Feb. 1	Discounts Received Dr. To Lakeside, Ltd. Being discount not allowed as per their letter January 29, 19x8.		2·77	2·77
(B) Feb. 4	Sundries Dr. C. Ridley (B.L. A/c) Discounts Allowed To C. Ridley (S.L. A/c) Being transfer of Sales Ledger Balance and Discount Allowed to Bought Ledger on settlement.		28·50 1·50	30·00

Should it happen, as in (B) above, that **either** the **debit** or **credit** aspect affects more than one Ledger Account, it is usual to prefix the word 'Sundries' to the entries, in this case to the debits.

C. Ridley's account in the **Bought Ledger** will then be as follows:

C. RIDLEY

DR.   CR.

Date	Details	J.O. Fo.	Amount	Date	Details	Fo.	Amount
19x8 Feb. 4 4	Sundries Sundries Bank Discount	1 C.B.2 2	£ 28·50 1·50 20·43 1·07 ———— £51·50	19x8 Feb. 1	Balance	b/d	£ 51·50 ———— £51·50

In posting from the Debit and Credit Journal to the Ledger Accounts, the word 'Sundries' again appears in the 'Details' Column. It is unnecessary, and would indeed be a waste of time, to repeat the whole of the information in the Ledger Account, when all that is required can be found on Fo. 1 of the Journal.

The two entries for the cheque £20·43, and discount £1·07, will, of course, be posted from the Cash Book in the ordinary way.

With both (*A*) and (*B*) we must observe that adequate narration is always an essential feature of Journal entries.

Example

A.B. purchased from C.D. a motor delivery van for cash £980 in April, 19x5, and in October he bought another for £1 210, giving the one bought in April in part payment, and paying the balance of £360 in cash. Show these entries in A.B.'s books of entry, and give the relevant Ledger Accounts.

Fo. 6

PURCHASE JOURNAL

Date	Supplier	Description	Inv. No.	Ledger Fo.	Total	Goods	Special Items
19x5 Apr.	C.D.	Motor Van	1	2	£ 980·00	£	£ 980·00
					Motors A/c Private Ledger Fo. 8 980·00		
Fo. 34 19x5 Oct.	C.D.	Motor Van	40	2	1 210·00		1 210·00
					Motors A/c Private Ledger F. 8 1 210·00		

Fo. 10

CASH BOOK

DR.   CR.

Date	Details	Fo.	Amount	Date	Details	Fo.	Amount
				19x5 Apr.	C.D.	2	£ 980·00
Fo. 25				Oct.	C.D.	2	360·00

Fo. 19

JOURNAL

19x5 Oct.	Sundries: Dr. Motors A/c C.D. Loss on Sale of Assets A/c Being Sale in part exchange of Ajax Van per C.D.'s invoice No. 40, September 29, 19x5	Fo. P.L.8 B.L.2 I.L.9	Dr. £ 850·00 130·00	Cr. £ 980·00

Fo. 2

PURCHASE LEDGER

C.D.

DR.   CR.

Date	Details	Fo.	Amount	Date	Details	Fo.	Amount
19x5 Apr. Oct.	Bank Sundries Bank	C.B.10 J.19 C.B.25	£ 980·00 850·00 360·00 £1 210·00	19x5 Apr. Oct.	Goods Goods	P.J.6 34	£ 980·00 1 210·00 £1 210·00

Fo. 8

PRIVATE LEDGER

MOTORS

DR.   CR.

Date	Details	Fo.	Amount	Date	Details	Fo.	Amount
19x5 Apr. Oct.	Goods Goods	P.J.6 34	£ 980·00 1 210·00	19x5 Oct.	Sundries	19	£ 980·00

In looking at this illustration, we see that the cost of the van
purchased in April is extended in the Purchase Journal into the
'Special Items' Column. It would be wrong to analyse it as
Goods, because it is apparently a Capital Asset. As such, it is
debited to Motors A/c in the Private Ledger of A.B. When the
second van is bought in October, exactly the same procedure is
followed. At this point, however, a record has to be made of the
disposal of the first van in part payment.

Having charged the business with two vans, we must, in effect,
give it credit in Motors Account for:

(a) The part exchange value of £850.
(b) Loss on Sale of £130.

We may only charge the former to C.D. as we have done in his personal account. The latter is a special kind of expense remaining to be borne by the business and will be shown separately in the Impersonal Ledger:

Fo. 9

LOSS ON SALE OF ASSETS

DR. CR.

Date	Details	Fo.	Amount	Date	Details	Fo.	Amount
19x5 Oct.	Sundries	J.19	£ 130·00				

It is desirable that we should notice from now on the utility for reference purposes of the Folio Column in each Ledger Account. The insertion of the folio numbers prefixed by the initial letter of the book of prime entry makes immediate reference a simple matter.

Example

Journalise the following transactions in the books of L. Denton:

Jan. 1 L. Denton commenced business with stock valued at £493, cash at bank £78, and fixtures value £55. £40 was owing to M. Robinson.

Mar. 10 Plant and machinery bought on credit from Langham Bros., value £523.

Apr. 11 K. Atkins, a debtor for £23, is known to be insolvent and the debt is written off as bad.

June 23 Goods valued £18·15 bought from Blake Bros. entered in the Purchase Day Book and posted in error to the debit of Blake Bros. Account in the Bought Ledger.

June 28 Cheque £15·17 posted to the debit of Jones Bros. instead of to the debit of Jones, Ltd.

The entries on *January* 1 are an instance of the use of the Journal for **opening** the books of a business. It is also apparent that the amount of L. Denton's Capital at this date is £586.

The Cash Book balance will be debited in the bank column of the **Cash Book,** and the £40 owing to M. Robinson credited to

his personal account in the **Bought Ledger.** The other items will
be posted to accounts in the **Private Ledger.**

The purchase of machinery on March 10 could quite well be
shown in the 'special items' column of the Purchase Journal, and
the present record is only an **alternative** to this.

JOURNAL

			Dr. £	Cr. £
Jan. 1	Sundries: To Sundries	Dr.		
	Cash at Bank		78·00	
	Stock		493·00	
	Fixtures		55·00	
	M. Robinson			40·00
	Capital			586·00
	Being Assets and Liabilities introduced this day.			
Mar. 10	Plant and Machinery	Dr.	523·00	
	To Langham Bros.			523·00
	Being purchase on credit of drilling machinery and lathe for tool shop.			
Apr. 11	Bad Debts	Dr.	23·00	
	To K. Atkins			23·00
	Being amount written off per collector's report dated April 1.			
June 23	To Blake Bros.			36·30
	Being goods purchased £18·15 posted in error to the debit of A/c and now adjusted			
June 28	Jones, Ltd.	Dr.	15·17	
	To Jones Bros.			15·17
	Being cheque posted in error to debit of Jones Bros.			

The entry on June 23 is interesting as showing the correction
of an error in **one Ledger Account,** that of Blake Bros.

Purchases Account in the Impersonal Ledger will have been
debited on June 30 with the total of the Purchase Day Book for
the month, which includes the item of £18·15.

At the same time, because of the error, there is also a **debit**
on a personal account in the Purchase Ledger of £18·15. Clearly
Blake Bros. should have been **credited** originally with £18·15,
and to adjust the position, it will now be necessary to journalise
a credit to them of double the amount, or £36·30. In so doing,
we shall cancel the debit error and record their position as
creditors for £18·15.

The point cannot be too strongly emphasised that ability to
journalise successfully presupposes a thorough understanding of

double entry principles. Transactions of the kind dealt with in the foregoing examples, while not so common as purchasing, selling and cash transactions, will inevitably arise in all businesses at some time or another, and call for initial record in the Debit and Credit Journal, in the manner illustrated.

TESTS AND QUESTIONS

1 Explain the uses of the Journal in the system of double entry book-keeping.

2 Explain the use of the Journal proper. What entries, other than the opening entry, would you expect to find in this book?

3 The following errors are discovered in the books of a business concern:

(a) £47·50 paid for new office furniture has been charged to office expenses.

(b) £39·18, representing a monthly total of discounts allowed to debtors, has been posted from the debit side of the Cash Book to the *credit* of Discount Account.

(c) An entry of £10, representing the retail value of goods returned to X & Co., wholesalers, has been made in the Returns Out-wards Book and posted. The amount should have been £7, the invoiced value of the goods in question.

Show the entries necessary to correct these errors. The original wrong entries are not to be deleted. Subject to this restriction, make the corrections in whatever form you consider most appropriate.

4 You are required to give the Journal entries necessary to correct the undermentioned errors in the books of a Limited Company:

(a) Cost of advertising the Prospectus, £2 200, charged to Adver-tising Account.

(b) Allowance of £50 made by a supplier of machinery entered in the Returns Outward Book and included in the total posted to Purchases Account.

(c) £500 received from a customer for goods yet to be delivered posted to the credit of Sales Account.

(d) Imprest of £20 handed to the Petty Cashier debited to General Expenses Account.

5   Give the Journal entries necessary to record the following facts in
    the books of I. Markham, a manufacturer:

    19x4
    Jan.   1 I. Markham commenced business with cash in hand, £36;
               cash at bank, £141; plant and machinery, £180; and stock
               value £200.
           28 Bought plant and machinery on credit from Speed & Co.,
               Ltd., value £130.
    Mar.   3 A debt for £25 owing by B. Sykes proves worthless.
           10 The plant and machinery purchased on credit from Speed
               & Co. was returned as not being according to specification.
           31 £25 interest on capital to be allowed.

6   Record by way of Journal entry the following in the books of A., a
    merchant:

    (a) X. is both a supplier and a customer. The debit on his Sales
        Ledger Account is £40, and the credit on his account in the
        Bought Ledger is £60.
            On February 28, 19x6, a cheque in full settlement is sent to
        him, less 2½% cash discount.
    (b) Purchase of office fixtures £100, and stationery, etc., £10, from
        Office Supplies, Ltd.
    (c) Provision on March 13, 19x6 (the date when A. closes his
        books) for interest at 5% per annum for six months in respect
        of a loan of £500 by Mrs. A.
    (d) Sale of delivery van of book value of £300 in part exchange at
        the price of £250, against a new van costing £750.

7   Give Journal entries to record or correct the following:
    19x6
    Jan.   6 £25 cheque received credited to John White, instead of
               James White, both being customers.
           14 Cuthbert agreed to accept 0·75 in £ in full settlement of the
               balance of £180 appearing on his account in the Bought
               Ledger at December 31, 19.5.
           17 Matthews, a customer, owed the business £200 on Decem-
               ber 31, 19x5. It is agreed to allow him £5 for window display
               expenses, and 5% gross for special trade discount.
           19 Arnold, a customer, to be charged by agreement £4 interest
               on his overdue account.
           24 Wilkins, a supplier, takes over plant and tools valued at
               £20 as part payment of the balance due to him of £32.

8   The book-keeper employed by John Horton handed you a Trial
    Balance which included on the debit side an item 'Suspense Ac-

count, £90·90.' He stated that this was the difference between the two sides of the Trial Balance which he could not trace. On investigation you find that the difference is caused by the following errors:

(a) The Sales Day Book has been over-cast on page 87 by £100.

(b) The Returns Outwards for November, amounting to £30·58 have been posted to personal accounts only.

(c) A cheque for £70·32 received from Barton Bros. has been posted to their Sales Ledger account as £73·20.

(d) A first and final dividend amounting to £5·88, received from the trustee in bankruptcy of Hubert Wilkins has not been posted to the Sales Ledger account. The full amount of the debt (£19) has been written off as bad during the year.

(e) A cheque for £12·24, paid to J. Smithson for goods supplied has been posted to his credit in the Sales Ledger.

Show the entries (Journal or Ledger) which are necessary to correct the above errors.

CHAPTER VIII

WRITING UP THE BOOKS

We have now become acquainted with the various books of prime entry and the Ledgers to which they serve as a basis, and we have realised in particular that the **double entry is completed within the Ledger**.

The examples that have been taken up to this point have largely dealt with the ordinary purchasing, selling and cash transactions of the business, and have been selected to illustrate the true meaning of double entry.

We ought now, therefore, to be in a position to look at other examples which include all these transactions and aim at the preparation of the Final Accounts, as they are termed, or the **Revenue Account** and **Balance Sheet**.

It is of the utmost importance that in working through them we try to put ourselves in the position of the Book-keeper, and consider **every transaction** from the standpoint of its effect on:

(*a*) The Profit or Loss result of the business, and

(*b*) Its Asset and Liability, or Capital position.

Example

On February 1, 19x1, R. Ready had the following Assets and Liabilities: Cash in hand £10; Cash at bank £200; Creditors: B. Bright £75 and C. Clowes £95; Debtors: R. Wright £60, and S. Tune £70; Furniture and fittings £180; Stock on hand £340.

Open the books by Journal entry, find and credit his capital, and then enter the following transactions in the proper subsidiary books, post to the Ledger and extract a Trial Balance at February 28, 19x1. The Cash Book and Personal Accounts should be balanced, and the balances brought down.

19x1			£
Feb.	1	Received cash from R. Wright	30·00
	2	Sold on credit to M. Moses goods	50·00
	4	Bought on credit from C. Clowes goods	120·00
	5	Paid wages, cash	12·00
	6	Drew cheque for personal use	25·00
		Cash sales for week	150·00
	9	Paid cash to bank	140·00
	12	Received cash from S. Tune £67·00	
		Allowed him discount 3·00	
			70·00
		Paid wages, cash	15·00
	13	Paid C. Clowes by cheque £90·00	
		Discount allowed 5·00	
			95·00
		Cash sales for week	87·00
	17	Sold on credit to R. Wright, goods	52·00
	19	R. Wright returned goods	10·00
		Paid wages, cash	16·00
	20	Cash sales for week	96·00
	22	Paid cash to bank	190·00
	27	Paid rent, cash	20·00
		Cash sales for week	82·00

Before we begin the work of opening the books for the month, it will be helpful to consider first the transactions and the business practice concerning them.

(a) The amount of the proprietor's capital is not stated, but as we know it to be the excess of the Assets over the Liabilities we can easily discover it, **and record it together with the other opening balances.**

(b) It is apparent that in the Cash Book there must be columns for 'Cash' as well as for 'Bank'. Cash Discounts also have to be provided for.

(c) Both Cash and Credit Sales are made. Only the **Credit Sales** will be recorded in the Sales Journal, i.e. in order to put on record the position of the customer as a debtor to the business, pending payment by him.

(d) There is no need to open columnar or analysis Purchase and Sales Journals. The one word 'goods' is the only indication we have of the purchases and sales as a whole.

R. READY

JOURNAL

Fo. 1

19x1 Feb. 1			Fo.	Dr. £	Cr. £
	Sundries	Dr.			
	To Sundries				
	Cash in Hand		C.B.2	10·00	
	Cash at Bank		2	200·00	
	R. Wright		S.L.20	60·00	
	S. Tune		25	70·00	
	Furniture and Fittings		P.L.65	180·00	
	Stock to Hand		70	340·00	
	To—B. Bright		B.L.15		75·00
	C. Clowes		10		95·00
	Capital		P.L.75		690·00
	Being Assets, Liabilities and Capital at this date.			£860·00	£860·00

The Journal entries as set out above enable us to post to the various Ledgers the balances outstanding on February 1.

Thus, the cash items will appear on the **debit** side of the Cash Book; accounts will be opened in the Sales Ledger for Wright and Tune, again as **debits**; and in the Purchase Ledger for Bright and Clowes, but on the **credit** side.

Similarly, **debit** balances will appear in the Private Ledger for Furniture and Stock, while R. Ready's Capital Account will be **credited** with £690.

Fo. 3

PURCHASE JOURNAL

Date	Supplier	Fo.	Total
19x1 Feb. 4	C. Clowes	B.L.10	£ 120·00
			I.L. Fo. 30

Note	Abbreviation
Cash Book	C.B.
Purchase Journal	P.J.
Sales Journal	S.J.
Sales Returns Journal	S.R.J.
Journal	J.
Bought Ledger	B.L.
Sales Ledger	S.L.
Impersonal Ledger	I.L.
Private Ledger	P.L.

CASH BOOK

Debit side

Date		Fo.	Discount	Cash	Bank
			£	£	£
19x1					
Feb. 1	Balances .			10·00	200·00
1	R. Wright .	J.1			
		S.L.20		30·00	
6	Cash Sales .	I.L.40		150·00	
9	Cash .	C			140·00
12	S. Tune .	S.L.25	3·00	67·00	
13	Cash Sales .	I.L.40		87·00	
20	Cash Sales .	I.L.40		96·00	
22	Cash .	C			190·00
27	Cash Sales .	I.L.40		82·00	
			£3·00	£522·00	£530·00
			I.L.46		
Mar. 1	Balances .	b/d		129·00	415·00

Credit side

Date		Fo.	Discount	Cash	Bank
			£	£	£
19x1					
Feb. 5	Wages .	I.L.55		12·00	
6	Drawings .	P.L.80			25·00
9	Bank .	C		140·00	
12	Wages .	B.L.10		15·00	
13	C. Clowes .	I.L.55	5·00	16·00	
19	Wages .	I.L.55			90·00
22	Bank .	C		190·00	
27	Rent .	I.L.60		20·00	
28	Balance .	c/d		129·00	415·00
			£5·00	£522·00	£530·00
			I.L.50		

Fo. 4

SALES JOURNAL

Date	Customer	Fo.	Total
19x1 Feb. 2 17	M. Moses R. Wright		£ 50·00 52·00
			£102·00
			I.L. Fo. 35

Fo. 5

SALES RETURN JOURNAL

(Returns Inwards)

Date	Customer	Fo.	Total
19x1 Feb. 19	R. Wright		£ 10·00
			I.L. Fo. 45

Having first written up the Books of Prime Entry **in respect of the transactions during the month,** and brought down the Cash and Bank Balances as instructed, we are able to post as we should in practice, from the Journals to the appropriate Ledger Accounts.

Let us begin with the **Personal** Ledgers, dealing first with that section relating to the Accounts of Suppliers, or **Bought Ledger.**

Fo. 10

BOUGHT LEDGER

C. CLOWES

DR.   CR.

Date	Details	Fo.	Amount	Date	Details	Fo.	Amount
19x1 Feb. 13 28	Bank Discount Balance	C.B.2 C.B.2 c/d	£ 90·00 5·00 120·00	19x1 Feb. 1 4	Balance Goods	J.1 P.J.3	£ 95·00 120·00
			£215·00				£215·00
				Mar. 1	Balance	b/d	120·00

Fo. 15

B. BRIGHT

Date	Details	Fo.	Amount	Date	Details	Fo.	Amount
Dr.							Cr.
				19x1 Feb. 1	Balance	J.1	£ 70·00

As no transactions have taken place on Bright's account, the opening balance on February 1 remains unchanged on February 28.

Next we may turn to the **Sales Ledger:**

Fo. 20

R. WRIGHT

Date	Details	Fo.	Amount	Date	Details	Fo.	Amount
Dr.							Cr.
19x1 Feb. 1 17	Balance Goods	J.1 S.J.4	£ 60·00 52·00	19x1 Feb. 1 19 28	Cash Returns Balance	C.B. S.J.R.5 c/d	£ 30·00 10·00 72·00
			£112·00				£112·00
Mar. 1	Balance	b/d	72·00				

Fo. 23

M. MOSES

Date	Details	Fo.	Amount	Date	Details	Fo.	Amount
Dr.							Cr.
19x1 Feb. 2	Goods	S.J.4	£ 50·00				

Fo. 25

S. TUNE

Date	Details	Fo.	Amount	Date	Details	Fo.	Amount
Dr.							Cr.
19x1 Feb. 1	Balance	J.1	£ 70·00	19x1 Feb. 12	Cash Discount	C.B.2	£ 67·00 3·00
			£70·00				£70·00

The **Impersonal,** or as it is sometimes termed, the **Nominal Ledger,** may now receive attention.

Within this, as we know, we shall expect to find the accounts dealing with the effect upon the business of the transactions entered into.

PURCHASES

Fo. 30

DR.   CR.

Date	Details	Fo.	Amount	Date	Details	Fo.	Amount
19x1 Feb. 28	Total for Month	P.J.3	£ 120·00				

CREDIT SALES

Fo. 35

DR.   CR.

Date	Details	Fo.	Amount	Date	Details	Fo.	Amount
				19x1 Feb. 28	Total for Month	S.J.4	£ 102·00

CASH SALES

Fo. 40

DR.   CR.

Date	Details	Fo.	Amount	Date	Details	Fo .	Amount
				19x1 Feb. 6	Cash	C.B.2	£ 150·00
				13	Cash	C.B.2	87·00
				20	Cash	C.B.2	96·00
				27	Cash	C.B.2	82·00
							£415·00

SALES RETURNS

Fo. 45

DR.   CR.

Date	Details	Fo.	Amount	Date	Details	Fo.	Amount
19x1 Feb. 28	Total for Month	S.R.J.5	£ 10·00				

Fo. 46

DISCOUNTS ALLOWED

DR.   CR.

Date	Details	Fo.	Amount	Date	Details	Fo.	Amount
19x1 Feb. 28	Total for Month	C.B.2	£ 3·00				

Fo. 50

DISCOUNTS RECEIVED

DR.   CR.

Date	Details	Fo.	Amount	Date	Details	Fo.	Amount
				19x1 Feb. 28	Total for Month	C.B.2	£ 5·00

Fo. 55

WAGES

DR.   CR.

Date	Details	Fo.	Amount	Date	Details	Fo.	Amount
19x1 Feb. 5	Cash	C.B.2	£ 12·00				
12	Cash	C.B.2	15·00				
19	Cash	C.B.2	16·00				
			£43·00				

Fo. 60

RENT

DR.   CR.

Date	Details	Fo.	Amount	Date	Details	Fo.	Amount
19x1 Feb. 27	Cash	C.B.2	£ 20·00				

Lastly, there is the **Private Ledger** to be considered.

Here we shall have first of all two **Asset Accounts**, for Furniture and Stock respectively, and one **Liability Account**, for Capital.

Fo. 65

FURNITURE AND FITTINGS

DR.   CR.

Date	Details	Fo.	Amount	Date	Details	Fo.	Amount
19x1 Feb. 1	Balance	J.1	£ 180·0				

Fo. 70

STOCK

DR.   CR.

Date	Details	Fo.	Amount	Date	Details	Fo.	Amount
19x1 Feb. 1	Balance	J.1	£ 340·00				

Fo. 75

CAPITAL

DR.   CR.

Date	Details	Fo.	Amount	Date	Details	Fo.	Amount
				19x1 Feb. 1	Balance	J.1	£ 690·00

If, however, we look at the Cash Book, we see that on February
6 **R. Ready**, the proprietor, drew a cheque £25 for his personal
use. This is a withdrawal from the business of:

(a) A part of the amount now standing to his credit on Capital
Account, or

(b) The profit which he estimates is being earned.

In either event, it must be debited in the Ledger in the Capital
Account above, or in a 'Drawings' Account opened for the
purpose:

Fo. 80

DRAWINGS

DR.   CR.

Date	Details	Fo.	Amount	Date	Details	Fo.	Amount
19x1 Feb. 6	Bank	C.B.2	£ 25·00				

Having now posted all the transactions to the Ledgers, and recorded **their dual aspect**, it is to be expected that arithmetical agreement has been obtained, in that the sum of the **Debit** Balances should equal the sum of the **Credit Balances on February 28, 19x1.**

Let us therefore extract the Balances on the Accounts and list them as Debits or Credits, according to their nature:

Ledger	Account	Fo.	Dr.	Cr.
			£	£
Cash Book	Cash	2	129·00	
	Bank	2	415·00	
Bought	C. Clowes	10		120·00
	B. Bright	15		75·00
Sales	R. Wright	20	72·00	
	M. Moses	23	50·00	
Impersonal	Purchases	30	120·00	
	Credit Sales	35		102·00
	Cash Sales	45		415·00
	Sales Returns	46	10·00	
	Discounts Allowed	48	3·00	
	Discounts Received	50		5·00
	Wages	55	43·00	
	Rent	60	20·00	
Private	Furniture and Fittings	65	180·00	
	Stock, February 1	70	340·00	
	Capital	75		690·00
	Drawings	80	25·00	
			£1 407·00	£1 407·00

In total the Double Entry is seen to be completed **within the Ledger Accounts**, regarding the Cash Book as a Ledger for this purpose.

This list, or summary of **Ledger Balances**, we call a **Trial Balance**. Its extraction at any time enables us:

(*a*) To satisfy ourselves of the arithmetical accuracy with which the routine work of writing up the Books of Prime Entry, and posting to the Ledgers, has been carried out.

(*b*) To provide a basis for the preparation of the Final Accounts, or **Revenue Account** and **Balance Sheet.**

Because of its importance, we must consider it at greater length.

TESTS AND QUESTIONS

1 N. Bell was in business as a wholesale merchant and on January 1,
   19x1, he had the following assets and liabilities: Cash in hand, £150;
   Bank overdraft, £2 680; Stock of goods, £7 400; Motor vans, £740;
   Fixtures and fittings, £920; Sundry Debtors: J. Betts, £640; E.
   Evans, £600; Sundry Creditors: T. Brown, £840; F. Shaw, £580.
      Enter the above and the following transactions into the proper
   subsidiary books, post to the Ledger and extract a Trial Balance.
   The Cash Book and, where necessary, the Ledger Accounts should
   be balanced and the balances brought down.

   Jan. 4 Received from J. Betts cheque for £628 in full settlement of
            his account for £640. Paid cheque to bank.
          6 Sold goods on credit to E. Evans, £1 200.
          9 Paid wages in cash, £63.
         11 Sold goods for cash, £143.
            E. Evans returned goods. Sent him credit note for £48.
         15 Sold a motor van for cash, £180.
         18 Paid cash into the bank, £200.
         23 Paid wages in cash, £63.
            Purchased on credit new motor van from the Albion
            Motor Co., Ltd., for £450.
         25 Received cheque from E. Evans for £1 740 in full settlement
            of the amount due from him. Paid cheque to bank.
            Purchased goods on credit from F. Shaw, £800.
         27 Paid T. Brown cheque for £820 in full settlement of the
            amount due to him on January 1.

   N.B.—No Trading and Profit and Loss Accounts or Balance Sheet
   are required.

2 On March 1, 19x1, A. Walker commences business with £5 000 in
   cash of which he pays £4 500 into the bank. Enter the following
   transactions in the books of original entry, post to Ledger Accounts
   and extract a Trial Balance.

   Mar. 2 Bought premises and paid £1 500 by cheque.
          4 Purchased on credit from J. Raleigh:
            30 gent's cycles at £25·50 each.
            45 ladies' cycles at £22·75 each.
            20 children's cycles at £17·25 each.
          5 Bought at an auction sale sundry goods for £268·00 and
            paid for them by cash.

Mar. 6 Sold to S. Taylor:
     1 gent's cycle at £30·75.
     1 ladies' cycle at £27·40.
     1 tandem at £42·50.

   8 Returned to J. Raleigh:
     10 children's cycles invoiced on the 4th and received a
     credit note.

  10 Paid J. Raleigh by cheque the amount due, less £41·25
     cash discount.

  12 Bought office furniture for cash £130·75.

  16 S. Taylor paid by cheque the amount due.

  18 Paid by cheque rent £77·25.
     Paid by cash wages £50·50.
     Paid by cash insurance £10·75.
     Cash sales for the period £597.

  20 Paid all cash into the bank except £50.

3 R. Simpson was in business as a wholesale cutler and jeweller. On
January 1, 19x6, his financial position was as follows: Cash in hand,
£140; Cash at bank, £350; Stock, £1 000; Fixtures and fittings, £160.
Sundry Creditors: M. Marsh, £150; D. Steele, £200. Sundry
Debtors: H. Robins, £275; J. Long, £175.

Enter the above and the following transactions into the proper
subsidiary books, post to the Ledger, and extract a Trial Balance.
The Cash Book and, where necessary, the Ledger Accounts should
be balanced and the balances brought down.

Jan. 2 Received from H. Robins on account, cheque for £200,
     which was paid to bank.

   3 Sold to D. Dennis & Co., Ltd.: Goods £40 less 10% trade
     discount.

   4 Paid wages in cash £60.

   6 Cash sales paid to bank, £300.

   7 Bought from Silversmiths, Ltd.: Goods £40 subject to
     trade discount of 15%.

   8 Paid M. Marsh by cheque £147·50 in settlement of his
     account of £150.

  11 Paid wages in cash £60.

  13 Cash sales paid to bank £250.

  15 Withdrew from bank for office cash £100.

  17 Sold to J. Long: on credit £30.

  18 Paid wages in cash £60.
     R. Simpson withdrew £30 for private purposes by cheque.

Jan. 18 Cash sales paid to bank £285.

   20 Received from J. Long in full settlement of the amount due
      from him on January 1, cheque for £203. Paid cheque to
      bank.

N.B.—No Trading and Profit and Loss Account or Balance Sheet
is required.

4 On January 1, 19x1, the financial position of R. Mason, gentleman's
   outfitter, is as follows: Cash in hand, £45·80; Stock, £3 750·00;
   H. Atherton (Dr.), £31·75; Fixtures and fittings, £750·00; A. Baker
   (Cr.), £390·00; Bank overdraft, £176·75. Find and credit his capital.
   During the month his transactions were as follows:

Jan. 4 Bought goods from G. Henry & Co., to the value of
      £812·80 less 12½% trade discount.

   6 Paid A. Baker the amount owing, less 5% cash discount.

   7 Returned to G. Henry & Co., goods to the gross value of
     £103·25.

   9 Sold goods to H. Atherton, £68·60.

   9 Received from G. Henry & Co. credit note for the net
     amount of goods returned.

   10 H. Atherton settled his account of January 1, after deduct-
      ing £1·75 cash discount.

   14 Bought new showcase £75·75 from W. Dixon.

   19 Sold goods to N. Dobbin £72·50.

   20 R. Mason paid £300 of his own money into the business
      Bank Account.

   23 Sold shop fittings for cash £27·60.

   26 Cash sales for the period £311·80.

   28 Paid all cash into bank except £50·00.

Enter the transactions in the appropriate subsidiary books—post to
the Ledger Accounts and extract a Trial Balance.

N.B.—Trading Account, Profit and Loss Account and Balance
Sheet are not required.

5 In the form of Cash Book provided, after properly heading each
   column, enter all the money transactions below and balance the
   Book.
      Journalise the opening balances and remaining transactions.
   (*Note:* Purchases and Sales Books may be used, if preferred.)
      Post the entries to the Ledger. Extract a Trial Balance.
      Close and balance the Ledger.

On October 1, 19x1, S. Strong reopened his books with the following balances in addition to his Capital Account:

	£
Cash	47·80
K. Knight & Co. (Cr.)	176·90
D. Day (Dr.)	225·75
Bank (overdraft)	217·90
Rent accrued, owing by S. Strong	20·00
Stock of goods	741·25

During the month his transactions were:

		£
Oct. 3	Received cheque from D. Day to settle account	220·00
5	Paid same into bank	220·00
8	Sold to D. Day: Goods	130·00
10	D. Day returned goods	4·20
13	Sundry cash sales	83·70
14	Paid into bank	100·00
16	Bought of K. Knight & Co.: Goods	91·75
19	Paid landlord by cheque	20·00
21	Paid K. Knight & Co. on account	150·00
22	Sold to D. Day sundry sports fittings and received cheque (banked)	43·75
26	D. Day's cheque returned dishonoured	43·75
27	Cash purchases to date	7·30
28	Drew cheque for self	25·00
30	Wages and expenses for month paid by cheque	50·40
	and in cash	11·50
31	Rent accrued	20·00
	Bank charges	1·75
	Interest on capital at 6% per annum calculated on balance at October 1, 19x1	—
	Stock of goods on hand valued at	763·25

6 On November 1, 19x1, John Maynard commenced business on his own account, trading under the style of The Bon Marché.

He paid £1 000 into the bank account of the business on that date, and also borrowed £500 from his father, Robert Maynard, to assist him in the venture. He paid £450 of this sum into the Bank.

The following transactions were entered into during the month
of November:

19x1		£
Nov. 1	Paid rent by cheque three months to January 31, 19x2	37·50
2	Obtained cheque book from bank	0·50
2	Bought material on credit:	
	Forrester & Co.	126·50
	Arnold & Sons	39·75
	H. Meyrick, Ltd.	112·95
3	Bought office fittings for cash	20·00
3	Drew cheque for cash	45·00
4	Sold goods on credit:	
	E. Walker	21·25
	J. Roberts	51·00
	L. Morley	47·45
	H. Longden	4·85
4	Paid wages in cash	28·25
11	Sent cheque to Forrester & Co.	125·00
	and obtained discount	1·50
16	Received cheque from Roberts	50·00
	and allowed discount	1·00
19	Received cheque from Morley	46·00
	and allowed discount	1·45
24	Paid wages in cash	28·25
27	Sent cheque to Arnold & Sons	39·00
	and obtained discount	0·75
30	Returned defective goods to H. Meyrick, Ltd.	9·25

Enter the above transactions in the proper books of prime entry,
post to the Ledger, and extract a Trial Balance at November 30.

7 W. Allen is in business as a wholesale and retail stationer. The
balances in his books on March 1 were:

	£	£
Cash in hand	19·45	
Cash at bank	88·75	
Stock	985·20	
A. Reid (Dr.)	91·45	
Capital		1 184·85
	£1 184·85	£1 184·85

Open the books by means of Journal entry. Enter the following transactions in the books of original entry, post to Ledger Accounts, and extract a Trial Balance:

Mar. 2 Bought of Barking & Co.:
          Envelopes £42·50.
          Writing Paper £68·60.
          Ink £12·90.
            Less 10% trade discount.

    4 Paid carriage in cash, £12·25.

    4 Sold to L. Lyons:
          Calendars £17·45.
          Foolscap envelopes £2·30.
          Blotting paper £8·65.

    5 A. Reid paid his account by cheque which was paid to the bank.

    8 L. Lyons returned envelopes invoiced on the 4th, and sent him credit note for £2·30.

    9 The bank returned Reid's cheque dishonoured.

   11 Paid Barking & Co. by cheque less 5% cash discount.

   15 Sold to H. Cooper:
          Quarto paper £3·15.
          Stencils £2·85.
          Envelopes £1·65.

   18 Cash sales for the period, £137·80.

   18 Paid in cash, wages, £43·55; rent, £21·00; insurance, £10·00.

   18 Paid all cash into bank except £12·00.

N.B.—No Trading Account, Profit and Loss Account, or Balance Sheet is to be prepared.

8 On January 1, 19x1, R. Baxter commenced business as a coal merchant with £1 650 in cash. On the same date he opened a current account at the bank and paid in £1 500. His transactions during the month follow:

Jan. 1 Bought a second-hand motor lorry by cheque, £256·50.
          Bought from the Victory Colliery Co., Ltd.:
          Coal £197.

    4 Cash sales £27·75.

    4 Sold to J. Yates, Coal £18·40.

    6 Paid Victory Colliery Co. £100 on account by cheque.

    8 Bought from The Agecroft Coal Co., Coke £168·50.

Jan. 10 J. Yates settled his account by cheque and allowed him
         5% cash discount.
      12 Sold to W. Jones, Coke £47·30.
      12 Paid carriage in cash £17.
      15 Settled the account of the Victory Colliery Co. by cheque
         and was allowed 5% cash discount on the original account.
      16 Cash sales £105.
      16 Paid sundry expenses in cash £53·60.
      16 Paid all cash into the bank except £20.

You are required to enter the above transactions in the books of
original entry, to post to Ledger Accounts, and to extract a Trial
Balance.
   No Trading Account, Profit and Loss Account, or Balance Sheet
is required.

9 Robert Salmon, a wholesale grocer, was, in January 1, 19x1, in the
   following financial position: Premises, £6 500; Fixtures and
   fittings, £500; Cash in hand, £215; Stock, £3 100; Cash at bank,
   £283; Debtors: A. Hardy, £70; G. White, £40; Creditors: Grocery
   Supplies Ltd., £276; Mills Brothers, £173.
      Open the Accounts necessary to record this position in the Ledger,
   and post, through correct books of original entry, the following
   transactions:

   19x1
   Jan. 2 Paid, by cheque, wages £80.
         3 Sold, on credit, to A. Hardy: Tinned fruit, £8; Biscuits, £9.
         5 Purchased, for cash, biscuits £65.
         6 Paid, by cheque, the amount due to Grocery Supplies,
           Ltd., less 2% cash discount.
           Cash sales to date £127.
         9 Purchased, on credit, from Grocery Supplies, Ltd., Goods,
           £117.
        11 Received cheque, which was paid into the bank, from A.
           Hardy, for the amount of his account to date less 5% cash
           discount.
           Purchased for cash, new showcase £75.
        14 Returned to Grocery Supplies, Ltd., ½ cwt. cheese supplied
           on the 9th inst. £5.
        16 Paid, by cheque, wages £75.
        16 Sold, on credit, to B. Ruston, Biscuits, £11.
        17 Purchased, on credit, from Loxley & Co., tea £52.
           Cash sales to date £117.

Jan. 16 Paid into bank from office cash £150.
 21 Agree to allow G. White £6 in consequence of defects in goods previously supplied to him.
 22 Paid, by cheque, to Mills Brothers, £150 on account.
 25 Robert Salmon pays into the bank, as additional capital, £500.

Balance the accounts as on January 25, 19x1, and extract a Trial Balance.

CHAPTER IX

THE TRIAL BALANCE

Two advantages have just been claimed for the Trial Balance. The first, that it is evidence of the arithmetical accuracy of the book-keeping work, clearly has reference to the dual aspect from which every transaction may be regarded, each transaction having been looked at from the twofold aspect upon which the double entry system relies.

Are we therefore justified in assuming that the routine work underlying the Trial Balance calls for no further comment? Is arithmetical accuracy alone all with which we need be concerned?

The answer to these two questions is 'no'.

Apparent proof of accuracy is not the same as conclusive proof, and we have to realise that errors may exist in the underlying work which the Trial Balance will not reveal.

If, for example, a **transaction has been altogether omitted** from the books, neither its **debit** nor its **credit** aspect can have been recorded.

Goods may have been purchased from Brown, a supplier, and an invoice duly received. But if, in course of checking prior to entry in the Purchase Journal, the invoice is lost or mislaid, nothing will ultimately appear to the **credit** of the **Supplier's Account** in respect of it. Similarly as it has never been entered in the Purchase Journal, it cannot form part of the Total Purchases for the month which are posted to the **debit** of Purchases Account.

Such an **error of omission** would be discovered only when the supplier's **Statement of Account** comes to hand.

Another example would be neglect to record in the Cash Book any discount deducted by a customer.

The customer would be credited with too little in his Personal Account, causing an Asset in the form of a Book Debt to be overstated, and **Discounts Allowed** Account would be under-debited, resulting in the **understatement** of an expense to the business.

There are also errors which we may describe as **compensating errors.** In this sense, an error in one direction is counterbalanced by an error in another direction of equal amount. Hence, again the lack of agreement is not disclosed by the Trial Balance.

The following are examples of **compensating errors:**

(*a*) The total of **Sales Account** on one page of the Impersonal Ledger is inadvertently carried forward £10 less than it should be, i.e. there is **short credit** of £10.

At the same time, the addition of Wages Account is made £10 too little, so that there is a **short debit** of £10.

(*b*) In extracting the balances on the Sales Ledger Accounts, an item of £110 is entered on the list of balances as £100, causing a **short debit** of £10, while a cheque for £10 from Jones, a customer, has been debited in the Cash Book but never posted to the credit of his account in the Sales Ledger. The **total book debts** are correctly shown in the List of Balances, **although the detail items are incorrect.**

We may also have to deal with **errors of principle.** Supposing £5 is paid by way of deposit in connection with the supply of Electricity to the business. This deposit is refundable if and when the business closes down, and therefore is an **Asset.** If the amount is debited to Heat, Light and Power Account in the Impersonal Ledger it will in all probability be written off as an **expense** for the particular period, resulting in an **overstatement of working expenses,** and an **understatement of Assets.**

Secondly, should a part of the Fixtures and Fittings be sold to a dealer when the offices are being modernised, and entered as a sale in the Sales Journal, Sales Account will be improperly inflated, **because the goods are not those in which the business is dealing.** Further, the Fixtures and Fittings Account will not record the reduction in value.

Here also the Trial Balance is of no help in the detection of the errors.

We must not, however, assume that its value as a basis for the preparation of the Final Accounts is seriously lessened. So far as accounts in the Impersonal and Private Ledger are concerned, these are not usually numerous, neither are the entries appearing therein, and great care is taken in practice to record the true facts.

Similarly when the Sales and Purchase Ledger Balances are extracted and totalled, it is usual for the work to be checked before the figures are finally accepted.

ERRORS WHICH THE TRIAL BALANCE WILL SHOW

If there is a 'difference' on the Trial Balance, search must be made for the probable cause.

We can compare the names of the accounts appearing in it with those in some previous Trial Balance, and note any omission. We can also scrutinise each item in the light of its description and the definition that:

(a) A Debit Balance is either an Asset or an Expense, and
(b) A Credit Balance is either a Liability or a Profit.

Thus if we regard Sales as a Profit, Sales Returns, or Returns Inwards should be considered as an Expense, or Debit Balance. If the returned goods remain in the warehouse unsold we could alternatively look on them as an Asset, but they would still be a Debit Balance.

It will not take long to go through the accounts in the Impersonal and Private Ledgers, if need be, to satisfy ourselves that they are apparently in order, and we should probably do this before re-examining the Sales and Purchase Ledger Accounts. Because they are so rarely met with, Credit Balances on the Sales Ledger and Debit Balances on the Purchase Ledger should also be considered as a likely source of error.

If nothing is thus brought to light, and assuming the (monthly) totals of the Books of Prime Entry have been checked to the Impersonal Ledger, the following steps can be taken:

(a) Check the additions (or casts) of the Books of Prime Entry.
(b) Check the postings in detail from the Books of Prime Entry to the Sales and Purchase Ledgers.

The two latter checks involve a great deal of time and labour, but should result in locating the error, and obtaining agreement in the Trial Balance.

Example

The following Trial Balance was extracted from the books of F. Briers on December 31, 19x1. Do you think that it is correct? If not, rewrite it in its correct form.

	Dr. £	Cr. £
Capital Account		1 000·00
Stock at January 1, 19x1	825·00	
Purchases and Sales	1 275·00	1 590·00
Returns Inwards		80·00
Returns Outwards	70·00	
Discounts Received	80·00	
Discounts Allowed		70·00
Motor Vans		175·00
Wages and Salaries	250·00	
Carriage		70·00
Rent and Rates	185·00	
Sundry Debtors	760·00	
Sundry Creditors		725·00
Cash in Hand	20·00	
Bank Overdraft	245·00	
	£3 710·00	£3 710·00

Although the total debits equal the total credits, the Trial Balance is very far from being correct.

It should instead appear as under:

	Dr. £	Cr. £
Capital Account		1 000·00
Stock at January, 1, 19x1	825·00	
Purchases	1 275·00	
Sales		1 590·00
Returns Inwards	80·00	
Returns Outwards		70·00
Discounts Received		80·00
Discounts Allowed	70·00	
Motor Vans	175·00	
Wages and Salaries	250·00	
Carriage	70·00	
Rent and Rates	185·00	
Sundry Debtors	760·00	
Sundry Creditors		725·00
Cash in Hand	20·00	
Bank Overdraft		245·00
	£3 710·00	£3 710·00

The adjustments made, and the reasons for them are:

(a) **Returns Inwards.** As an expense or Asset (of which we spoke on page 120) this is a Debit Balance.

(b) **Returns Outwards**, i.e. to suppliers. These are sometimes called Purchase Returns, and are a Credit Balance.

(c) **Discounts Received.** As a profit to the business, the amount represents a Credit Balance.

(d) **Discounts Allowed.** Clearly an expense, and so a Debit.

(e) **Motor Vans** are an Asset of the business and will be a Debit Balance in the Private Ledger.

(f) **Carriage.** The cost of carriage is a business expense, and a Debit in the Impersonal Ledger.

(g) **Bank Overdraft.** As a liability due to the bank this must be a Credit Balance in the Cash Book.

CHAPTER X

FOUR-COLUMN TRIAL BALANCE

The purpose of this form of Trial Balance is to assist us further in the preparation of the Profit and Loss Account and Balance Sheet. It demonstrates in a manner which is not apparent in the ordinary form of Trial Balance with which we have dealt, the fact that:

(a) A **Debit** Balance is either an **Asset** or an **Expense,** and

(b) A **Credit** Balance is either a **Liability** or a **Profit.**

Let us redraft the Trial Balance of R. Ready shown on page 109, in **four-column form:**

Account	Ledger	Fo.	Revenue Dr.	Revenue Cr.	Capital Dr.	Capital Cr.
			£	£	£	£
Cash	Cash Book	2			129·00	
Bank		2			415·00	
C. Clowes	Bought	10				120·00
B. Bright		15				75·00
R. Wright	Sales	20			72·00	
M. Moses		23			50·00	
Purchases	Impersonal	30	120·00			
Credit Sales		35		102·00		
Cash Sales		40		415·00		
Sales Returns		45	10·00			
Discounts Allowed		46	3·00			
Discounts Received		50		5·00		
Wages		55	43·00			
Rent		60	20·00			
Furniture and Fittings	Private	65			180·00	
Stock		70	340·00			
Capital		75				690·00
Drawings		80			25·00	
			£536·00	£522·00	£871·00	£885·00

Commencing Stock, although an Asset, is entered in the **Revenue** column, because it represents goods in which the business is dealing. The Stock on hand at February 28, 19x1, will be recorded in:

(a) The Revenue column (Credit), and
(b) The Capital column (Debit),

thus enabling us to record:

(a) The true Profit, and
(b) The existence of the Asset of Stock at this date.

SUMMARY

	Dr. £	Cr. £
Revenue	536·00	522·00
Capital	871·00	885·00
	£1 407·00	£1 407·00

What we have now done is to show in the **first two columns** all those items which are of a Revenue character, and which alone will concern us in ascertaining Profit or Loss.

In the **third and fourth columns** are found the accounts which relate to Assets except closing Stock, and Liabilities, and as such compose the Balance Sheet of the business.

TESTS AND QUESTIONS

1 Can the arithmetical agreement on the Debit and Credit Columns in a Trial Balance be considered conclusive proof of the accuracy of the book-keeping work?
    Illustrate your answer with at least three suitable examples.

2 Write short notes on:
    (a) Errors of omission
    (b) Errors of commission
    (c) Compensating errors
    giving two examples of each.

3 On taking out a Trial Balance from a set of books, a book-keeper found that the Dr. side exceeded the Cr. by £9.

Assuming that this 'difference' was due to a single mistake, mention as many types of error as you can think of, each different in principle, any one of which could have caused it.

4 On preparing a Trial Balance from a set of books the sides are found not to agree, the Dr. total being £2 530·20, and the Cr. £2 580·60. You are convinced that nothing has been omitted and that all the figures are arithmetically correct, all postings, additions, etc., having been independently checked.

What is the probable nature of the error made and what will be the correct totals of the Trial Balance?

5 The following errors were discovered in a set of books kept by Double Entry:

(a) An item of £52 in the Sales Day Book posted to the customer's account as £50·20.

(b) Bank interest amounting to £60 charged by the bank on an overdraft, entered on the debit side of the Cash Book in the bank column.

(c) An item of £15 for goods returned by a customer entered in the Returns Outwards Book and omitted to be posted.

(d) A payment by cheque of £10 to X,Y., entered in the Cash Book on the credit side in the cash column.

State by what amount the totals of the Trial Balance disagreed.

6 The Assets Balances in a Trial Balance amount to £8 500, the Capital (less Drawings) to £4 000, and the Gross Income or Profits to £6 000. The Total Debit Balances amount to £12 000. The only adjustment not appearing in the Ledger is Closing Stock valued at £1 000. What is the profit for the year, and what is the amount of the liabilities? Show your workings.

7 (a) Explain shortly the value of preparing at any given date a Trial Balance from the books of a business.

(b) Amend the following Trial Balance as you think necessary to correct same.

TRIAL BALANCE

November 30, 19x2

	Dr. £	Cr. £
J. Livingstone, Capital		1 000·00
Wages	268·00	
Purchases	1 249·00	
Sales		3 108·00
Rent Paid		50·00
Discount Received		12·00
Electricity		16·00
Salaries	52·00	
Carriage	5·00	
Plant and Machinery	1 201·00	
Leamington Bank, Ltd., Overdraft	47·00	
Cash in hand	6·00	
L. Pawson (supplier)		61·00
F. Thomas (supplier)		19·00
V. Wyles (customer)	33·00	
S. Watson (customer)	105·00	
P. Robbins (customer)	11·00	
Stock, December 1, 19x1		926·00
Furniture and Fixtures, December 1, 19x1		325·00
	£2 977·00	£5 517·00

8   State what 'difference' would be caused in the books of a business
    by each of the following errors:

   (a) The omission from the list of debtors' balances, compiled for
       the purpose of the Trial Balance, of a debt of £12·25, due from
       P. & Co.

   (b) Omission to post from the Cash Book to the Discount Account
       the sum of £5·35, representing discounts allowed to debtors
       during July.

   (c) Omission to make any entry in respect of an allowance of
       £8·50 due to Q. & Co. in respect of damaged goods.

   (d) Posting an item of wages paid, correctly entered as £31·75 in
       the Cash Book, as £31·25 in the Ledger Account.

(e) Posting £2, being cash received from the sale of an old office typewriter, to the debit side of 'Office Equipment' Account.

Note.—These errors are to be taken as affecting different sets of books having no relation one to another.

9 (a) Define the term 'Trial Balance'.

  (b) If the Debit and Credit sides of a Trial Balance agree in amount is this conclusive evidence that the whole of the Book-keeping has been correctly done? If not, why not?

  (c) From the following list of balances, extracted from the books of M. Brake prepare a Trial Balance as on March 31, 19x2:

BALANCES, MARCH 31, 19x2

	£
Capital, M. Brake	13 000·00
Drawings, M. Brake	1 200·00
Purchases	11 564·50
Sales	23 914·65
Stock, April 1, 19x1	7 624·45
Sundry Creditors	2 715·75
Bills Payable	3 000·00
Furniture and Fittings	250·00
Carriage on Purchases	115·40
General Expenses	1 246·46
Wages	6 351·60
Salaries	1 286·55
Bank Loan (secured by a Mortgage on the Premises)	3 500·00
Freehold Premises	6 000·00
Sundry Debtors	6 214·14
Returns Inwards	321·25
Bank Charges and Interest	261·46
Postage and Stationery	114·35
Carriage on Sales	384·53
Discounts Allowed	633·25
Discounts Received	16·84
Cash at Bank	245·60
Cash in hand	23·70
Bills Receivable	2 310·00

10 The following Trial Balance contains certain errors. You are required to discover them and draw up a correct Trial Balance.

	Dr. £	Cr. £
H. Jones, Capital Account		6 000·00
Current Account (Cr.)		1 091·00
S. Brown, Capital Account		4 000·00
Current Account (Dr.)	57·00	
Salaries and Wages	3 140·00	
Rent and Rates	520·00	
Sales, less Returns		22 556·00
Purchases, less Returns	17 245·00	
Stock	5 472·00	
Trade Debtors	10 314·00	
Trade Creditors		3 591·00
Fixtures and Fittings	550·00	
Manufacturing Expenses	926·00	
Manufacturing Expenses (unpaid)	102·00	
Office Expenses	341·00	
Carriage Inwards	559·00	
Carriage Outwards		253·00
Bank Overdraft		1 956·00
Interest on Overdraft		42·00
Bad Debts written off	112·00	
Bad Debts Reserve	250·00	
Cash in hand	15·00	
	£39 546·00	£39 546·00

11 The following is the 'Trial Balance' of Diminishing Returns owned
by X.Y. at December 31, 19x1:

	Dr. £	Cr. £
Capital		650·00
Bank	126.00	
Machinery	452·00	
Fixtures	78·00	
Stock, January 1, 19x1		340·00
Purchases	2 242·00	
Wages	1 135·00	
Salaries	312·00	
Rent	100·00	
Sales		4 612·00
Repairs	57·00	
Bad Debts	24·00	
Heat and Light	48·00	
Bills Receivable	118·00	
Debtors	852·00	
Creditors		475·00
	£5 544·00	£6 077·00

Amend the Trial Balance, taking the following into account:

(a) No entry had been made in the ledger in respect of a bill for £24 discounted with the bank on December 20, 19x1. Discounting charges (£1) had, however, been debited to the customer's account.

(b) The Sales Day Book had been undercast £89.

(c) The bank confirmed the overdraft at the sum shown on December 31, 19x1.

(d) X.Y.'s private drawings of £208 had not been posted to the Ledger.

(e) A sale of £10 had not been posted to the account of I. Jones, a customer.

12 At December 31, 19x1, the accountant of A.B.C., Ltd., has failed to balance his books of account. The difference has been carried to the debit of a Suspense Account.

Subsequently, the following errors are discovered:

(a) The total of the Sales Day Book for June has been posted to Sales Account in the Impersonal Ledger as £2 784·25. The Day Book total is £2 748·25.

(b) Cash discounts allowed for the month of November, £37·10, and Discounts received, £19·85, have been posted to the wrong sides of the Ledger Account.

(c) An allowance to a customer of £1·95 has been posted to the debit of his account in the Sales Ledger.

(d) A book debt of £14·55, due by L., a customer, has been omitted from the list of Sales Ledger balances.

(e) Cash drawings of the proprietor, amounting to £20, have not been posted to the Ledger.

(f) Goods purchased costing £21·10 were posted to the credit of the Supplier's Ledger Account, and also to the credit of 'Sundry Purchases' Account in the Bought Ledger.

After the discovery and correction of the errors mentioned, the books balanced. You are required:

1 To show the Suspense Account as it originally appeared.

2 To make the requisite corrective entries.

CHAPTER XI

WHAT IS PROFIT OR LOSS?

Question

The profit made seems to be represented by an increase in the Assets of the business during the period. Is this always the case?

Answer

Yes. The word 'Profit' has no meaning except in the sense of an increase of Net Assets. You could just as truly say that Profit represents an increase in Capital. Put in another way, if the Capital invested at the commencement is a liability of the business, the liability is greater at the end of the period to the extent of the Profit earned.

Question

What, then, is a Loss?

Answer

A shrinkage in the Net Assets, or the extent to which they fall short of the initial Capital. If the latter had at one time comprised £100 worth of stock which owing to a general drop in prices had to be sold for £90 cash, an Asset of £90 would replace one of £100 and a Loss of £10 would have been incurred.

Such a loss would be described as a **Revenue Loss,** because stock is a part of the **Current Assets** of the business, or its Trading property. But if **Fixed Assets,** like Plant and Machinery, are sold at a figure below their book value, a **Capital Loss** is said to have been sustained.

Question

Referring again to the last example (page 123), the proprietor had withdrawn £25 from the business for his personal use, and yet you put the item in the third, or **Asset** column of the Trial Balance.

Should it not have been entered in the first or **Expense** column?

Answer

No, and for this reason. In the majority of businesses the owners will withdraw periodically either cash or goods (sometimes both) for their private use. These withdrawals are probably made to cover their living expenses, and have no relation whatever to the **expenses of the business.** We may regard them as withdrawals **on account of accruing profits.**

Therefore they properly appear elsewhere than in the Revenue columns of the Trial Balance. To enter them in the third or **Asset** column is the only alternative and is justified in point of fact if we look upon the initial Capital as a **Liability.** In withdrawing money or goods from the business, the proprietor has really reduced the Capital invested in the first place, assuming no Profits, or insufficient Profits, have been earned to cover the withdrawals.

Question

Should drawings then be set against **Profits,** rather than against Capital?

Answer

Often it is found convenient to proceed in this way. The Capital Account, as we have seen, is credited with whatever the proprietor first introduces. Any periodic drawings are then debited to a separate, or **Drawings Account.** This is sometimes called a **Current Account.** Subsequently when the figure of profit is ascertained it is put to the credit of Drawings Account, and any resultant balance probably represents the proprietor's under or over estimate of the profits. Of course, withdrawals may be made on account of Capital, and would be debited to Capital Account, but these are somewhat exceptional.

Question

Am I right in thinking that the Trial Balance, whether in the ordinary or in the Four-Column Form, gives the whole of the information needed for preparing the Final Accounts?

Answer

No. Even in the simple case of R. Ready, in the last example, certain **adjustments** may have to be made. It is true, however, to say, as we did, that it provides a **basis** for their preparation.

Question

What are these adjustments?

Answer

It will be better for us to consider them after we have become familiar with the ordinary form of **Revenue Account and Balance Sheet,** because they affect both.

The main additional factor we have to take into account is, however, that of **Stock in Trade.**

In ascertaining our profit figure, it is not enough to compare the cost of goods purchased with the proceeds of goods sold. Since a minimum amount of stock has always to be held by the business this will in any event be part of the cost of purchases, but clearly it cannot appear in the sales **until it is sold.** Thus, at any particular date, e.g. the date to which the business makes up its accounts, allowance must be made for the existence of the stock **then on hand,** and its proper value.

In the case of a new business, if we thought in terms of **quantities** only, we might say **purchases** equal **sales** plus **stock on hand at the end** of the period. Therefore closing stock **must** be included in the second column of the Trial Balance, and as it is a part of the property of the business at the same date, it **appears also** in the third or **Asset** column, i.e. in the former as a credit, and in the latter as a debit.

CHAPTER XII

THE REVENUE ACCOUNT

The Trading Account
The Profit and Loss Account
The Appropriation Account

What has just been discussed enables us to proceed to this first section of the Final Accounts.

Our task is to determine, in a suitable way, the Profit or Loss which has resulted from the carrying on of the ordinary transactions of the business.

We have always to remember with regard to the Final Accounts that they must be clear and informative, and free from unnecessary detail.

The period in respect of which they are drawn up will vary according to the requirements of the proprietor. In many cases it is customary to prepare them at yearly intervals, or at the date of the business's financial year end. This may be December 31, March 31, the end of the busy season, or some other date when perhaps there is least pressure of work on the office staff.

The **Revenue Account** is usually divided into three sections:

(*a*) The Trading Account.
(*b*) The Profit and Loss Account.
(*c*) The Appropriation Account.

For our present purpose it is the first two sections which are important.

In all three sections, however, we find that the **form** adopted is that of the **ordinary Ledger Account,** using the **Dr.** and **Cr.** symbols which are a feature of the latter.

TRADING ACCOUNT

The purpose of this account is to determine what is called the
gross profit or **loss**.

In it, after making due allowance for stocks carried at the
beginning and the end of the period, we compare in a merchanting business the proceeds of sales with the cost of goods sold.

Example

On January 1, 19x7, A. Graham had a stock of goods value
£1 216. His purchases for the year amounted to £10 340, and
his sales to £15 000. Transport charges on incoming goods
amounted to £208. He valued his stock on December 31, 19x7,
at £1 764. Show his Trading Account.

TRADING ACCOUNT
Year ended December 31, 19x7

DR.			CR.
	£		£
Stock, January 1 19x7	1 216·00	Sales	15 000·00
Purchases £10 340·00		Stock, December 31 19x7	1 764·00
Carriage Inward 208·00			
	10 548·00		
Gross Profit	5 000·00		
	£16 764·00		£16 764·00

It is important we should notice the following points:

(*a*) The account is headed 'Year ended December 31, 19x7',
implying that it is a survey of the transactions throughout
the year.

(*b*) The cost of purchases is increased by the transport charges
paid, and represents **delivered cost** to the business. Apart
from this no other kind of expense whatever is included.

(*c*) **Gross Profit** is seen to be the excess of sales over the purchased cost of the goods sold. It is the first stage in the
determination of the final, or net, profit.

Stock in Trade

Sometimes a difficulty may arise as to the measurement of the quantity and value of the **Stock** at **December 31, 19x7,** which is shown above at £1 764.

We saw on page 132 how necessary it was to take it into account by means of an actual stocktaking.

In this process the goods on hand will be counted, weighed, measured, etc., listed on stock sheets and priced at purchased cost. They cannot be valued at the higher selling price because they are not yet sold, and may never be sold. It is reasonable to value them at cost price, because in doing so we are merely carrying forward **from one period into another** a part of the Cost of Purchases.

It may be that at the date of stocktaking the market price (or present buying price) is less than the cost price. Provided, however, that there is no selling deficiency, i.e. the cost price, together with any selling expenses yet to be incurred, does not exceed the selling price, no adjustment is required. The business is not to be penalised only because it failed to buy at the bottom of the market.

A final point to note is that in the Trading Account the ratio of **gross profit** to **sales** or **turnover** is an important one in all businesses. Expressed as a percentage it amounts in this case to $33\frac{1}{3}\%$ of the Sales.

Let us now consider the **closing entries** in the Ledger Accounts concerned.

PRIVATE LEDGER

STOCK

Dr.							Cr.
Date	Details	Fo.	Amount	Date	Details	Fo.	Amount
19x7 Jan. 1	Balance	b/d	£ 1 216·00	19x7 Dec. 31	Transfer to Trading A/c		£ 1 216·00
Dec. 31	Transfer to Trading A/c		1 764·00	Dec. 31	Balance	c/d	1 764·00
19x8 Jan. 1	Balance	b/d	1 764·00				

(a) On January 1, 19x7, **stock then on hand** of course appears as
a Debit Balance and is transferred on December 31 to the
debit of the Trading Account.

(b) At the same time the closing stock figure of £1 764 is debited
above and posted to the **credit** of Trading Account.

(c) The debit of £1 764 is then brought down on January 1,
19x8.

As in making these entries in the **Stock Account** we are trans-
gressing the rule that no first entry shall be made in any Ledger
Account, it may be preferred to use the **Debit and Credit Journal**
as the proper Book of Prime Entry. It use for this purpose was
referred to on page 91. The record in this Journal would then be:

			Dr. £	Cr. £
19x7 Dec. 31	Trading A/c, 19x7 Stock Being Transfer of Stock at January 1, 19x7	Dr.	1 216·00	1 216·00
19x7 Dec. 31	Stock Trading A/c, 19x7 Being Stock at this date transferred	Dr.	1 764·00	1 764·00

We could also journalise the transfers from the other Accounts
which will be found in the Impersonal Ledger. Unless we do so,
the closing entries will appear as follows:

PURCHASES

DR.							CR.
Date	Details	Fo.	Amount	Date	Details	Fo.	Amount
19x7 Dec. 31	Total Pur- chases for Year		£ 10 340·00	19x7 Dec. 31	Transfer to Trading A/c		£ 10 340·00

CARRIAGE INWARDS

DR.							CR.
Date	Details	Fo.	Amount	Date	Details	Fo.	Amount
19x7 Dec. 31	Total Expenses for Year		£ 208·00	19x7 Dec. 31	Transfer to Trading A/c		£ 208·00

As regards **Sales** the transfer will be made from the **debit** of Sales Account to the credit of Trading Account.

SALES

DR.   CR.

Date	Details	Fo.	Amount	Date	Details	Fo.	Amount
19x7 Dec. 31	Transfer to Trading A/c		£ 15 000·00	19x7 Dec. 31	Total Sales for Year		£ 15 000·00

In a **manufacturing** business, on the other hand, the Trading Account will be in somewhat different form. In addition to purchases, **wages** paid to workpeople employed in the actual production of the goods will be debited.

Purchases here will include in the main **raw materials** and component parts.

As **gross profit** in a **merchanting** business is ascertained after comparing the proceeds of sales with the cost of goods sold, similarly in a **manufacturing** business the proceeds of sales are compared with the **Direct Cost,** or Prime Cost, of production, which covers **both purchases and workpeople's wages.**

Our justification for dealing with it in this way may be stated as follows:

(*a*) **Merchanting business.** Every sales order booked involves a direct and proportionate increase in Purchases.

(*b*) **Manufacturing business.** Every sales order calls for not only a direct increase in purchases, but also a direct increase in workpeople's wages.

In (*b*) apart from these direct expenses of production, there are also the general factory expenses to be considered. These include rates on the factory premises, repairs to plant and machinery, power costs for operating the plant, and so on. It would be incorrect for us to include these in the Trading Account unless we are instructed to do so, because their inclusion would convert the Account into a Manufacturing, or Working Account.

PROFIT AND LOSS ACCOUNT

This follows immediately after the Trading Account, of which it is really a continuation.

It commences with the balance brought down from the Trading Account, which as we have seen is a **gross profit** if a **credit** balance, or a **gross loss** if a **debit** balance.

Its purpose is to ascertain the final or **net profit** of the business for the period by including:

(a) The remaining **expenses,** other than those already dealt with in the Trading Account.
(b) The **incidental sources** of **income,** such as
   Cash Discounts received,
   Bank Interest received, etc.

In form it is precisely similar to the Trading Account, the expenses or debits appearing on the left-hand side, and the incidental sources of income or credits on the right-hand side.

As regards both debits and credits in the Profit and Loss Account, care must be taken that:

(a) The expenses are those **of the business only** (*excluding* such items as Proprietor's drawings, or private payments made on his behalf).
(b) **The whole of the expenses** relating to the period under review are properly brought in.

We shall see at a later stage the importance of the latter point, but meanwhile let us look at the form and construction of the Profit and Loss Account.

Example

From the items set out below select those which should appear in the Trading (or Goods) and Profit and Loss Account, prepare those accounts (only) showing the Gross Profit and the Net Profit or Loss.

	£
Capital	2 400·00
Freehold Premises	1 350·00
Stock at January 1, 19x9	650·00
Debtors	360·00
Creditors	512·00
Purchases	3 500·00
Sales	5 000·00
Returns Inwards	20·00
Discounts Allowed	52·00
Salaries	220·00
Trade Expenses	153·00
Rates and Taxes	90·00
Fixtures and Fittings	62·00
Cash at Bank	450·00

The stock on hand at December 31, 19x9, was £215.

TRADING AND PROFIT AND LOSS ACCOUNT
Year ended December 31, 19x9

Dr.			Cr.
19x9	**£**		**£**
Stock, January 1	650·00	Sales £5 000·00	
Purchases	3 500·00	*Less* Returns 20·00	
Gross Profit c/d	1 045·00		4 980·00
		Stock, December 31 19x9	215·00
	£5 195·00		£5 195·00
Salaries	220·00	Gross Profit b/d	1 045·00
Trade Expenses	153·00		
Rates and Taxes	90·00		
Discounts Allowed	52·00		
Net Profit	530·00		
	£1 045·00		£1 045·00

The remaining items in the list, with which we have not dealt, are of a Capital nature, and will appear in the Statement of Assets and Liabilities, or Balance Sheet of the business.

The information below the 'Gross Profit Line' comprises the **Profit and Loss Account** proper.

The transfers from the Accounts in the **Impersonal** Ledger will
be made as follows:

SALARIES

Dr.							Cr.
Date	Details	Fo.	Amount	Date	Details	Fo.	Amount
19x9 Dec. 31	Total Salaries for Year		£ 220·00	19x9 Dec. 31	Transfer to Profit and Loss A/c		£ 220·00

TRADE EXPENSES

Dr.							Cr.
Date	Details	Fo.	Amount	Date	Details	Fo.	Amount
19x9 Dec. 31	Total for Year		£ 153·00	19x9 Dec. 31	Transfer to Profit and Loss A/c		£ 153·00

RATES AND TAXES

Dr.							Cr.
Date	Details	Fo.	Amount	Date	Details	Fo.	Amount
19x9 Dec. 31	Total for Year		£ 90·00	19x9 Dec. 31	Transfer to Profit and Loss A/c		£ 90·00

DISCOUNTS ALLOWED

Dr.							Cr.
Date	Details	Fo.	Amount	Date	Details	Fo.	Amount
19x9 Dec. 31	Total for Year		£ 52·00	19x9 Dec. 31	Transfer to Profit and Loss A/c		£ 52·00

Alternatively, instead of making the transfers direct to the
Profit and Loss Account, we may use the **Debit and Credit**

Journal, with the result that the following Journal entries will appear as **closing entries:**

19x9 Dec. 31			Dr. £	Cr. £
	Sundries			
	Profit and Loss A/c	Dr.	515·00	
	Sundries			
	Salaries			220·00
	Trade Expenses			153·00
	Rates and Taxes			90·00
	Discounts allowed			52·00
	Being transfer of Expense Account balances to Profit and Loss Account as above.			

If the latter method be adopted the word 'Sundries' will describe the credit entries in each of the Ledger Accounts, in place of 'Transfer to Profit and Loss Account'.

APPROPRIATION, OR NET PROFIT AND LOSS ACCOUNT

As its name implies, this third section deals with the ascertained Net Profit or Loss, and its distribution among the proprietors of the business.

Thus in a partnership firm the Net Profit figure will here be divided in the ratio in which the partners share profits and losses.

In the case of a Limited Company, the appropriation account shows how the Net Profits are divided in dividend to the shareholders according to their respective rights and interests.

The necessity for such an account rarely, if ever, arises where the position of a sole trader is under consideration, the Net Profit being carried direct to the Capital or Current Account of the proprietor, as already explained.

TESTS AND QUESTIONS

1 What do you understand by (a) Capital Expenditure; (b) Revenue Expenditure?

State some items coming under each of these headings in the case of a Company carrying on business as manufacturers of aeroplanes.

2 What is the object in preparing a Trading Account as distinct
  from a Profit and Loss Account? Explain what information may
  be obtained from the former and its importance to a trader.

3 What do you understand by a 'Nominal Account'?
    State some exceptions to the general rule that such accounts are
  closed when the Profit and Loss Account has been prepared,
  indicating the reasons for any balances which may remain.

4 What are the reasons for dividing the ordinary revenue account of a
  business into two sections, the Trading Account and the Profit and
  Loss Account?

5 What is the object of calculating gross profit and net profit? Does
  gross profit measure the prosperity of a business?

6 (a) What may be the advantages to a business of having: (i) a
      Cash Received Book, (ii) a Cash Paid Book, (iii) a Private
      Cash Book, instead of a Single Cash Book only?

  (b) The stock of goods held by Edward Newman on January 1,
      19x6, consisted of 1 000 units valued at £0·50 each.

    At December 31, 19x6, 800 units were held in stock, of which the
    cost price was £0·50 per unit, and the then market value £0·40 per
    unit.

    Show how the Stock Account would appear in Newman's
    Ledger for the year 19x6.

7 A fire occurred on the premises of a merchant on June 15, 19x2,
  and a considerable part of the stock was destroyed. The value of
  the stock salved was £450.

    The books disclosed that on April 1, 19x2, the stock was valued
  at £3 675, the purchases to the date of the fire amounted to
  £10 494 and the sales to £15 650.

    On investigation it is found that during the past five years the
  average gross profit on the sales was 36%.

    You are required to prepare a statement showing the amount the
  merchant should claim from the Insurance Company in respect of
  stock destroyed or damaged by the fire.

8 On January 5, 19x7, Ambrose sold goods to Applejohn.

    The goods had cost Ambrose £100, and the selling price was
  50% on cost, payment being due on monthly account less 2% for
  cash.

    On January 28, 19x7, Applejohn returned a part of the goods,
  and Ambrose sent him a credit note for £30.

    The amount due was paid by cheque on February 28, 19x7, but
  three days later the cheque was returned by the bank unpaid, and
  ultimately £0·75 in the £ was received from Applejohn and
  accepted in full settlement.

Show:

(*a*) Applejohn's Account in the books of Ambrose;

(*b*) What profit or loss Ambrose made on the whole transaction.

9 A business has three departments, A, B and C. You are asked to calculate the working profit in each department, by reference to the following:

	£
Opening Stocks, B	1 280·00
Opening Stocks, C	640·00
Closing Stocks, B	1 320·00
Closing Stocks, C	650·00
Purchases	6 000·00
Wages	1 800·00
General Expenses	1 250·00
Sales, B	6 800·00
Sales, C	3 200·00

All purchases are made for A department in the first instance. A department (which has no sales) processes the goods and then re-issues them to B and C departments at fixed prices.

The issues to B were valued at £5 000 and to C at £2 400.

25% of the wages are charged to B, 20% to C, 10% to general expenses, and the balance to A.

The general expenses are recharged as follows:

Department A, 7% on output value,

Department B, 10% on sales value,

Department C, 7% on sales value,

any difference being carried to the Profit and Loss Account.

10 PQ carries on business as a merchant, but, although he has taken stock regularly at the end of December in each year, he has not kept proper books of account. He keeps a Cash Book, Petty Cash Book and Personal Ledger.

If requested by him to ascertain the result of his trading for the past year, explain briefly how you would proceed.

CHAPTER XIII

THE BALANCE SHEET

Together with the Revenue Account, we have described this as a part of the Final Accounts of the business. It has been not inaptly defined as 'a flashlight photograph of the position of affairs of the business at a particular date'.

More precisely we can speak of it as a Statement of Assets and Liabilities, including the balance of the Revenue Account made up to the date at which the Balance Sheet is prepared.

That it is a Statement of Assets and Liabilities justifies us in confining our attention to the 'Capital' columns of the four-column Trial Balance, the **debit balances** in which were seen to represent Assets, and the **credit balances, Liabilities.**

The fact that it includes the ascertained balance on the Revenue Account implies that this balance, if a Credit, will be shown as a Liability and if a Debit, as an Asset.

In other words, the business having an **initial liability** to its proprietor for the amount of Capital invested by him, has now a **further liability** in respect of the profit earned. Had a loss been sustained, it would be a Conventional Asset, or Asset in name only, i.e. it would appear on the Assets side of the Balance Sheet as representing the extent to which **the Assets as a whole were deficient in relation to the Capital.**

It is important for us to remember that the Balance Sheet is the complement to the Revenue Account and is indeed an essential part of the Final Accounts, for this reason. When the business was begun Capital was invested in it, perhaps in the first place in the form of cash. Almost at once this cash would be spent in the acquisition of various forms of property, of the kind we have defined as Fixed Assets, or Current Assets.

The former represented property which the business must possess as part of its equipment; the latter consisted of property in which the business was dealing.

If the Current Assets were therefore so dealt in by the proprietor or his manager as to produce a Profit, ascertained by the preparation of a Revenue Account, it would clearly be very desirable to draw up a further Balance Sheet at **the end of each trading period,** showing just what Assets existed in the hands of the business at that date. Provided no additions to or withdrawals from Capital had taken place, and each Asset held was reasonably and properly valued in each succeeding Balance Sheet, any increase in the Total Assets would represent a **profit,** and conversely any decrease a **loss.**

In the latter case, as the loss appeared in the Balance Sheet as an 'Asset', it could quite well be deducted from the **liability** of the business to its proprietor on **Capital** Account, disclosing at that point a **loss of Capital,** which, of course, is in line with the facts.

THE FORM OF THE BALANCE SHEET

We have seen that the Revenue Account is prepared very much in the form of the ordinary Ledger Account.

In form, it is a summarised Ledger Account to which all the balances appearing in the 'Revenue' columns of the Trial Balance are transferred at the end of the financial year of the business. By so doing, an ultimate balance (either of Profit or Loss) is struck.

But we still have to deal with the balances appearing in the 'Capital' columns. It is these latter remaining balances, **and the balance of the Revenue Account,** which are entered in a 'sheet of balances' or **Balance Sheet.**

We could, if we wished, show this Balance Sheet in the form of an ordinary Ledger Account, debiting to it the Assets, and putting the Liabilities on the credit side.

The opposite, however, is the almost universal practice in this country, the Debit and Credit sides being reversed. Thus, Liabilities are shown on the left-hand or 'Debit' side of the Balance Sheet, and Assets on the right-hand or 'Credit' side, and this is true whether the business be owned by a sole trader, a partnership firm, or a Limited Company.

As a result, in reading the Balance Sheet in the ordinary way, from left to right, we begin with the Liabilities, and then turn to a study of the Assets out of which they are to be met.

We can also regard the Balance Sheet as a **'classified summary'** of the Ledger Balances remaining on the books after the preparation of the Revenue Account, and including the balance of this latter Account.

THE BALANCE SHEET AND THE TRIAL BALANCE CONTRASTED

While both are drawn up at a particular date, the former includes only those balances which are, or have become **Assets** and **Liabilities**; the latter includes as well the various Impersonal Ledger balances relating to **expenses** and **gains.**

The Balance Sheet is a properly marshalled statement of the Assets and Liabilities, setting them out in their order of Realisability or Priority. The Trial Balance merely lists the whole of the balances in the order in which they happen to appear in the Ledgers.

Further, the purpose of the Balance Sheet is to give information to the proprietor of the business as to its financial position, whereas the Trial Balance is extracted primarily to prove the arithmetical accuracy of the book-keeping work.

Finally, the Balance Sheet always includes the value of the Stock on Hand at the end of the period; the Trial Balance, unless in four-column form (and not necessarily then) does not show this Asset.

Let us now take two illustrations involving some of the points we have been discussing:

Example

From the following items construct the Balance Sheet of L. Redfern as on December 31, 19x1.

	£
Capital as at January 1, 19x1	2 000
Motor vans as at December 31, 19x1	2 200
Cash at bank as at December 31, 19x1	700
Profit for the year	3 000

	£
Land and buildings as at December 31, 19x1	4 100
Drawings for the year	1 500
Stock of Goods, December 31, 19x1	2 300
Loan from A. Herbert	4 000
Debtors as at December 31, 19x1	2 000
Sundry Creditors as at December 31, 19x1	3 800

In this first case, it may be helpful if we list the items as Assets
(Debits) or Liabilities (Credits), i.e.:

	Dr. £	Cr. £
Capital, January 1, 19x1		2 000·00
Motor vans, December 31, 19x1	2 200·00	
Cash at bank, December 31, 19x1	700·00	
Profit for the year		3 000·00
Land and Buildings, December 31, 19x1	4 100·00	
Drawings	1 500·00	
Stock of Goods, December 31, 19x1	2 300·00	
Loan from A. Herbert		4 000·00
Debtors as at December 31, 19x1	2 000·00	
Sundry Creditors as at December 31, 19x1		3 800·00
	£12 800·00	£12 800·00

L. REDFERN

BALANCE SHEET AS AT DECEMBER 31, 19x1

Liabilities	£	£	Assets	£	£
Loan from A. Herbert	4 000·00		Cash at Bank		700·00
Sundry Creditors	3 800·00		Debtors		2 000·00
		7 800·00	Stock of Goods		2 300·00
Current Account:			Motor Vans		2 200·00
Profit for year	3 000·00		Land and Buildings		4 100·00
Less Drawings	1 500·00				
	1 500·00				
Capital Account:					
As at January 1 19x1	2 000·00				
		3 500·00			
		£11 300·00			£11 300·00

We may then proceed as follows, remembering:

(a) That a Balance Sheet is always prepared at some definite date.

(b) That the balances on the various Accounts of which it is made up are **not** transferred to it as is the case with the Revenue Account.

It should be noted that:

(a) The Assets are stated in their order of realisability beginning with the liquid asset of 'Cash at Bank.'

(b) Cash, Debtors and Stock represent **Current Assets,** while Motor Vans and Land and Buildings are **Fixed Assets.**

(c) Although **Profit** and **Drawings** have been shown in a Current Account they might equally well have been recorded in Capital Account only.

Example

From the following particulars construct the Balance Sheet of T. Tomlinson as on March 31, 19x2:

Capital April 1, 19x1, was £5 000. The loss for the year to March 31, 19x2, was £1 200 and his drawings were £220. On March 31, 19x2 the Stock was £2 480, and the Bank Overdraft £1 320, the Debtors £3 260, the Loan from F. Weston £2 200, the Fixtures and Fittings £1 480, Creditors £2 900, Cash in Hand £50, Machinery £2 730.

If we have studied the first illustration carefully, it should not be necessary to list the balances again before constructing the Balance Sheet.

Looking at the information given, we see, however, that a **trading loss** of £1 200 has been sustained, and in addition there are drawings of £220. The initial Capital has thus **decreased** by £1 420.

As regards the Liabilities, we may note here that the first two relate to **cash advances,** the item 'Creditors' referring to the Purchase Ledger Accounts of suppliers for **goods** or **services.**

Having considered separately the Trading and Profit and Loss Accounts, and the Balance Sheet, we may now, as in a practical case, prepare each of them from an ordinary two-column Trial Balance.

T. TOMLINSON

BALANCE SHEET AS AT MARCH 31, 19x2

Liabilities	£	£	Assets	£	£
Bank Overdraft	1 320·00		Cash in Hand		50·00
Loan from			Debtors		3 260·00
F. Weston	2 200·00		Stock		2 480·00
Creditors	2 900·00		Fixtures and Fittings		1 480·00
		6 420·00	Machinery		2 730·00
Capital Account:					
April 1, 19x1	5 000·00				
Less Loss,					
year to					
March					
31, 19x2					
1 200·00					
Drawings					
220·00					
	1 420·00	3 580·00			
		£10 000·00			£10 000·00

Example

From the following balances prepare the Trading Account, Profit and Loss Account, and Balance Sheet of J. Farmer, a retailer, for half year ended June 30, 19x1:

	£	£
Petty Cash	50·00	
Sundry Creditors		493·00
Cash at Bank	986·00	
Furniture, Fixtures and Equipment	400·00	
Purchases	8 417·00	
Sales		11 618·00
Stock June 30, 19x1	1 117·00	
Office Expenses	45·00	
Rent and Rates	997·00	
Lighting and Heating	186·00	
Advertising	75·00	
Delivery Expenses	66·00	
Capital		2 000·00
Drawings	1 560·00	
Carriage on Purchases	212·00	
	£14 111·00	£14 111·00

Stock on June 30, 19x1, £1 084.

J. FARMER

PROFIT AND LOSS ACCOUNT
Six Months ended June 30, 19x1

DR.   CR.

	£	£		£	£
Stock, Jan. 1, 19x1		1 117·00	Sales		11 618·00
Purchases	8 417·00		Stock, June 30, 19x1		1 084·00
Carriage on Purchases	212·00				
		8 629·00			
Gross Profit c/d		2 956·00			
		£12 702·00			£12 702·00
Rent, Rates and Taxes		997·00	Gross Profit, b/d		2 956·00
Lighting and Heating		186·00			
Advertising		75·00			
Delivery Expenses		66·00			
Office Expenses		45·00			
Net Profit, carried to Capital A/c		1 587·00			
		£2 956·00			£2 956·00

J. FARMER

BALANCE SHEET AS AT JUNE 30, 19x1

DR.   CR.

	£	£		£	£
Sundry Creditors		493·00	Petty Cash	50·00	
Capital Account	2 000·00		Cash at Bank	986·00	
Add Net Profit for half year to date	1 587·00				1 036·00
			Stock		1 084·00
	3 587·00		Furniture, Fixtures and Equipment		400·00
Less Drawings	1 560·00				
		2 027·00			
		£2 520·00			£2 520·00

We should note that as the Trading Account and the Profit and Loss Account are only divisions of the Revenue Account, they may conveniently be shown together, as above, in one statement.

TESTS AND QUESTIONS

1 What effect would the following errors made by a book-keeper have upon (a) the Trial Balance, (b) the annual accounts of a business:

   (i) An item of £50 for goods sold to C.D. posted from the Sales Journal to the credit of C.D.'s Ledger Account.
   (ii) An item of £12, representing the purchase of a desk, placed in the general expenses column of the Purchase Journal.
   (iii) A sum of £15, representing interest allowed by the banker, entered in the correct column on the credit side of the Cash Book.

2 Enumerate the assets you would expect to find on the Balance sheet of A.B., a motor-car manufacturer, grouping them into the different classes.
   Why is the distinction between different types of asset important?

3 At December 31, 19x1, the Cash Book of Simmonds, a sole trader, shows an overdraft of £98. The following cheques had been drawn and entered in the Cash Book on December 30, but were not presented for payment until January 4, 19x2.

	£
Grey	61·00
Maddox	34·00
Wilson	10·00

   Bank charges of £8 for the half-year ended December 31, 19x1, were entered in the Cash Book in the first week of January only.
   A cheque for £35, received from Foxton, a customer, and duly banked, was returned dishonoured on December 24, but Simmonds had omitted to make the appropriate entry in the Cash Book.
   Prepare a Reconciliation, showing the Bank Pass Book balance at December 31, 19x1.

4 From the following particulars draw up the Balance Sheet of B. Wilton as on December 31, 19x1: Land and buildings, £1 000; Machinery, £325; Motor vans, £120; Fixtures and fittings, £70; Stock on hand at December 31, 19x1, £950; Sundry debtors, £856; Cash in hand, £29; Sundry creditors, £1 820; Bank overdraft, £1 200; Loan from A. Mather, £200; Capital as at January 1, 19x1, £230; Loss for the year, £100.
   State briefly your opinion of the financial position of B. Wilton.

5 A.B., an engineer, decides to erect a new machine in his works. He dismantles an old machine and uses material therefrom to the value of £50 in the erection of the new machine. Additional

materials are purchased from outside sources at a cost of £150, and the wages amount to £200.

Explain how the foregoing items would be dealt with in his books.

6 In the form of Cash Book provided, after properly heading each column, enter all the money transactions below and balance the book.

Journalise the opening balances and remaining transactions. (Note: Purchases and Sales Books may be used, if preferred.)

Post the entries to the Ledger. Extract a Trial Balance.

Draw up a Profit and Loss Account and Balance Sheet.

On May 1, 19x7, D. Robinson, nurseryman, reopened his books with the following balances in addition to his Capital Account: Cash, £40; Rent outstanding, £80; Bank overdraft, £470; M. Merritt (Cr.), £232; S. Service (Dr.), £327; Stock, £1 565.

During the month his transactions were:

		£
May 3	Received cheque from S. Service and paid into Bank	300·00
5	Sold to S. Service:	
	Rose bushes	146·00
	Rose standards	139·00
	Misc. plants	127·00
7	S. Service's cheque returned dishonoured	300·00
10	S. Service paid in cash (banked)	275·00
14	Bought of M. Merritt:	
	Fruit trees	356·00
	Shrubs	42·00
18	Paid M. Merritt by cheque to settle account to 1st inst.	230·00
21	Returned to M. Merritt damaged shrubs	4·00
25	Cash sales	48·00
26	Bought for cash sundry plants at auction	17·00
27	Paid rent outstanding by cheque	80·00
29	Drew cheque for self	80·00
31	Wages and expenses for month:	
	Paid by cheque	120·00
	And in cash	52·00
	Bank charges	6·00
	Rent accrued	40·00
	Interest on capital at 6% p.a.	
	Stock on hand valued at	1 701·00

7 The following balances were extracted from the books of D. Wright on December 31, 19x1. You are required to prepare a

Trading Account, Profit and Loss Account and Balance Sheet as on that date.

	Dr. £	Cr. £
Cash in Hand	17·00	
Bank Overdraft		175·00
Stock, January 1, 19x1	6 794·00	
Purchases and Sales	14 976·00	26 497·00
Wages	3 719·00	
Insurance	155·00	
Bank Charges	110·00	
Furniture and Fittings	1 115·00	
Returns Inwards and Outwards	309·00	237·00
Sundry Drs. and Crs.	1 753·00	615·00
Land and Buildings	20 000·00	
Discount		154·00
Capital		21 270·00
	£48 948·00	£48 948·00

Stock at end £1 169·00.

8   From the following Trial Balance of J. Lowe, prepare Trading and Profit and Loss Accounts for the year ended March 31, 19x2, and a Balance Sheet as on that date.

   The stock on hand at March 31, 19x2, was valued at £5500·00.

	£	£
Purchases	21 300·00	
Carriage Inwards	350·00	
Sales		29 600·00
Stock, April 1, 19x1	4 000·00	
Trade Expenses	850·00	
Fixtures and Fittings	2 000·00	
Discounts Allowed	900·00	
J. Lowe: Capital		6 000·00
Returns Inwards	750·00	
Cash in Hand	150·00	
Sundry Debtors	2 400·00	
Salaries	1 200·00	
J. Lowe: Drawings	2 500·00	
Discounts Received		400·00
Sundry Creditors		4 000·00
Cash at Bank	2 700·00	
Rent	500·00	
Rates	400·00	
	£40 000·00	£40 000·00

9 The following Trial Balance was extracted from the books of
   R. Parr on December 31, 19x1:

	Dr. £	Cr. £
Capital		35 000·00
Drawings	1 450·00	
Stock at January 1, 19x1	26 000·00	
Purchases and Sales	45 000·00	65 000·00
Returns Outwards		600·00
Returns Inwards	1 000·00	
Salaries	4 750·00	
Trade Expenses	2 050·00	
Bad Debts	230·00	
Discount Account (balance)		350·00
Sundry Debtors	35 750·00	
Sundry Creditors		19 600·00
Insurance	220·00	
Fixtures and Fittings	1 850·00	
Motor Vans	2 650·00	
Rent, Rates and Taxes	3 550·00	
Bank Overdraft		3 950·00
	£124 500·00	£124 500·00

The value of the stock on hand was £17 950.

You are required to prepare Trading and Profit and Loss
Accounts for the year ended December 31, 19x1, and a Balance
Sheet as on that date.

10 The following balances were extracted at April 30, 19x2, from the
   books of C.D.:

   (a) Prepare therefrom a Trading and Profit and Loss Account for
       the year ended on that date, and also a Balance Sheet.

   (b) Do the results of the business for the year justify the drawings
       of £350 by C.D.?

	£
Office Salaries	628·00
Insurance	61·00
Discounts Received	33·00
Sales	7 350·00
Bad Debts	69·00
Plant and Machinery	430·00
Commission	127·00
Investment Interest Received	30·00
Stock, May 1, 19x1	1 110·00
Repairs	98·00
Sundries	46·00
Goods Returned by Customers	100·00
Discounts Allowed	115·00
Rent and Rates	322·00
Purchases	4 290·00

	£
Sundry Debtors	143·00
Travelling Expenses	263·00
Wages and National Insurance	3 004·00
General Insurance	34·00
Carriage Inwards	87·00
Sundry Creditors	1 426·00
C.D.: Capital, May 1, 19x1	3 250·00
Cash at Bank	109·00
Coal, Gas and Water	177·00
Goods Returned to Suppliers	74·00
Investment in Utopia, Ltd.	600·00

The stock at April 30, 19x2, was valued at £1 275·00.

11 The following is the Trial Balance extracted at December 31, 19x2, from the books of S. Printer, who carries on business as a manufacturer of sports equipment:

	Dr. £	Cr. £
Petty Cash Book	28·00	
Nominal Ledger:		
Carriage Outwards	504·00	
Carriage Inwards	266·00	
Travelling Expenses	2 169·00	
Discount Allowed	933·00	
Discount Received		218·00
Repairs and Incidentals	820·00	
Rent, Rates and Taxes	872·00	
Factory Wages	10 655·00	
Heating and Lighting	137·00	
Sales, less Returns		30 750·00
Factory National Insurance	318·00	
Packing and Dispatch Expenses	1 252·00	
Purchases, less Returns	10 546·00	
Salaries and National Insurance	2 735·00	
Private Cash Book		853·00
Private Ledger:		
Stock, January 1, 19x2	3 915·00	
S. Printer: Capital at January 1, 19x2		10 000·00
S. Printer: Drawings	1 200·00	
Office Fixtures and General Equipment January 1, 19x2	1 567·00	
Equipment Sold		136·00
Equipment Purchased	608·00	
Bank Interest Account	46·00	
Sales Ledgers:		
Accounts Receivable	6 002·00	
Purchase Ledger:		
Accounts Payable		2 616·00
	£44 573·00	£44 573·00

The stock at December 31, 19x2, was valued at £5 200.

You are required to:

(a) Prepare a Trading and Profit and Loss Account for the year ended December 31, 19x2, and a Balance Sheet at that date.

(b) State the percentages of Gross Profit and of Net Profit to Turnover.

(c) Show the Office Fixtures and General Equipment Account as it would appear in the Private Ledger.

12 The following is the Trial Balance extracted from the books of J.B. as at December 31, 19x1.

	Dr. £	Cr. £
Private Ledger:		
Capital, January 1, 19x1		4 137·00
Drawings	1 000·00	
Stock, January 1, 19x1	2 035·00	
Fixtures and Fittings, January 1, 19x1	2 119·00	
Bills Payable		268·00
Bills Receivable	238·00	
Nominal Ledger:		
Purchases	5 911·00	
Sales		10 782·00
Discounts Allowed	223·00	
Discounts Received		104·00
Packing Expenses	192·00	
Office Expenses	74·00	
Salaries	826·00	
Repairs	58·00	
Lighting and Heating	87·00	
Rates	146·00	
Rent	200·00	
Wages (workpeople)	1 644·00	
Sundry Expenses	61·00	
Cash Book		781·00
Petty Cash Book	27·00	
Creditors (Personal Ledger)		1 433·00
Debtors (Personal Ledger)	2 664·00	
	£17 505·00	£17 505·00

The stock on hand at December 31, 19x1, was valued by J.B. in the sum of £3 157.

Prepare Trading and Profit and Loss Account, and Balance Sheet.

13 The following 'Statement of Affairs' have been drawn up to give
the financial position, as on March 31, 19x1, and March 31, 19x2,
respectively, of A. Brown, who keeps his books on a single entry
basis:

STATEMENT OF AFFAIRS, MARCH 31, 19x1

	£		£
Capital	6 192·00	Fixtures	250·00
Creditors	742·00	Stock	2 305·00
		Debtors	4 176·00
		Cash	203·00
	£6 934·00		£6 934·00

STATEMENT OF AFFAIRS, MARCH 31, 19x2

	£		£
Capital	5 933·00	Fixtures	230·00
Creditors	817·00	Stock	2 562·00
		Debtors	3 777·00
		Cash	181·00
	£6 750·00		£6 750·00

Brown has transferred £100 a month regularly from his business
banking account to his private banking account by way of drawings, and he has taken £25 worth of stock for his private use. The
alteration in the value of the fixtures represents an amount written
off by way of depreciation.

Calculate Brown's trading profit for the year.

14 The only books kept by Brown are Personal Ledgers. At January 1
his position is as follows:

	£		£
Cash	17·00	Creditors	635·00
Debtors	3 109·00	Capital	3 023·00
Stock	102·00		
Equipment at cost	430·00		
	£3 658·00		£3 658·00

At December 31 following, he informs you that the following are
the figures concerning his Assets and Liabilities:

	£
Cash	15·00
Bank (overdraft)	230·00
Stock	98·00
Debtors	3 036·00
Creditors	502·00

He has had his equipment valued, and thinks that it is now only
worth £350. He has taken notes as to his drawings, and informs you
that he has spent £332 for household purposes, etc., £40 for a life
assurance premium, and £10 for fire insurance for business assets. In
addition, he has taken home goods, of which the cost price was
£9 and the sale price £12.

Prepare a Statement showing Brown's profit for the year, and
his general position at December 31.

15   BALANCE SHEET

	£		£
Creditors	721·00	Freehold Premises	1 560·00
Capital	3 150·00	Machinery and Plant	420·00
		Stock	876·00
		Debtors	982·00
		Cash	33·00
	£3 871·00		£3 871·00

The above is a copy of Samuel Wood's Balance Sheet as on
December 31, 19x1. The only books kept are a Cash Book and a
Ledger. The following is a summary of his receipts and payments
for the year ended December 31, 19x2:

Receipts		*Payments*	
	£		£
Cash on account of		Creditors for Goods	
Credit Sales	4 276·00	Purchased	3 954·00
Cash Sales	1 863·00	Wages	743·00
Capital paid in	200·00	General Expenses	627·00
		Additions to Machin-	
		ery	160·00
		Drawings	536·00
	£6 339·00		£6 020·00

On December 31, 19x2, the amount due to Creditors was £816, and the Debtors and Stock amounted to £918 and £854 respectively. You are required to prepare Trading and Profit and Loss Accounts for the year ended December 31, 19x2, and a Balance Sheet as on that date, after making adjustments in respect of the following:

(*a*) Depreciation of 10% is to be written off the Machinery and Plant, including additions during the year.

(*b*) £150 is to be provided as a Reserve for Doubtful Debts.

(*c*) The sum of £38 for goods supplied to the proprietor was included in the Debtors' balances at December 31, 19x2.

CHAPTER XIV

ADJUSTMENTS IN THE FINAL ACCOUNTS

Question

You said (on page 131) that certain adjustments may be necessary in preparing the Final Accounts, and that the Trial Balance does not show what they are. Can we consider them now?

Answer

As we have dealt with the simple form of Revenue Account and Balance Sheet, in which no adjustments were called for, we may now look a little more closely at the problem of ascertaining **true Profit and Loss** as it arises in practice.

In the first place, our task is not merely to prepare the Final Accounts from the information given in the books of the business as they may stand. We must examine the Ledger Accounts, particularly the accounts in the Impersonal or Nominal Ledger, with a view to seeing that they are **complete so far as concerns the period under review.**

Question

Is there any likelihood of their being incomplete?

Answer

When we speak of the function of the Revenue Account, for example, as the statement of the Profit or Loss over a definite period, it is essential that we include in it **all the expenses incurred as well as the whole of the gross income** of the business.

If any expenses **attributable to the period** were inadvertently omitted, the final figure of Profit would be untrue, and would be **overstated.** Similarly, Profit is **understated** if we neglect to bring in every kind of income, however incidental to the main purpose of the business, which has been **earned** during the period and for which it may properly take credit.

Question

Can you give me examples of such items, and explain why they are termed 'adjustments'?

Answer:

One of the biggest single items of expense in a manufacturing business is **wages** paid to workpeople. In an ordinary case wages may be paid on Fridays in respect of the week ended on the preceding Wednesday. The wage sheets or cards for the week have to be checked and certified, the pay roll prepared, deductions made for National Insurance, and so on. Consequently, if the financial year ended on a Thursday, wages for a whole week and one day would be outstanding, no payment would have been made, and there would be no Credit entry in the Cash Book, and no Debit entry in the Wages Account for the amounts involved when the books were closed.

In effect, the **expense** figure for wages would be less than the true amount, and the fact that the workpeople were **creditors** of the business would be ignored. The former clearly has a bearing on the **Revenue Account** and the latter on the **Balance Sheet**. Therefore we must make an adjustment raising the wage figure to its true level (an additional Debit), and at the same time record the liability for wages in the Balance Sheet (an additional Credit).

Another instance arises in connection with the Book Debts, or **'Sundry Debtors'**, as we have more recently described them.

At the end of the financial year, a certain amount will be due from customers under this head for goods sold to them. The value of these goods appears as 'Sales' in the **Trading Account**, as we have seen, and is the main source of Profit. Unless we are quite convinced that our customers are willing and able to pay what they owe, a part of the Book Debts may become **Bad Debts**, and any loss that is likely to arise in this way must be charged by way of **estimate** against the Profit earned in the period. Otherwise, such estimated loss, if and when it becomes an actual or ascertained loss, is a burden on the Profits of the **subsequent** trading year. Neglect to reserve an estimated sum for Bad or Doubtful Debts has then the effect of **overstating Profits,** and **overstating Assets also,** in that they appear in the Balance Sheets of the business at more than they will ultimately realise.

The adjustment required in this case is to **debit** a sum to **Revenue** by way of 'Provision for doubtful debts', along with the debts actually written off as Bad during the period.

The corresponding Credit balance so created can be shown on the Liabilities side of the Balance Sheet, or better, as a **deduction** from the total Sundry Debtors on the Assets side, thereby reducing them to their estimated collectible value.

Question
With all these adjustments, then, both the Revenue Account and the Balance Sheet are affected?

Answer
Yes, either as a Debit to Revenue and a Credit on the Balance Sheet, with what is called a **Liability Provision**, or as a Credit to Revenue and a Debit on the Balance Sheet, in the form of an **Asset Provision.** The following are illustrations:

Example

Merryweather & Co. pay a rent of £250 per annum for their business premises, which are rated at £225 per annum. The local rates are £0·8 in the £ payable half yearly in advance on March 31 and September 30.

The rent is payable on the usual quarter days, but on September 30, 19x6, the firm sublet a part of the premises to Tenant & Co. at £50 per annum, the first half-yearly payment being due on March 31, 19x7.

The Rent and Rates Account in Merryweather's books was as follows on January 1, 19x6:

19x6 Jan. 1	Balance b/d, Rates prepaid	£ 45·00	19x6 Jan. 1	Balance b/d, Rent due December 25	£ 62·50

You are required:

(a) To write up the account for the year, bringing down any necessary balances at December 31, 19x6.

(b) To state in which section of the Final Accounts for the year 19x6 these balances would appear, giving reasons in brief.

Before we begin, let us take the information given, and consider it. The following points must be borne in mind:

(a) The financial year end of the business is December 31, 19x6.

(b) In the year ended on that date we shall expect to find in the **Profit and Loss Account**:

    1 An expense for rent payable of £250.

    2 An expense for rates of £180 (£0·8 in £ on £225).

    3 A profit for rent receivable from Tenant & Co. of £12·50 (3 months at £50 per annum).

(c) And in the **Balance Sheet**:

    4 An Asset or Debit Balance of £45 representing **rates paid in advance for the 3 months to March 31, 19x7.**

    5 A similar **Asset** of £12·50, being rent accrued due at December 31, 19x6.

The Rent and Rates Account in the Impersonal Ledger will then appear as on p. 164 assuming all payments are made on the due dates.

We notice in the above account that two columns may usefully be provided for rent and rates respectively, and that the *two provisions* carried down appear as the opening figures for the year 19x7. Since they are Debit Balances they may rightly be described as **Asset Provisions.**

It is not usually the practice to journalise these provisions (as by entry in the Debit and Credit Journal) and to this extent we find one exception to the general rule that 'nothing should be recorded in a Ledger Account which has not first appeared in a Book of Prime Entry.'

One more illustration may be taken of a provision, which is in the reverse direction.

Example

During 19x5, his first year of business, a merchant wrote off Bad Debts amounting to £100, and at December 31 made a provision for Bad and Doubtful Debts, amounting to £50.

During 19x6, a final dividend, £30, was received in respect of one of the debts (£40) written off in 19x5, further debts amounting to £60 were written off, and at December 31, 19x6, the merchant

MERRYWEATHER & CO.

RENT AND RATES

Dr.

Date		Rent £	Rates £
19x6			
Jan. 1	Balance b/d, Rates prepaid		45·00
2	Cash, Rent	62·50	
Mar. 25	Cash, Rent	62·50	
31	Cash, Rates 6 months to September 30, 19x6		90·00
June 24	Cash, Rent	62·50	
Sept. 29	Cash, Rent	62·50	
30	Cash, Rates 6 months to March 31, 19x7		90·00
Dec. 25	Cash, Rent	62·50	
31	Transfer to Profit and Loss A/c, Rent Receivable	12·50	
		£325·00	£225·00
19x7			
Jan. 1	Balance b/d: Rent accrued due / Rates prepaid	12·50	45·00

Cr.

Date		Rent £	Rates £
19x6			
Jan. 1	Balance b/d, Rent due December 25	62·50	
Dec. 31	Provision for 3 months' Rent accrued due from Tenant & Co. at this date at £50·00 per annum c/d	12·50	
31	Provision for 3 months' Rates paid in advance c/d		45·00
31	Transfer to Profit and Loss A/c: Rent Payable / Rates	250·00	180·00
		£325·00	£225·00

considered it prudent to make a provision against existing debts of 60% for one of £40, and 30% for one of £30.

In addition it was estimated that a final dividend of £0·75 in the £ would be received in 19x7 in respect of a debt standing in the books at £28.

You are required to produce, for the two years, the Bad Debts Account, Provision for Bad and Doubtful Debts Account, and (as far as possible) Profit and Loss Account.

IMPERSONAL LEDGER
BAD DEBTS

DR.		£			CR. £
19x5 Dec. 31	Sundry Customers' Debts written off	100·00	19x5 Dec. 31	Transfer to Profit and Loss A/c	100·00
19x6 Dec. 31	Sundry Customers' Debts written off	60·00	19x6 Jan. 1	Cash, Final Dividend of £0·75 in £ on debt of £40·00 written off in 19x5	30·00
			Dec. 31	Transfer to Provision for Bad and Doubtful Debts A/c	30·00
		£60·00			£60·00

IMPERSONAL LEDGER
PROVISION FOR BAD AND DOUBTFUL DEBTS

DR.		£			CR. £
19x5 Dec. 31	Provision c/d, being provision at this date	50·00	19x5 Dec. 31	Transfer to Profit and Loss A/c.	50·00
19x6 Dec. 31	Transfer from Bad Debts A/c	30·00	19x6 Jan. 1	Provision b/d	50·00
31	Provision c/d, being provisions at this date: X. 60% of £40·00 £24·00 Y. 30% of £30·00 9·00 Z. 25% of £28·00 7·00	40·00	Dec. 31	Transfer to Profit and Loss A/c	20·00
		£70·00			£70·00
			19x7 Jan. 1	Provision b/d	40·00

PROFIT AND LOSS ACCOUNTS (EXTRACT)

Year ended December 31, 19x5

Dr.		Cr.
	£	
Bad Debts, including Provision	150·00	

Year ended December 31, 19x6

	£	
Bad Debts, less Recoveries, and and including Provision	20·00	

In this illustration, we are instructed to open separately an account for the Provision for Bad and Doubtful Debts.

The recovery of £30 during 19x6 serves to reduce the expense of £60 for debts written off during that year, and the balance is transferred at the year end to the Provision Account. The Provision required at December 31, 19x6, is brought down as a **Credit Balance** on January 1, 19x7, and may as such be termed a **Liability Provision.**

TESTS AND QUESTIONS

1 Explain briefly the object of a bad debts reserve. Upon what basis is it usually formed? How does it affect the Profit and Loss Account and the Balance Sheet? Illustrate your answer with a specimen account.

2 During the year ended December 31, 19x9, C. P. Kilham made the following bad debts: A.B., £13·13; X.Y., £5·49; and R.Z., £12·91.

    Submit the entries Kilham should make when closing his books as on December 31, 19x9.

3 X. sets up in practice as a doctor on January 1, 19x2. During 19x2 he received fees amounting to £3 545, and at the end of the year £237 was owing to him. During 19x3 the fees received amounted to £3 831, and at the end of the year £364 was owing to him. His expenses amounted to £1 265 in 19x2 and £1 320 in 19x3, there being no liabilities outstanding at the end of either year.

    Ascertain his profit for each of these years.

4 On October 1, 19x5, the Bad Debts Reserve Account of a business stood at £3 768. During the ensuing twelve months bad debts amounting to £3 389 were written off. On June 30, 19x6, a payment of £80 was received on account of a debt which had been treated as irrecoverable two years previously. The debts outstanding at September 30, 19x6, were examined, and the book-keeper

was instructed to make a reserve of £3 400 to cover the anticipated loss.

You are required to show the Ledger Account or Accounts as they appear after the closing of the books had been completed.

5 On January 1, 19x6, H. Jacks owed J. Dixon £220. On March 31 Jacks purchased goods from Dixon valued at £246, of which he returned goods to the value of £16 on April 3. On April 6 Jacks paid Dixon £120 on account. On July 1 Dixon received notice of the bankruptcy of Jacks, and on October 5 he received first and final dividend of £0·35 in the £ from the Trustee in Bankruptcy. Show the account of H. Jacks in the Ledger of J. Dixon as it should appear after Dixon had balanced his books at December 31, 19x6.

6 The Rates Account of G. Baker is shown in his Ledger as follows:

RATES ACCOUNT

19x4

Dec. 31 To Balance, in advance, b/f £16.

19x5

May 31 To Cash, half-year to September 30, 19x5, £34·50.

Nov. 18 To Cash, half-year to March 31, 19x6, £34·50.

Balance the account by transfer to Profit and Loss Account at December 31, 19x5, bringing forward the appropriate amount in advance.

7 At December 31, 19x1, the Ledger of T. Atkins contained the following balances for debts due to him:

	£
Arthur	36·08
Charles	15·50
Henry	14·09
Percy	20·50

The estate of Arthur is being administered in Bankruptcy, and it is feared, pending realisation, that not more than £0·50 in the £ will be recoverable. Henry has died and his estate has no assets whatever. For the sake of prudence 5% is to be reserved on the debts of Charles and Percy.

Show the four accounts, together with Bad Debts Account and Reserve for Doubtful Debts Account. Journal need not be given.

8 In 19x2 a trader, X., wrote off as a bad debt £19·77, the balance of an account due to him by Y.

In 19x3 Y. paid the debt in full. Show by means of Journal entries how the recovery of this debt would be dealt with in closing X.'s books for 19x3, on the assumption that:

(a) The cash received was posted to the credit of Y.'s account.

(b) The cash was posted to a nominal account.

9 The payments made by X., Ltd., to its travellers on account of
   commission and salaries during 19x4 amounted to £1 547·18 and
   during 19x5 to £1 752·67. The amounts accrued and unpaid under
   this heading were as follows:

	£
December 31, 19x3	36·96
December 31, 19x4	41·18
December 31, 19x5	22·89

   Draw up a statement showing the amount to be charged against
   profits in 19x4 and 19x5 respectively, and show what would have
   been the effect of accidentally omitting to make the proper reserve
   at the end of 19x4.

10 The Rent and Rates Account in the Ledger of Riley Bros. showed
   that on December 31, 19x5, the rent for the quarter to Christmas
   was outstanding, and that the rates for the half-year ending
   March 31, 19x6, amounting to £76·37 had been paid. During the
   ensuing year the following payments relating to rent and rates were
   made:

		£
Jan. 4	Rent for Christmas quarter	90·00
Mar. 29	Rent for Ladyday quarter	90·00
June 26	Rates for half-year ending September 30, 19x6	74·73
July 7	Rent for Midsummer quarter	90·00
Sept. 30	Rent for Michaelmas quarter	90·00
Dec. 28	Rent for Christmas quarter	90·00

   The rates for the half-year ending March 31, 19x7, which amounted
   to £80·89 were paid on January 6, 19x7.
      You are required to show the Rent and Rates Account as it
   would appear after the books for the year ended December 31,
   19x6 had been closed. Make any calculation in months.

11 The financial year of Sanctions, Ltd., ended on December 31,
   19x5.
      At that date, the following balances appeared, among others, in
   their Impersonal Ledger:

   Rates, £225 (15 months to March 31, 19x6).
   Wages, £7 098 (to December 27, 19x5).
   Stationery, Advertising, etc., £864.
   Bad and Doubtful Debts, written off, £126.

      The wages for the week ending January 3, 19x6, were £63.
      Stationery stocks for which an adjustment is required amounted
   to £117.

The Sundry Debtors totalled £5 660, and a reserve is to be made of 5% for doubtful debts, and 2% for discounts.

Show the Ledger Accounts involved after giving effect to the above.

12 X.Y., who owed £200 to A.B. for goods supplied on June 1, 19x4, became unable to pay his debts in full and offered a composition of £0·25 in the £ to his creditors and this was accepted. A cheque for the dividend was received by A.B. on December 1, 19x4.

When X.Y. called his creditors together, A.B. had on his premises a machine belonging to X.Y. and claimed a right of lien in respect thereof. This was admitted and the machine was valued at £80. A.B.'s claim was consequently reduced by this amount.

A.B. decided that instead of selling the machine he would retain it as part of his plant. When making up his annual accounts on December 31, 19x4, the balance of X.Y.'s account was written off as a bad debt.

You are required to show, by means of Journal entries and Ledger Accounts, how the foregoing transactions would be recorded in A.B.'s books.

13 In the books of Harry Holborn at December 31, 19x6, the financial year end, the Ledger Account for 'Heat, Light, Power and Water' shows a Debit Balance of £253. Investigation discloses the following points:

(a) A deposit of £10 (returnable on cessation of supply) was paid on April 1, 19x6, in respect of electric power.

(b) The charge for electric power is made quarterly, and the last debit in the account is for the three months to November 30, 19x6. The demand note for the three months to February 28, 19x6, amounted to £36.

(c) A half-year's water rate, amounting to £14, was debited to the account in October, 19x6, in respect of the period to March 31, 19x7.

Make such adjustments in the Ledger Account as appear to you to be necessary and state how, if at all, they would be shown in Holborn's Balance Sheet at December 31, 19x6.

14 On January 1, 19x3, A. and B. go into business as advertising consultants, on the footing that each contributes £1 000 cash as capital, profits and losses to be shared equally.

The £1 000 provided by A. is borrowed by him privately from his bankers at 8% p.a. interest.

It is agreed that B., who devotes his whole time to the business, shall receive prior to the ascertainment of profit a management salary of £1 250 p.a.

Office accommodation is acquired on February 1, 19x3, at a rent of £300 p.a., payable quarterly, the first payment to be made on March 31, 19x3.

Furniture and fittings are purchased on the latter date from O.F., Ltd., for a sum of £72 cash, and B. introduces other similar equipment of a value of £36 to be credited to his Capital Account.

Apart from the above items, at December 31, 19x3, there has been received in cash by A. and B. as consultants' fees the sum of £6 150, and at that date fees totalling £340 are outstanding and due to them.

Office salaries, heating, lighting, etc., amounted to £575 during the period, and A. and B. incurred travelling and entertaining expenses of £763 in connection with visits to clients, all of which has been duly paid.

Prepare a Revenue Account of the business of A. and B. for the year ended December 31, 19x3, and a Balance Sheet at that date.

CHAPTER XV

DEPRECIATION

We have seen in the preceding chapter how very important it is that all matters affecting the ascertainment of true profit shall be properly taken into account whenever an attempt is made to produce a Trading and Profit and Loss Account and Balance Sheet. Thus, any outstanding income, even though not actually received in cash, and any expense incurred but not yet paid must, if relating to the period under review, be provided for either as an **Asset or a Liability Provision.**

In so doing, we are taking steps to ensure **the genuineness of the profit figure** which the Revenue Account discloses, but we should not forget that the **Balance Sheet** drawn up at the end of the period likewise calls for attention. If the Balance Sheet is concerned with the proprietor's Capital, and the property or Assets by which it is represented, it is just as necessary to consider the correctness of the values put upon these Assets. Generally speaking, it is sufficient for the Assets as a whole to be shown at their 'going concern' values, i.e. at a figure which reflects their worth to the business as an established concern, producing a normal and reasonable profit on the total Capital invested. By way of contrast we can speak of **break-up** values of the property, representing its realisable value if sold in the market for what it will fetch. Between the two, there is a very wide gap, particularly noticeable with **Fixed Assets,** as distinct from **Current Assets.**

Examples of Current Assets, as we know, are:

(a) Stock in Trade, and
(b) Book Debts,

and we have seen that they are typical of the property **in which the business is dealing from day to day.** The Stock held by the business must be capable of sale at the prevailing market price; Book Debts must also be capable of collection from customers at their full value, subject to any provision made for debts which are considered to be doubtful.

We can, therefore, appreciate that as regards Current Assets, the test of their **realisable value** is all-important, and their **book value** (as shown in the Books of Account) should be in line with it.

In the case of **Fixed Assets,** however, being property **purchased for retention** and **not** for resale, altogether different considerations apply. Of this class of property, examples are:

(a) Plant and Machinery,

(b) Motor Vehicles for delivering goods to customers.

Without them, the business cannot begin to function, and they are clearly an essential part of its Capital equipment.

Because they represent property **used** for the purpose of the business, we have to recognise that there is in them **an element of impermanence,** and although they are retained within the business, a limit must be set to their **effective working life,** or the period of time during which they can be economically operated. Beyond that period, no matter how carefully they have been repaired and overhauled, it will be probably be found that charges for renewals and replacements of parts to an increasingly large extent have to be met, so much so, that quite apart from the risk of their becoming obsolete, or out of date, **these Assets as a whole must be replaced.**

The effective working life will naturally vary as between one class of Fixed Asset and another; sometimes it may be from 20 to 30 years, while with motor vehicles, 3 years is often the maximum period during which useful service can be rendered to the business.

As a result, we can recognise a progressive shrinkage in value of these classes of property, which we term **depreciation,** and it is very important that we take a note of it as **a shrinkage of value caused by the use of the property for the purpose of profit-earning.**

We can even take the matter further, and argue that against the profits earned in each trading year should be put as an expense the depreciation estimated to have taken place.

In other words, we may say that the loss in value is just as truly a business expense as the wages paid to workpeople, or the charge for rent and rates.

The real working expenses will be understated if the factor of depreciation is ignored year by year, and ultimately, when the machinery is worn out, or obsolete, the proprietor of the business will have to introduce fresh Capital to replace it, or else shut down.

This point of view brings us to the second reason for charging depreciation. Net Profit as ascertained by the preparation of the Trading and Profit and Loss Account is the yield upon the Capital invested, and may be wholly withdrawn by the proprietor in the form of cash. If depreciation is charged as a business expense, this Profit figure will be accordingly reduced, and also the amount of **cash withdrawable from the business** on account of it. Put in yet another way, cash or its equivalent, representing the charge for depreciation, will be retained within the business, and may, over a period of time, accumulate to provide the moneys required for eventual replacement.

For these reasons, it is the general practice to depreciate or **write down** the Fixed Assets, usually on a percentage basis, at all times when the Final Accounts are to be prepared.

The result is that we have:

(a) **A Debit to Profit and Loss Account,** and

(b) **A Credit to the particular Asset Depreciation Account.**

The two methods most generally employed are:

1 The Straight Line, or Fixed Instalment method.
2 The Diminishing Balance, or Reducing Instalment method.

They both have this in common, that a percentage of either the cost or book value of the Asset is written off against profits period by period, with or without allowance for any **residual** or **scrap** value.

The former, or straight line method relies on writing off yearly a part of the **original or purchase cost.** When the Asset is bought its effective working life is estimated as being a certain number of years, and the cost is recovered rateably over this period.

Example

Sanders and Son have a motor lorry which cost £1 185 on January 1, 19x5. Depreciation is to be provided on the Straight Line method over a period of 3 years when it is expected that it will be bought back by the supplier for £300. Show the Ledger Account of the Asset and the Asset Depreciation Account in the firm's books.

At December 31, 19x5, the lorry would appear in the Balance Sheet as under:

Assets

	£	£
Motor Lorry, at cost	1 185·00	
Less Depreciation	295·00	
		890·00

i.e. its **book value** would then be £890 only.

PRIVATE LEDGER
MOTOR LORRY

DR.   CR.

Date	Details	Fo.	Amount	Date	Details	Fo.	Amount
19x5 Jan. 1	Cash, Purchase cost		£ 1 185·00	19x5 Dec. 31	Balance	c/d	£ 1 185·00
			£1 185·00				£1 185·00
19x6 Jan. 1	Balance	b/d	1 185·00	19x6 Dec. 31	Balance	c/d	1 185·00
19x7 Jan. 1	Balance	b/d	1 185·00	19x7 Dec. 31 31	Cash Transfer to disposal of motor lorry A/c		300·00 885·00
			£1 185·00				£1 185·00

MOTOR LORRY DEPRECIATION

Dr.   Cr.

Date	Details	Fo.	Amount	Date	Details	Fo.	Amount
19x5 Dec. 31	Balance	c/d	£ 295·00	19x5 Dec. 31	Transfer to Profit & Loss A/c		£ 295·00
19x6 Dec. 31	Balance	c/d	590·00	19x6 Jan. 1 Dec. 31	Balance Transfer to Profit & Loss A/c	b/d	295·00 295·00
			£590·00				£590·00
19x7 Dec. 31	Transfer to disposal of motor lorry A/c		885·00	19x7 Jan. 1 Dec. 31	Balance Transfer to Profit & Loss A/c	b/d	590·00 295·00
			£885·00				£885·00

DIMINISHING BALANCE METHOD

In this case, a fixed percentage is written off the book value of
the Asset as it appears at the commencement of each year. This
method is sometimes used by smaller firms. Most firms would
keep a detailed register for each particular motor car or lorry
and for each item of plant and machinery.

Example

At January 1, 19x6, the balance on the Plant and Tools Account
was £4 730. During the year a lathe was purchased costing £575,
and on March 31, 19x7, three drilling machines which cost £900
when purchased 3 years ago were sold for £520.

Show the Asset Account, reckoning depreciation at 10% per
annum on the Diminishing Balance method.

PRIVATE LEDGER
PLANT AND TOOLS

Dr.   Cr.

Date	Details	Fo.	Amount	Date	Details	Fo.	Amount
19x6			£	19x6			£
Jan. 1	Balance	b/d	4 730·00	Dec. 31	Profit & Loss A/c Depreciation 10% of £4 730·00		
June 30	Cash Lathe		575·00				473·00
				31	Balance	c/d	4 832·00
			£5 305·00				£5 305·00
19x7				19x7			
Jan. 1	Balance	b/d	4 832·00	Dec. 31	Cash 3 Drilling Machines sold		520·00
				31	Profit & Loss A/c. Loss on sale		136·10
				31	Profit & Loss Depreciation 10% on £4 832·00		483·20
				31	Balance	c/d	3 692·70
			£4 832·00				£4 832·00
19x8							
Jan. 1	Balance	b/d	£3 692·70				

N.B.—

Cost 3 years ago	900·00	
1st year 10%	90·00	
	810·00	
2nd year 10%	81·00	
	729·00	
3rd year 10%	72·90	
	656·10	
Selling price	520·00	
Loss:	£136·10	

At December 31, 19x6, the following would appear in the Balance Sheet:

Assets

Plant and Tools	£	£
At 1.1.19x6	4 730·00	
Add Additions at Cost	575·00	
	5 305·00	
Less Depreciation at 10% per annum	473·00	
		4 832·00

Although this is the net book value it does not show the aggregate cost and depreciation provided which 'best practice' would consider desirable.

The reducing instalment method is open to the criticism that Fixed Assets so depreciated tend to be dealt with in groups, and that with ordinary rates of depreciation its slowness in writing down the values is not sufficiently recognised. If the life of the asset is short the percentage required may be prohibitively high; e.g. to depreciate a tool having a life of 3 years only would require a 90% rate.

Sometimes the Debit and Credit Journal is used so as to avoid making a Prime Entry in the particular Ledger Account:

Example

19x6 Dec. 31			Dr. £	Cr. £
	Profit and Loss A/c	Dr.	473·00	
	Plant and Tools Depreciation A/c.			473·00
	Being depreciation at 10% p.a. now written off.			

As the illustration shows, an account for Depreciation as a business expense may be opened in the Impersonal Ledger, but the Debit Balance on it must ultimately be transferred to Profit and Loss Account.

TESTS AND QUESTIONS

1 How is the shrinkage in the value of fixed assets provided for in accounts kept on the double entry principle?

Illustrate your answer by showing an account relating to an asset which has been written down in accordance with your suggestions.

2 Explain briefly, but as clearly as you can, why it is generally necessary, when preparing the accounts of a business, to make provision for depreciation of the fixed assets.

If you know of any exceptions to this general rule, mention them and give your reasons.

Note.—Goodwill is, for the purpose of this question, not to be regarded as a fixed asset.

3 On January 1, 19x1, a business purchased a motor delivery van for £800.

Show how the account would appear in the books of the business for the four following years assuming that depreciation is written off (*a*) by the fixed instalment method, and (*b*) by the diminishing balance method, the rate of depreciation being 20% in each case.

State, giving your reasons shortly, which method of depreciation you consider is more appropriate for an asset of this sort.

4   On January 1, 19x2, Dix, Ltd., purchased machinery costing £240. For the years 19x2, 19x3 and 19x4 depreciation was written off at the rate of 5% on the diminishing balance. During 19x5, it became apparent that the machinery would not be of service after December 31, 19x6, and for these latter two years the fixed instalment method was substituted. In December, 19x6, the machinery realised £15 on sale. You are required to write up the Machinery Account from the commencement, reckoning depreciation to the nearest £.

5   X., Ltd., purchased a seven-year lease of certain shop premises for £8 000. A further sum of £2 000 was expended in various alterations, and it was estimated that at the end of the lease the cost of restoring the premises to their original condition (for which the company were liable) would be about £500.

Show the Ledger Account for the first two years, providing for depreciation.

6   From the following particulars, write up the Machinery Account for the year ended November 30, 19x6.

The balance from the previous year was £26 882.

On May 31, 19x6, new machinery was purchased for £1 264, and wages amounting to £24 were paid for its erection. The old machinery replaced by the above was sold for £144, which was its written-down value on November 30, 19x5.

Depreciation at the rate of $12\frac{1}{2}$% per annum is to be written off.

7   The Balance Sheet of P.Q. & Co., Ltd., drawn up as on March 31, 19x7, showed plant and machinery valued, after writing off depreciation, at £25 500.

Depreciation had been written off regularly, from the dates of purchase of the various items, at the rate of 10% per annum on the diminishing value.

On June 1, 19x7, a motor, which had been bought on November 1, 19x2, for £750, was sold for £250 and replaced by a new one costing £1 100.

Show the Plant and Machinery Account as it would appear in the Company's books for the year ended March 31, 19x8, after writing off the appropriate depreciation for the year.

8   C.D. purchased factory premises (subject to a lease of 10 years from June 30, 19x0) from the Liquidator of H., Ltd., on June 30, 19x4, the purchase price being £3 000.

To enable him to complete the purchase, he borrowed £1 650 from Happy Bank, Ltd., the loan being repayable in three years by equal annual instalments of principal, reckoning interest at 10% per annum.

Provide depreciation on the fixed instalment basis, and show the Property Account and the Loan Account in C.D.'s books for the three years to June 30, 19x7.

9 On January 1, 19x4, a manufacturer acquired a machine at a cost of £1 200.

During 19x4 repairs to the machine cost £50 and a new attachment, which cost £250, was added to it.

The repairs during the year 19x5 amounted to £180.

It was decided to depreciate the machine at the rate of 10% per annum on the reducing instalment method.

From the foregoing particulars you are required to write up the Machinery Account for the two years ended December 31, 19x5.

10 The following is the Trial Balance extracted from the books of J. Falconer at December 31, 19x6:

	Dr. £	Cr. £
Salaries	2 414·00	
Discounts Received		132·00
Repairs and Renewals	318·00	
Sales		18 505·00
Carriage Outwards	163·00	
Creditors		674·00
Wages	6 116·00	
Sundry Expenses	86·00	
Sundry Debtors	3 445·00	
Commission	196·00	
Capital, January 1, 19x6		7 200·00
Stock, January 1, 19x6	1 572·00	
Discounts Allowed	578·00	
Returns Outwards		295·00
Plant and Machinery, January 1, 19x6	1 460·00	
Cash in Hand	2·00	
Purchases	7 336·00	
Rates	175·00	
Warehouse Expenses	537·00	
Office Fixtures, etc., January 1, 19x6	220·00	
Cash at Bank	1 200·00	
Rent of Premises	188·00	
Drawings	1 000·00	
Bad Debts Reserve, January 1, 19x6		200·00
	£27 006·00	£27 006·00

You are required to prepare:

(a) Trading and Profit and Loss Account for the year to December 31, 19x6.

(b) Balance Sheet at December 31, 19x6, showing per cent net Profit to Capital at January 1, 19x6.

(c) The following adjustments are necessary:

(1) The stock on hand at December 31, 19x6, was valued at £1 769.

(2) 3 months rates are prepaid in the sum of £35.

(3) The rent of premises is £250 per annum, payable quarterly, and has been paid to September 29, 19x6.

(4) Depreciation is to be charged at 5% on plant and machinery, and 10% on office furniture, etc.

11 Give the Journal entries necessary to record the following transactions:

Dec. 2 Bought fixtures and fittings value £345 on credit from S. Maxton and Sons.

15 A cheque value £76·25 received from Perkins, Ltd., was wrongly posted to Brampton Bros.' Account.

19 Exchanged one motor-car value £120 for three typewriters value £22 each and the balance in cash.

31 Plant and machinery is to be depreciated by £73.

31 O. Carfax, a debtor for £55, having become insolvent, pays £0·2 in the £ settlement of the amount owing.

12 A firm acquired a 25 years' lease of its business premises for £18 000. The firm's bankers advanced £12 000 towards the purchase price on the security of the lease.

Repayment of the Bank loan is made by quarterly instalments of £250 which the bank debit to the firm's current account together with interest at the rate of 10% per annum.

You are required to make the entries in the firm's books at the end of the first year to record the above arrangements, including depreciation of the lease according to the method you consider most suitable in the circumstances.

CHAPTER XVI

PARTNERSHIP

In the chapters that have gone before we have considered the business to be owned by a sole proprietor, or, as he is termed, a **sole trader.** This was the earliest form of proprietorship, and still exists in the typical small business, often of the merchanting and distributive type.

With the growth in the size of the business unit, the Capital required to provide the necessary equipment and to finance ordinary trading is usually found to be in excess of the resources of any one individual. A further handicap must be recognised in the fact that, in the event of the business failing, the proprietor is liable to his last penny for the payment of his business creditors. His liability is said to be **unlimited,** in contrast to that of the shareholders in a Limited Company, which is restricted to the amounts, if any, unpaid on the shares they have contracted to take.

Between these two extremes we have the partnership relation which, just as in the case of the Sole Trader, involves each partner in unlimited liability as regards the whole of the debts of the **partnership firm.**

It is a very suitable form of business proprietorship where:

(a) A large amount of Capital is not required.
(b) Liabilities to suppliers and others are unlikely to be considerable.
(c) The business is of a size in which each partner can take part in the general supervision.

For these reasons, partnerships are often found in the professions and in the smaller merchanting and manufacturing businesses.

PARTNERSHIP ACT 1890

A measure of statutory control was imposed by this Act, which defines partnership as **the relation which subsists between persons carrying on business in common with a view to profit.**

Before the passing of the Companies Act 1967 not more than twenty persons could be partners but this limitation has now been withdrawn. The Act of 1890 provides certain rules which, in the absence of written or verbal arrangement between the partners, can be applied in defining the duties of the partners to each other, and their responsibility to persons outside the firm with whom they have business dealings.

As it is in all respects desirable to make special arrangements in each individual case, and to have a permanent record of what is agreed upon, a **Deed, or Articles of Partnership,** is often drawn up by which each of the partners consents to be bound. These also provide for such modifications of the Act of 1890 as may be thought necessary.

The Deed may state:

(a) The term for which the partnership is entered into.

(b) The nature of the business to be carried on.

(c) The amount of Capital to be introduced and in what circumstances it may be withdrawn.

(d) The ratio in which Profits and Losses shall be shared.

(e) How much each partner shall be entitled to draw on account of accruing profits.

(f) Whether Interest shall be allowed on Partners' Capitals.

(g) The salaries, if any, to be paid to individual partners.

As regards (a), if no term is stated, or the partnership is continued without any fresh agreement after the original term has expired, it is said to be a **Partnership at Will.**

Of the above, items (c), (d), (e), (f) and (g) have a special bearing on the **accounts,** and must therefore be considered separately.

CAPITAL

The Capital brought in may take the form of cash, or property in kind, such as machinery, buildings, stock, etc.

In any event, the agreed value must be credited to the Partner's **Capital Account**, and the proper Asset Account debited. If the Capitals are **fixed** the profit shares and drawings on account thereof will be dealt with in separate **Current Accounts.** The form of the latter is exactly similar to what was described on page 147.

PROFITS AND LOSSES

Partners may share Profits and Losses on any agreed basis. In the last resort the Partnership Act provides that they are entitled to share equally. Sometimes Profits and Losses may be divided in the ratio of the Fixed Capitals; in other cases where one partner takes a more active part than another, he may be rewarded with a bigger proportionate share.

DRAWINGS

It is better to agree at the outset upon a limit for each partner's drawings. As the cash so withdrawn depletes the circulating Capital, interest may be charged thereon from the date withdrawn to the end of the firm's financial year. Drawings may be in the form of goods as well as cash, in which event **Purchases Account** will usually be credited and the partner's Current Account debited.

INTEREST ON CAPITALS

Prior to the division of the Net Profit, the Deed may provide for charging Interest on the Capital of each partner. If this were not done in a case where, for example, Capital Accounts were unequal, but Profits and Losses were divided equally, the partner having the larger (or largest) Capital would lose.

Such Interest on Capital is in no sense a business expense, and would be debited in the Appropriation, or Net Profit and Loss Account.

PARTNERSHIP SALARIES

A management salary may be paid to one or more of the partners if they devote more time to the business than their co-
partners, or if they are **active** as distinct from **sleeping** partners.
The latter may be regarded as those who have contributed
Capital, but take no part in the daily supervision of affairs.

Salaries paid or payable to the partners will, like interest on
Capital, be debited in the Appropriation Account. They are, in
effect, and as regards each partner, a part of the ascertained
profit due to him as a proprietor.

PARTNERS' ADVANCES

If a partner, to assist the firm, advances cash by way of **loan**,
it is probable that he will require it to be treated in the books in
a manner different from the **Capital** invested by him. The amount
should therefore be credited to a separate **Loan Account.**

The Act of 1890 provides that the partner making the **advance**
shall be entitled to interest thereon at the rate of 5% per annum
from the date of the advance.

GOODWILL

Goodwill is a business Asset, which may be defined as the worth
inherent in an established business producing a normal and
reasonable profit on the Capital employed in it.

It is **worth** or **value** over and above that represented by the
Tangible Assets, such as buildings, plant, stock and book debts,
and can so be termed an **Intangible** Asset.

If the business were sold, it would clearly be to a purchaser's
advantage to pay something for the right to enjoy a continuity
of the profits arising, and this is well brought out in the case of
a **partnership.**

An incoming partner can be expected to pay the existing
partners for the goodwill represented by his profit share, and an
outgoing partner is entitled to have goodwill taken into account
in determining the sum due to him. The Deed of Partnership

will often indicate how the value of the goodwill is to be ascertained, in these and similar circumstances, as by reference to past profits or an estimate of future maintainable profits.

Example

A. joins B. in partnership on January 1, 19x5. The Capital is provided as to £5 000 by A., who is a dormant partner, and £500 by B., who devotes his whole time to the business and is wholly dependent on it.

Assuming the gross receipts for 19x5 are £20 000, and the working expenses £9 000, prepare a Revenue Account incorporating these items, and also the distribution of profit, allowing 5% Interest on Capital, and dividing the balance equally.

A. AND B.

PROFIT AND LOSS ACCOUNT
Year ended December 31. 19x5

DR.				CR.
	£			£
Working Expenses	9 000·00	Gross Receipts		20 000·00
Balance, Net Profit c/d	11 000·00			
	£20 000·00			£20 000·00
Interest on Capital:		Net Profit b/d		11 000·00
A. 5% on £5 000·00	250·00			
B. 5% on £500·00	25·00			
	275·00			
Balance:				
A. ½ share £5 362·50				
B. ½ share 5 362·50				
	10 725·00			
	£11 000·00			£11 000·00

In the above we see the benefit to A. of charging interest on Capital.

The interest due to each partner and the amount of his profit share can be carried direct to Capital Account, or alternatively credited to a Current Account.

Example

Rogers and Shaw enter into partnership on January 1, 19x7, and agree to divide Profits and Losses equally, after charging Interest on Capital at 4% per annum.

On December 31, 19x7, the following Balances are extracted from their books:

	Dr. £	Cr. £
Rogers: Capital		3 000·00
Drawings	1 156·00	
Shaw: Capital		2 000·00
Drawings	1 156·00	
Sales		14 257·00
Discounts Received		81·00
Purchases	5 413·00	
Discounts Allowed	187·00	
Salaries	1 497·00	
Wages	2 500·00	
Sundry Debtors	4 200·00	
Rates	75·00	
Printing and Stationery	292·00	
Travelling Expenses	596·00	
Bad Debts	24·00	
Repairs and Renewals	133·00	
Cash in Hand	11·00	
Bank Overdraft		34·00
Subscriptions	8·00	
Bank Charges	10·00	
Legal Charges	15·00	
Audit Fee	21·00	
Sundry Creditors		662·00
Factory and Warehouse Premises	1 234·00	
Plant and Machinery	1 506·00	
	£20 034·00	£20 034·00

The stock at December 31, 19x7, was valued by the partners at £1 125.

You are required:

(*a*) To prepare Trading and Profit and Loss Account for the year to December 31, 19x7, and a Balance Sheet at that date.

(*b*) To state the percentage of Gross Profit to turnover.

(*c*) To show the Partners' Current Accounts.

The following adjustments are necessary:

1   Provide £50 for wages accrued due.
2   Provide 1% on the amount of the Sundry Debtors for Bad and Doubtful Debts.
3   Provide £100 depreciation in respect of Plant and Machinery.

ROGERS AND SHAW

TRADING AND PROFIT AND LOSS ACCOUNT
Year ended December 31, 19x7

		£		£
Purchases		5 413·00	Sales	14 257·00
Wages	£2 500·00		Stock, December 31, 19x7	1 125·00
Add Provision	50·00			
		2 550·00		
Gross Profit c/d, 33⅓% to turnover		7 419·00		
		15 382·00		15 382·00
Salaries		1 497·00	Gross Profit b/d	7 419·00
Travelling Expenses		596·00	Discount Received	81·00
Printing and Stationery		292·00		
Discounts Allowed		187·00		
Repairs and Renewals		133·00		
Rates		75·00		
Bad Debts	£24·00			
Add Provision	42·00			
		66·00		
Audit Fee		21·00		
Legal Charges		15·00		
Bank Charges		10·00		
Subscriptions		8·00		
Depreciation of Plant and Machinery		100·00		
		3 000·00		
Net Profit c/d		4 500·00		
		7 500·00		7 500·00
Interest on Capitals:			Net Profit b/d	4 500·00
Rogers, 4% on £3 000·00		120·00		
Shaw, 4% on £2 000·00		80·00		
		200·00		
Rogers, ½ share	£2 150·00			
Shaw, ½ share	2 150·00			
		4 300·00		
		£4 500·00		£4 500·00

Note.—In practice, the Provisions are seldom shown separately in the Revenue Account, e.g. Wages would be shown in the one sum of £2 550 only.

ROGERS AND SHAW

BALANCE SHEET AS AT DECEMBER 31, 19x7

Liabilities		£	*Assets*		£
Sundry Creditors	£662·00		Cash in Hand		11·00
Wages Due	50·00		Sundry Debtors	£4 200·00	
		712·00	*Less* Provision	42·00	
Bank Overdraft		34·00			4 158·00
Current Accounts:			Stock in Trade		1 125·00
Rogers:			Plant and		
Interest on			Machinery	£1 506·00	
Capital	£120·00		*Less* Depreciation	100·00	
One half profit	2 150·00				1 406·00
	2 270·00		Factory and Warehouse		
Less Drawings	1 156·00		Premises		1 234·00
		1 114·00			
Shaw:					
Interest on					
Capital	80·00				
One half profit	2 150·00				
	2 230·00				
Less					
Drawings	1 156·00				
		1 074·00			
Capital Accounts:					
Rogers	£3 000·00				
Shaw	2 000·00				
		5 000·00			
		£7 934·00			£7 934·00

ROGERS

PRIVATE LEDGER
ROGERS—CURRENT ACCOUNT

DR.					CR.
19x7		£	19x7		£
Dec. 31	Drawings	1 156·00	Dec. 31	Interest on Capital	
31	Balance c/d	1 114·00		4% on £3 000·00	120·00
			31	One half Profit, year to date	2 150·00
		£2 270·00			£2 270·00
			19x8		
			Jan. 1	Balance b/d	1 114·00

SHAW—CURRENT ACCOUNT

Dr.					Cr.
19x7 Dec. 31	Drawings	£ 1 156·00	19x7 Dec. 31	Interest on Capital, 4% on £2 000·00	£ 80·00
31	Balance c/d	1 074·00	31	One half Profit, year to date	2 150·00
		£2 230·00			£2 230·00
			19x8 Jan. 1	Balance b/d	1 074·00

In this example we should be careful to note how the provisions for **wages, doubtful debts** and **depreciation** are dealt with in the Balance Sheet.

TESTS AND QUESTIONS

1 Give some reasons why interest is generally charged against the drawings of individual members of a firm, and also credited to their Capital Accounts.

2 Give two reasons why interest on Capital Accounts should be taken into account in dividing the profits of a partnership.

  Mention a case, if you know of one, where one of these reasons does not apply.

3 Earle and Yeoman contemplate the establishment of a dairy to be carried on by them in partnership. Earle is to provide nine-tenths of the capital required, but, having no practical knowledge of the work, is not expected to take much active part in it. Yeoman is experienced in this direction and upon him will devolve the management of the undertaking.

  If consulted by them with regard to the financial provisions to be embodied in the Partnership Deed, enumerate your suggestions.

4 In the absence of agreement, to what extent are partners entitled to interest on capital in and loans to the firm?

  Illustrate your answer by reference to the following:

	£
A. Capital	10 000·00
B. Capital	5 000·00
A. Loan	3 000·00

Profits of the firm (before charging any interest), £2 500.

5 On January 1, 19x6, A. and B. entered into partnership but
   without any formal deed of partnership. A. provided £10 000 as
   capital, and B. provided £500. On July 1, 19x6, A. advanced £2 000
   on loan to the firm.

   Accounts were prepared and disclosed a profit of £6 000 for the
   year to December 31, 19x6, but the partners could not agree as to
   how this sum should be divided between them. A. contended that
   the partners should receive 5% interest on capital and that he
   should receive 6% interest on his loan to the firm, and the balance
   then available should be divided equally. B. contended that, as
   he did most of the work, he should be paid a salary before any
   division of profit was made.

   You are required to show how the profits of the firm should be
   divided and to state what different division, if any, would be made
   if A. had written a letter to B. agreeing that a partnership salary
   of £1 500 should be paid to him.

6 A., a sole trader, prepared accounts as on March 31, 19x4, when
   his Capital Account showed a balance of £9 000. On April 1 he
   took in B., as a partner on the terms that before B.'s entry a
   Goodwill Account for £4 000 should be raised, that B. should bring
   in £3 000 in cash as his capital, interest at 5% per annum should be
   allowed on Capital Accounts and the balance of profit be divided
   between A. and B. in the proportion of 3 to 1.

   The profit for the year to March 31, 19x5, before charging
   interest, was £4 050. Show the division of this between A. and B.
   Show also what the division would have been had no provision
   been made as to goodwill, the other arrangements being as stated
   above.

7 X. and Y. are partners, and they admit Z. as a partner, profits to
   be shared as follows: X. four-ninths, Y. three-ninths, Z. two-
   ninths.

   Y. is credited with a partnership salary of £300 per annum, and
   X. and Y. guarantee that Z.'s share of profits shall not be less than
   £2 000 in any year.

   The profits for the year ended December 31, 19x9, prior to providing for Y.'s salary, amounted to £8 208.

   Prepare the Appropriation section of the firm's Profit and Loss
   Account.

8 A., a sole trader owning an established business, took B. into
   partnership on January 1, 19x3, at which date the goodwill of the
   business was agreed to be worth £6 000. A.'s capital (exclusive of
   goodwill) was £10 000, and B. brought in £3 000 as his capital.

Interest on Capital Accounts was to be allowed at 5%, and A. and B. were to divide the remaining profit in the ratio of 2 to 1.

The profit for 19x3 before charging interest, was £5 600.

Calculate the division of this sum between A. and B. on the alternative assumptions that:

(1) Goodwill was ignored on B.'s entering the business.
(2) Goodwill was taken into account at its correct value.

9 Bright and Smart carry on business in partnership, sharing profits in the proportion of three-fifths and two-fifths respectively.

On January 1, 19x6, the Capital Accounts showed the following credit balances: Bright, £8 000; Smart, £6 000.

The Partnership Agreement provides that the partners shall be allowed interest on capital at 5% per annum and that Bright shall be entitled to a salary of £600 per annum and Smart to one of £400 per annum. During the year ended December 31, 19x6, the partners' drawings were: Bright, £550; Smart, £425.

The profit for the year, prior to making any of the foregoing adjustments, was £3 500.

You are required to write up the Profit and Loss Appropriation Account and to show how the Capital Accounts of the partners would appear on the Balance Sheet at December 31, 19x6.

10 A. and B. entered into partnership on January 1, 19x6, sharing profits and losses equally.

A. contributed £5 000 as capital, comprising £2 000 in cash, and fixtures and plant valued at £3 000.

B. could only introduce £1 000 in cash, but it was agreed he should be given credit in the sum of £1 500 for his sales connection, and also receive a salary at the rate of £170 per annum.

On June 30, 19x6, B. paid in an additional £500, and at the same date C. entered the firm, paying £1 600 for a quarter share of the profits and goodwill and bringing in £1 000 cash as his capital, all of which it was agreed should be left in the business.

A. and B. continued to share profits in the same relative proportions as before, and it was arranged that as from the date of C.'s entry, B.'s salary should cease, but 5% per annum interest on capitals should be allowed.

The profits for the year to December 31, 19x6, prior to charging such interest and B.'s salary, were £1 170. Draw up a Statement showing the division of this amount between the partners, making any necessary apportionments on a time basis, and open Ledger Accounts to record the whole of the foregoing.

11 Alfred White and George Gardiner, in partnership as merchants,
    extract from their books the undermentioned Trial Balance at
    December 31, 19x5:

	Dr. £	Cr. £
Capital Accounts:		
White		5 000·00
Gardiner		3 000·00
Stock, January 1, 19x5	4 000·00	
Discounts Received		100·00
Salesmen's Salaries	1 000·00	
Rent	400·00	
Rates	200·00	
Carriage Inwards	1 000·00	
Sales		20 000·00
Balance at Bank	800·00	
Drawings:		
White	500·00	
Gardiner	300·00	
Trade Creditors		2 400·00
Purchases	15 000·00	
General Expenses	500·00	
Fixtures and Fittings	1 800·00	
Trade Debtors	5 000·00	
	£30 500·00	£30 500·00

Notes.—(1) One year's interest at 5% is due on the Capital Ac-
              count of each partner but otherwise the Partnership
              Act, 1890, applies.
          (2) Stock December 31, 19x5, £5 000.
          (3) Of the rates paid, one payment, £50, was for the half-
              year ended March 31, 19x6.
          (4) Depreciate Fixtures and Fittings by 10%.

You are required to produce Trading and Profit and Loss Account
for the year 19x5 with Balance Sheet as at the end thereof.

12 James and John entered into partnership as merchants on January
    1, 19x6. James brought in cash £500 and stock-in-trade £1 000;
    John brought in cash £300 and a motor lorry £700. The agreement
    provided that John was to have a salary from the firm of £250 per

annum and that each partner might draw (on account of salary and profit) £100 per month; otherwise the terms of the Partnership Act, 1890, were to apply.

At the end of 19x6 the following Trial Balance was extracted from the books:

TRIAL BALANCE, DECEMBER 31, 19x6

	Dr. £	Cr. £
Capital Accounts		2 500·00
Debtors	950·00	
Cash	25·00	
Carriage Inwards	500·00	
Bank		135·00
Stock	1 000·00	
Rent Paid	550·00	
Sales		16 000·00
Motor Lorry	700·00	
Carriage Outwards	130·00	
Discounts Received		575·00
Petty Cash Expediture	52·00	
Purchases	11 500·00	
Drawings	2 400·00	
Creditors		697·00
Discounts Allowed	50·00	
Rates Paid	200·00	
Salaries (not Partners)	850·00	
Fixtures and Fittings (cost)	1 000·00	
	£19 907·00	£19 907·00

Notes.—(1) Stock December 31, 19x6, valued at £1 800.

(2) Rent accrued but not paid, £50.

(3) Rates paid in advance, £40.

(4) Depreciate the motor lorry at 10% per half-year on the diminishing balance system, and the Fixtures and Fittings at 5% per half-year on original cost.

(5) Bank charges not yet entered in books, £50.

Prepare Trading and Profit and loss Accounts for 19x6 and a Balance Sheet at the end of the year.

13 The following Trial Balance has been extracted as at March 31,
    19x7, from the books of C. Spargo and W. Penna—partners
    sharing profits and losses in the proportion of 2 to 1 respectively.

	Dr. £	Cr. £
Stock, April 1, 19x6	3 690·00	
Purchases and Sales	36 892·75	49 469·97
Bad Debts written off	291·67	
Plant and Machinery (cost (£7 000)	6 650·00	
Furniture and Fittings (cost £1 200)	1 164·00	
Returns	371·56	297·54
Discounts	351·71	403·69
Drawings: C. Spargo	560·00	
W. Penna	380·00	
Debtors and Creditors	5 620·00	4 872·68
Light and Heat	397·80	
Rent, Rates and Taxes	650·63	
Insurances	131·50	
Salaries	1 215·68	
Wages	6 394·93	
General Expenses	445·62	
Bad Debts Reserve		200·00
Commissions		363·97
Capital: C. Spargo		5 800·00
W. Penna		3 800·00
	£65 207·85	£65 207·85

Value of stock on March 31, 19x7, £1 793.

You are asked to draw up Trading and Profit and Loss Accounts
for the year, using the following data for making necessary
adjustments:

(a) Depreciate plant and machinery 10% on cost.

(b) Depreciate furniture and fittings 5% on cost.

(c) Amount of insurance pre-paid, £31·75.

(d) Amount of wages due but unpaid, £111·65.

(e) The Bad Debts Reserve is to be increased to an amount equal
    to 5% of debtors' balances.

(f) Amount of commissions due but not received—£34·94.

(g) Capital Accounts to be credited with interest at 5% per
    annum.

(No interest to be charged on drawings.)
No Balance Sheet is to be drawn up.

Instead, you are to show the following accounts in full for the year ended March 31, 19x7:

(i) Plant and Machinery Account.

(ii) Insurance Account.

(iii) Bad Debts Reserve Account.

(iv) Commission Account.

14 The firm of John Smith & Sons, makers of engineering equipment, consists of John and Magnus Smith. They share profits equally, after each has been credited with interest at 5% on his capital at the beginning of the year.

At January 31, 19x7, the end of the firm's financial year, the following are the balances in the Ledger:

	£	£
Purchases: Raw Materials	18 562·00	
Finished Goods	860·00	
General Office Expenses	934·00	
Returns Inwards	413·00	
Creditors, including an unsecured loan of £500, maturing in 19x9		2 617·00
Bad Debts Provision		205·00
Stock: Raw Materials	3 906·00	
Finished Goods	101·00	
Wages (Factory)	18 687·00	
Salaries (Factory)	1 252·00	
Rent, Insurance, etc. (Factory)	1 246·00	
Rent, Insurance, etc. (Factory), Prepaid	25·00	
Net Rents from Workmen's Cottages		97·00
Fire Expense	750·00	
Carriage Outwards	909·00	
Factory Equipment and Machinery	14 315·00	
Factory Equipment and Machinery Depreciation Provision		2 000·00
Cash	14·00	
Sales		45 200·00
Interest Paid on Overdraft, etc.	61·00	
Debtors	4 135·00	
Capital: John Smith		12 420·00
Magnus Smith		3 740·00
Drawings: John Smith	837·00	
Magnus Smith	371·00	
Bank		1 099·00
	£67 378·00	£67 378·00

The stock of raw materials at January 31, 19x7 was valued at
£4 310. There were then no finished goods on hand.

The 'Fire Expense' Account shows the balance of a heavy loss
from fire in 19x2. £150 of this amount is now to be written off.

£22 of bank overdraft interest is accrued and has not been
allowed for.

The Equipment Depreciation Provision is to be increased by
£315.

A claim for £150 has been made against the firm under the
Redundancy Payments Act 1965.

Prepare suitable Final Accounts and Balance Sheet.

CHAPTER XVII

THE CRITICISM AND INTERPRETATION OF ACCOUNTS

Much of what has been already written concerns the recording of business transactions from the earliest stage in the Books of Prime Entry to the preparation of the Final Accounts.

We must never lose sight of the fact that accounts are kept in order that they may assist the proprietor or manager of the business, and it will be time well spent to consider the work we have done from the point of view of those who are to make use of it.

If the accounts, or any part of them, have no meaning to us, they can have no meaning to others, and we must try to regard the records made as telling a story of what has happened, and telling it in a clear and intelligible manner.

A very simple instance of this is seen in the ordinary **Ledger Account**. Having regard to the subject-matter of the account as indicated by its heading, we should be able to describe not only the nature of the entries appearing in it, but also the final result of the transactions, both from the personal and the impersonal aspect.

Example

Overleaf is a customer's account as shown in the Sales Ledger. At the beginning of the year £50 was owing by him, and a month later he returned goods to the value of £10, further goods being supplied to him on February 28.

On March 10, he remits a sum of £20, which is stated to be 'on account'—in itself often a sign of weakness. Despite this, goods are again invoiced to him on May 3, and on June 4 a cheque is received for the balance of what was due as far back as January 1.

H. BROWN

| DR. | | | | | | | | CR. |
Date	Details	Fo.	Amount	Date	Details	Fo.	Amount
19x7			£	19x7			£
Jan. 1	Balance	b/d	50·00	Feb. 1	Returns		10·00
Feb. 28	Goods		25·00	Mar. 10	Cash on A/c		20·00
May 3	Goods		15·00	June 4	Bank		19·50
June 7	Bank, cheque				Discount		0·50
	returned		19·50	Aug. 8	Bank, First		
7	Discount		0·50		and Final		
					Dividend		
					of £0·25		
					in the £		15·00
				31	Bad Debts		45·00
			£110·00				£110·00

The bank subsequently reports that the cheque has not been met, and Brown is accordingly debited with the amount of the cheque **and** discount.

Between then and August 8, he either compounds with his creditors as a whole, or is made bankrupt. A first and final dividend of £0·25 in the £ is received, and £0·75 in the £ has to be written off as a Bad Debt.

CRITICISM OF THE FINAL ACCOUNTS

It is, however, in regard to the Trading and Profit and Loss Account and Balance Sheet, as representing the logical conclusion of the book-keeping work, that the principal points for criticism arise.

To deal firstly with the **Trading Account**, the following may have to be considered:

(a) How does the **sales** figure compare with that of the previous year, or other period, and how far have alterations in selling prices contributed to any difference noted?

(b) Similarly as regards **purchases** and the cost of materials bought.

(c) Are the **closing stocks** much in excess of those held at the beginning of the year, and if so, in a manufacturing business, to what extent do they consist of raw material or the finished product? In the former case, have purchases been made in anticipation of a rise in the price of materials? In the latter case, is the turnover partly seasonal so that a large part of the stock is sold early in the following trading period? What is the average stock carried, and what is its relation to the turnover?

(*d*) Does the business earn a fairly consistent rate of Gross Profit, expressed as a percentage to turnover? If less than the usual Gross Profit is earned, is it because selling prices have declined or because the closing stock is valued at the then market price which is below the original cost?

Should the Gross Profit percentage rise, is the cause to be found in more favourable selling prices, or in an improper inflation of closing stock values?

The following illustration may be helpful:

Example

At January 1, 19x7, T. Peters had a stock of 1 000 articles then valued at £1 per unit. During the year he purchased 10 000 articles at the same average cost. To arrive at his selling price he adds 50% to cost, his Gross Profit thus being 33⅓%. The sales amount to 9 000 articles. Show his Trading Account for the year assuming:

1 Selling prices were advanced 10%, stock values remaining constant, and

2 Stock values at December 31, 19x7, had fallen by 10%, which is to be provided for.

In the first case the Trading Account shows a Gross Profit of 39·4%, as follows:

DR.				CR.	
	Units	£		Units	£
Stock, Jan. 1, 19x7	1 000	1 000·00	Sales (at £1·65 per unit)	9 000	14 850·00
Purchases	10 000	10 000·00			
Gross Profit (39·4% to Sales)		5 850·00	Stock (at cost, £1·00 per unit)	2 000	2 000·00
	11 000	£16 850·00		11 000	£16 850·00

In the second case, the stock provision will appear as a separate
expense contra in the Profit and Loss Account:

DR.   CR.

	Units	£		Units	£
Stock, Jan. 1, 19x7	1 000	1 000·00	Sales (at £1·50 per unit)	9 000	13 500·00
Purchases	10 000	10 000·00	Stock (at current market price)	2 000	1 800·00
Gross Profit (33⅓% to Sales)	—	4 500·00	P/L A/c contra, Stock Provision	—	200·00
	11 000	£15 500·00		11 000	£15 500·00

THE PROFIT AND LOSS ACCOUNT

This section of the Revenue Account includes, as we have seen,
the **indirect** or 'overhead' expenses of the business.

To a large extent these do not vary in sympathy with the sales
or turnover figure, and therefore it is always necessary to watch
carefully the individual items, and the total to which they amount.

Broadly speaking, the Profit and Loss Account is concerned
with the reconciliation of **Gross** and **Net Profit.** Stated in another
way, Gross Profit may be said to consist of (*a*) the indirect expenses and (*b*) Net Profit.

INDIRECT EXPENSES

To assist scrutiny, some suitable arrangement of these expenses
is most desirable. **Subheadings** may be inserted, such as:

1 **Production Expenses**
   Factory Rent, Rates, etc.
   Repairs to Plant.
   Depreciation of Plant, etc.
2 **Selling and Distribution Expenses**
   Travellers' Salaries and Commission.
   Travelling Expenses.
   Rent of Show Rooms, etc.
3 **General or Administrative Expenses**
   Office Salaries.
   Bank Interest.
   Depreciation of Office Furniture, etc.

A classification of the Profit and Loss Debits in this way is much more helpful than a mere haphazard listing of the balances on the various Ledger Accounts.

NET PROFIT

This is of importance because it represents:

1 The amount which the proprietor may withdraw in the form of cash, **and still leave his Capital intact.**
2 The net yield on the Capital invested, which may conveniently be stated as **a percentage return on that Capital.**

The net earnings of the business can only be ascertained after including all expenses, and all forms of income, as we saw in Chapter 14, and clearly the proprietor will expect to receive something in excess of the rate of interest obtainable from the investment of an equivalent amount of capital in, say, gilt-edged securities. How much more will largely depend on the degree of risk to which his business Capital is exposed in each particular case.

THE BALANCE SHEET

A point constantly to be borne in mind is that the Revenue Account and the Balance Sheet must be read together. Each serves to explain and interpret the other. As an example, if a profit is disclosed at the end of the period, it must be reflected in an increase of the Net Assets. If a loss has been sustained, these Assets will be less at the end of the period than they were at the beginning. Further, when depreciation is charged in the Profit and Loss Account, not only will the profit figure be reduced, but the book value of the Fixed Asset in question will similarly be reduced in the Balance Sheet.

The Balance Sheet is concerned with showing the position of the business **at a particular date.** That position may substantially alter on the day after its preparation, or it may be materially different on the day before it was prepared. The most informative

Balance Sheet is that which gives the typical or average state of affairs.

In criticising a Balance Sheet we may well begin with the **Liabilities.**

Who is interested in the business as a provider of Capital? Apart from the libability to the proprietor on Capital Account, there may be amounts due to trade creditors, and to bankers. The latter liabilities rank ahead of the former, and the proprietor must wait until all these claims are met before he can recover any part of his original investment.

The proportion of the Proprietor's Capital to other liabilities should also be noted. If relatively large sums are due to suppliers and others, the position must be further investigated by reference to the total Assets available, and their division between **Fixed,** and **Current or Floating Assets.**

Just as liabilities may be divided as between Fixed or Deferred Liabilities—those in favour of the proprietors, and Current Liabilities—or the claims of creditors, so it is from the Current or Floating Assets that the creditors primarily look for payment.

We have already considered the distinction between Fixed and Current Assets, but as a final illustration, the following introduces other points:

The Balance Sheet of T., a haulage contractor, at February 28, 19x6, is as set out below.

	£		£
T. Capital:		Leasehold Warehouse, Offices, Sheds, etc., at cost, March 1, 19x0	3 511·00
Balance forward £7 350·00		Motor Vehicles, Wagons, etc., at cost, *less* Depreciation, March 1,	
Add Profit for year 1 750·00		19x5 £5 700·00	
9 100·00		*Less* Depreciation 2 037·00	
Less Drawings 1 600·00	7 500·00		3 663·00
Trade Creditors	2 118·00	Stocks of Fuel, Oil, Waste, etc., as estimated by T.	495·00
Accrued Expenses	432·00	Book Debts, Gross	2 606·00
Western Bank, Ltd.	269·00	Insurance prepaid	15·00
		Cash in Hand	29·00
	£10 319·00		£10 319·00

You are required:

(a) To comment carefully upon the position disclosed.

(b) To draw up a statement showing the amount of the:

   (i) Fixed Assets.

   (ii) Net Current Assets.

(a) Criticism of Position Disclosed

The **Profit** for the year is rather more than 20% on the Capital. Before accepting it, we should look at the **Assets** of the business and the basis of their valuation.

The first item, **Leasehold Warehouse, Office, etc.,** is stated at cost six years ago. No provision for depreciation has been made by reference to the term of the lease.

By contrast, **Motor Vehicles and Wagons** have been depreciated, but we do not know the rate. A proper figure for depreciation would probably be from 15 to 20% of the original cost, i.e. on the straight line method (see page 174).

The **Stocks** are shown 'as estimated.' Estimates may be of two kinds, good and bad, and information should be sought as to whether the quantities or values, or both, have been estimated, and whether the values are in line with cost or market price, whichever was the lower at the date of the Balance Sheet.

As the Book Debts are described 'gross', their full face value has clearly been taken, and there is no provision for Doubtful Debts. The amount should be related to the value of sales during the year, or in January and February.

It would thus seem that the profit for the year is over-stated because of possible over-valuations of the Assets mentioned.

Lastly, there is a pressing need for the collection of the Book Debts to provide moneys out of which to pay the trade creditors and accrued expenses. The extent of this urgency will in part depend on the limit set to the Overdraft facilities.

(b) Statement of Fixed Assets and Net Current Assets

This may be drawn up as follows:

(i) Fixed Assets.

	£
Leasehold Warehouse, Offices, Shed, etc., at cost March 1, 19x0	3 511·00
Motor Vehicles, Wagons, etc., at cost, less depreciation	3 663·00
Total Fixed Assets	**£7 174·00**

(ii) Net Current Assets (or net working capital)

	£
Stocks of Fuel, Oil, etc., as estimated	495·00
Book Debts (gross)	2 606·00
Insurance prepaid	15·00
Cash in hand	29·00
	£3 145·00

Deduct—

	£	£
Trade Creditors	2 118·00	
Accrued Expenses	432·00	
Western Bank, Ltd.	269·00	2 819·00
Total net current assets		**326·00**
Fixed Assets		7 174·00
Net Current Assets		326·00
		£7 500·00

Representing

	£
Capital introduced by proprietor	7 500·00

The insurance prepaid is an asset at the date of the balance sheet. If the business was discontinued it could be recovered from the insurance company and if the business carries on then the following period will receive the benefit of it.

TESTS AND QUESTIONS

1 A trader's Capital appears on the 'liabilities' side of his Balance Sheet. In what sense is it true that the Capital is a liability of the business?

  What would you infer if the trader's Balance Sheet (assumed correctly drawn up) showed his Capital on the 'Assets' side?

2 Give an example of one of each of the following:
  (a) Fixed Asset.
  (b) Current Asset.
  Explain the difference (if any) in the purposes for which such Assets are held by a trader or manufacturer.

3 Suppose that you have been newly appointed to an administrative position in a wholesale merchanting business. What data would you call for, and what tests would you apply to this, in order to find out if the general financial position of the business is sound and healthy?

4 The following is an account taken from the Sales Ledger of Herbert Charleston. Explain clearly what information this account gives you.

LEONARD BRYAN

DR.			£	19x4		CR. £
19x4				Feb. 3	Returns	21·00
Jan. 1	Balance		102·00	April 4	Cheque	401·00
Mar. 3	Goods		336·00		Balance carried forward	16·00
			£438·00			£438·00
April 4	Balance forward		16·00	Sept. 22	Cheque	164·00
June 23	Goods		141·00			
Aug. 3	Interest Charged		7·00			
			£164·00			£164·00
Sept. 26	Cheque Dishonoured		164·00	Nov. 15	Bad Debts A/c	164·00
			£164·00			£164·00

5 Briefly explain the meaning of the items shown in the following Ledger Account.

E. SIMPSON—CAPITAL ACCOUNT

DR.					CR.
19x2		£	19x2		£
June 30	Cash Drawings	200·00	Jan. 1	Balance	3 636·00
Sept. 30	Purchases, Motor		June 30	Cash	500·00
	car for self	1 060·00	Sept. 30	Freehold Pro-	
Nov. 30	Balance	4 116·00		perty	1 225·00
			Nov. 30	A. Graham	15·00
		£5 376·00			£5 376·00

Note.—On November 20, A. Graham, a creditor, for goods supplied had agreed to accept a cash payment of £0·5 in the £ in full discharge of his account of £30.

6 Each year a firm calculates the following percentages:

   (a) Gross profit per cent on sales.

   (b) Net profit per cent on gross profit.

   (c) Net profit per cent on capital.

   What information do you think is obtained from these calculations?

7 From the under-mentioned figures which were extracted from the books of a manufacturer you are asked to prepare an account or statement in a form which will give the proprietor the maximum information as to his trading results, including the percentages of the various items to turnover, and to state what conclusions can be drawn from the figures:

	Year ended September 30,	
	19x4	19x5
	£	£
Purchases of Material	5 823·00	6 494·00
Wages: Productive	5 064·00	6 768·00
Non-productive	620·00	984·00
Returns Inwards	472·00	1 903·00
Discount Received	180·00	36·00
Salaries	1 560·00	1 584·00
Selling Expenses	1 720·00	2 784·00
Discount Allowed	420·00	492·00
Works Expenses	3 176·00	3 456·00
Office Expenses	370·00	420·00
Stock at commencement of year	2 189·00	2 876·00
Sales	20 472·00	25 903·00

The stock of material at September 30, 19x5, was valued at £1 882.

8 The following accounts showing the result of a year's trading, with comparative figures for the preceding year, have been submitted to the proprietor of a manufacturing business, who has forwarded them to you for criticism. Re-arrange the accounts in the form you consider will give the maximum information (showing also the percentages of the various debits on turnover), and state any conclusions which can be drawn from the figures.

TRADING AND PROFIT AND LOSS ACCOUNTS

	Year ended Dec. 31,			Year ended Dec. 31	
	19x0 £	19x1 £		19x0 £	19x1 £
Stock	2 105·00	2 001·00	Sales	20 000·00	18 000·00
Purchases	5 576·00	5 524·00	Stock	2 001·00	1 495·00
Wages (Productive)	5 500·00	5 400·00			
Works Expenses	960·00	909·00			
Gross Profit c/d	7 860·00	5 661·00			
	£22 001·00	£19 495·00		£22 001·00	£19 495·00
Rent and Rates	700·00	720·00	Balance b/d	7 860·00	5 661·00
Wages (Non-productive)	800·00	990·00			
Salaries	1 808·00	1 818·00			
Travellers' Commission and Expenses	920·00	900·00			
Office Expenses	272·00	270·00			
Bad Debts	200·00	414·00			
Net Profit	3 160·00	549·00			
	£7 860·00	£5 661·00		£7 860·00	£5 661·00

9 Criticise, under the appropriate headings, any five of the items of the Balance Sheet of B. M. Downfield. In your opinion, is his financial position satisfactory? Give reasons for your answers.

BALANCE SHEET OF B. M. DOWNFIELD FOR 19x5–19x6

Liabilities			Assets		
		£			£
Sundry Creditors		12 500·00	Cash		1 300·00
Bank		3 200·00	Bills Receivable		2 680·00
Capital		1 040·00	Sundry Debtors		3 200·00
			Stock		6 860·00
			Plant	£2 000·00	
			Add Cost of Repairs	200·00	
					2 200·00
			Fittings, Cost Price in 19x0		500·00
		£16 740·00			£16 740·00

10 In the course of your audit of the accounts of a Trading Company
    the following comparisons are noted:

| | 19x9 | 19x0 |
	£	£
Sales	40 000·00	30 000·00
Stocks, closing	10 000·00	14 000·00
Gross Profit	8 000·00	7 800·00
General Expenses	2 500·00	1 800·00
Selling Expenses	1 000·00	1 100·00
Discounts to Customers	400·00	450·00
Bad and doubtful debts	200·00	100·00
Debtors	10 000·00	11 000·00
Trade and Sundry Creditors	5 000·00	3 000·00

Comment on the figures set forth above and indicate what, if any,
special inquiries you consider the facts necessitate.

CHAPTER XVIII

LIMITED COMPANIES, AND THE COMPANIES ACTS, 1948 AND 1967

The limited company, as an artificial body corporate, owes its existence to registration under the provisions of the Companies Act, 1948, and must be considered apart from changing generations of shareholders. The latter, when subscribing for shares, are able to limit their liability to the nominal or 'face' value of the shares taken by them. An applicant for 100 shares of £1 each has, when his offer is accepted by the company, a liability to pay £100 *and no more*, even if the company should in future be unable to meet the claims of its creditors. The creditors have contracted with the company, to which alone they can look for payment.

Thus limited liability has furnished an immense stimulus to the development of business because:

(a) *The company*, unlike the Sole Trader, or Partnership firm, can obtain capital funds from a very large number of persons.

(b) *The individual shareholder* can take as many, or as few shares as he desires, and when once he has paid for them is protected from any further liability.

PUBLIC AND PRIVATE COMPANIES

All Companies incorporated under the Companies Acts, 1948 and 1967, are bound by its provisions and comprise two main classes:

Public Companies and Private Companies.

A Private Company is one which, by its Articles, or Regulations:

(a) Restricts the number of its shareholders (exclusive of employees or ex-employees) to fifty.

(*b*) Restricts the right freely to transfer shares issued by it.

(*c*) Forbids any appeal to the public to subscribe for its shares or debentures.

A broad distinction is that a Public Company is one in which the public are substantially interested as providers of capital, whereas in a Private Company management and proprietorship are often identical, the company having been formed chiefly to obtain the benefit of limited liability rather than the provision of new money.

Restrictions on the transfer of shares in a Private Company may mean that a would-be seller must first offer his shares to an existing shareholder, or accept a price determined in accordance with the Articles, etc.

THE MEMORANDUM AND ARTICLES OF ASSOCIATION

Any seven or more persons, or where the company to be formed will be a Private Company, any two or more persons may form an incorporated Company by subscribing their names to a Memorandum of Association and otherwise complying with the requirements of the Companies Act.

The Memorandum of Association is, in effect, the Charter of the Company, and must state:

(*a*) The name of the company, with 'Limited' as the last word of the name.

(*b*) The situation of the Registered Office of the company.

(*c*) The objects of the company.

(*d*) That the liability of the members is limited.

(*e*) The amount of the Share Capital with which the company proposes to be registered, and the division thereof into shares of a fixed amount.

No subscriber of the Memorandum may take less than one share.
As regards the Memorandum, note:

(*a*) The name chosen for the new company must not so closely resemble that of an existing company as to deceive or cause confusion in the mind of the public.

The proposed name may in the first instance be submitted to the Registrar of Companies.

(b) The applicants for registration must state the objects which it is proposed to carry out. The company may only act in fulfilment of the objects stated. If the substratum of the business disappears, particularly where the company is a Public Company, it is only right that the directors should not be able to turn unhindered to some quite unrelated form of business with the residue of the funds originally subscribed.

Usually the opportunity is taken to provide for eventualities by adding to the main object a number of others which may be regarded as reasonably incidental to it.

(c) The Capital stated in the Memorandum of Association is variously styled the Registered, Authorised or Nominal Capital, but may be altered from time to time by the company in general meeting.

Articles of Association, or a series of regulations prescribed for the company, may be registered with the Memorandum, but failing this, a model set of articles, known as Table A (and given as an appendix to the Companies Act, 1948), is applicable.

The Articles may be likened to the rules of a club or society, and provide for the general conduct of the company's affairs.

All members of the company are bound by the Articles in force, even if they subsequently acquire their shares by purchase in the market, and were not original subscribers.

The Articles may be altered or added to by passing a special resolution of members in general meeting, a three-fourths majority being required and not less than 21 days' notice of the intention to propose the resolution as a special resolution having been given.

The Articles will concern the following, *inter alia*:

Shares. Issue, transfer and voting rights.
Directors. Appointment, powers and remuneration.
Meetings. Procedure, and business thereat.
Finance. Preparation and circulation of Accounts, payment of dividends, etc.

SHARE CAPITAL

Shares, as units of proprietorship, may be generally classified as Ordinary and Preference Shares. The latter carry a fixed rate of dividend and are known as e.g. 6% Preference Share. Preference Shareholders have a priority for this dividend to the extent there are profits available. Ordinary Shares, subject to the placing to reserve of any part of the profits, take what remains, and may earn very large dividends in prosperous years. The Ordinary Shareholders have thus the opportunity of capital appreciation through an increase in market price.

With Cumulative Preference Shares any arrears of dividend are carried forward to the ensuing period.

Redeemable Preference Shares are those which are to be redeemed either out of *profits*, or from the proceeds of a fresh issue of *capital*: otherwise the shareholder of any class may only realise his investment by sale in the market.

The two latter classes represent variations of the simple Preference Share, and are usually of importance in the case of a Public Company, whose appeal to the investor it is desired to frame in the broadest possible way.

Voting Rights are commonly restricted to the Ordinary Shareholders. Preference Shareholders may enjoy voting rights during any period when their dividend is unpaid.

It must be carefully observed that with both Public and Private Companies the boon of limited liability is only conferred on the understanding that the capital fund of the company is maintained intact.

The capital must not be returned to shareholders in dividend.

Dividends should only be paid out of profits periodically ascertained by preparing accounts, and as recommended by the directors and approved by the members in general meeting.

The Articles may give the directors power to pay *interim* dividends.

Dividends are usually paid according to the amounts from time to time *paid-up* on the Shares.

DEBENTURES

In addition to issuing shares, a company may issue debentures, which are acknowledgments of *loans* made to the company. The debenture-holder, unlike the shareholder, is a *creditor*, with all a creditor's remedies.

Debentures issued by companies incorporated under the Companies Act are usually redeemable at a future date. Meantime the debenture-holder is entitled to receive interest at a fixed rate per cent whether or not profits exist out of which to pay it.

A further feature of debentures is that the holders are almost always *secured* creditors. This means that the company pledges or charges some part of its property (e.g. its factory premises) in favour of such creditors specifically, who may, on default by the company, appoint a Receiver (Receiver for debenture-holders), realise the security to the best advantage and repay themselves out of the proceeds.

It will thus be appreciated that an issue of debentures, because of the minimum risk of loss to the holder, may enable money to be *borrowed* at a rate of interest relatively low in comparison with the rate of dividend paid on Preference and Ordinary *Shares*.

BOOKS OF ACCOUNT

Statutory Books

The Companies Act, 1948, requires every company to keep proper books of account to record its:

(*a*) Cash receipts and payments.
(*b*) Trading purchases and sales.
(*c*) Assets and liabilities.

Proper books of account are such as are necessary to give a true and fair view of the state of the company's affairs and to explain its transactions.

The *Statutory Books* of the company similarly required, chiefly comprise:

(*a*) The Register of Members.
(*b*) The Register of Charges (e.g. Debentures).
(*c*) The Register of Directors and Managers.
(*d*) Separate Minute Book for meetings of directors, and of shareholders.

The Register of Members is the principal statutory book, in which particulars are to be kept of members, their share-holdings, transfers, etc.

Access to the Register of Charges is clearly a help to an unsecured creditor or other person giving credit to the company, enabling him to see what part of the company's property is already charged.

ACCOUNTS AND AUDIT

The directors of both Public and Private Companies must once in each year lay before the company in general meeting a Profit and Loss Account made up to a date not earlier than the date of the meeting by more than nine months.

A Balance Sheet made up to the same date must also be presented, together with a report of the directors as to their dividend recommendations and the general state of the company's affairs.

The Balance Sheet must contain a summary of the Authorised and Issued Share Capital of the company, and particulars of the general nature of its Assets and Liabilities. The Companies Act, 1948, in its Eighth Schedule as amended by the Second Schedule of the 1967 Act, lays down detailed requirements as to the contents of Balance Sheets and Profit and Loss Accounts.

Every company must at each annual general meeting appoint an Auditor, or Auditors, who must in general belong to a body of accountants recognised by the Board of Trade. The Auditors are to report to the members on the accounts examined by them, and have a right of access at all times to the books, accounts and vouchers of the company.

Example No. 1

From the following particulars, prepare a Balance Sheet of Wick, Ltd., at November 30, 19x6, grouping the Assets and Liabilities in the form you think most desirable:

	£
4% Debentures	20 000·00
Cash at bank	4 911·00
General Reserve	10 000·00
Calls in arrear on Ordinary Shares	100·00
Stock-in-Trade	34 009·00
Goodwill, at cost	30 000·00
40 000 5% Preference Shares	40 000·00
80 000 Ordinary Shares	80 000·00
Doubtful Debts Provision	500·00
Contingent Liability on Bills discounted	250·00
Preliminary Expenses, not written off	600·00
Sundry Debtors	12 350·00
Freeholds, at cost	32 750·00
Creditors	5 962·00
Profit and Loss Account, December 1, 19x5 (Cr.)	5 000·00
Plant and Machinery, at cost, less depreciation, provided to date (£20 000) December 1, 19x5	54 600·00
Deposit with Local Authority	9 800·00
Debenture Discount, not written off	200·00
Additions to Plant and Machinery at cost	742·00
Profit for the year, *less* Dividends on Preference Shares	7 600·00
Depreciation for the year	10 000·00

The Authorised Capital of the company is 50 000 5% Preference Shares of £1, and 100 000 Ordinary Shares of £1.

Note:
(a) Preliminary Expenses represent those incurred in connection with the formation of the company, stamp duty on the authorised capital, solicitors' and accountants' charges, etc.
(b) Discount on Debentures is a concession made by the company to the debenture-holders at the time of issue. The

Solution to Example No. 1:

WICK, LTD.
Balance Sheet at November 30, 19x0

Share Capital	Authorised £	Issued and Fully Paid £	£
5% Preference Shares of £1·00	50 000·00	40 000·00	
Ordinary Shares of £1·00	100 000·00	80 000·00	
	150 000·00	120 000·00	
Deduct Calls in Arrear		100·00	
			119 900·00
Reserves			
General		10 000·00	
Profit and Loss Account		12 600·00	
			22 600·00
Share Capital and Reserves			142 500·00
Loan			
4% Debentures repayable			20 000·00
Current Liabilities			
Trade Creditors			6 962·00
			£169 462·00

Fixed Assets	Cost £	Depreciation £	Net Book Value £
Freehold land	32 750·00	—	32 750·00
Plant and Machinery	75 342·00	30 000·00	45 342·00
Total Fixed Assets	£108 092·00	£30 000·00	78 092·00
Current Assets			
Stock			34 009·00
Debtors, less doubtful debts provision (£500·00)			11 850·00
Local Authority Deposit			9 800·00
Cash and Bank Balance			4 911·00
			60 570·00
Intangible Assets			
Goodwill			30 000·00
Preliminary Expenses			600·00
Discount on Debentures			200·00
			30 800·00
			£169 462·00

Note: There is a Contingent Liability of £250·00 in respect of Bills discounted.

amount of cash received from them was to this extent less
than their claim for ultimate repayment, viz. £20 000.

(c) There should also be presented the corresponding amounts
at the end of the immediately preceding financial year for
all items shown in the balance sheet.

Example No. 2

The following is the Balance Sheet at June 30, 19x0, of Bleak,
House & Co.:

	£	£		£
Sundry Creditors		8 440·00	Cash	120·00
Bankers		18 600·00	Sundry Debtors	20 780·00
			Stock-in-Trade	42 140·00
Capital Accounts:				
B. Bleak	74 000·00		Plant and Machinery	63 000·00
H. House	29 000·00		Goodwill	4 000·00
		103 000·00		
		£130 040·00		£130 040·00

The partners shared profits and losses as to three-fifths to B.
Bleak and as to two-fifths to H. House.

A Limited Company, Bleak House, Ltd., was formed to
acquire the business as from July 1, 19x0, the purchase consideration being £106 000. All the Assets and Liabilities were
taken over at book values, except as regards the Goodwill and
the Plant and machinery, which last were valued for the purpose
of the Sale and Purchase Agreement at £58 000.

In respect of the amount due to him, B. Bleak received 20 000
5% Preference Shares of £1 each in the new company, and the
balance in cash.

H. House received the whole of his share in £1 Ordinary
Shares, allotted at par, except for £3 200 paid to him in cash.

In addition to the foregoing, 30 000 Preference Shares were
issued to the public at par for cash, and 60 000 Ordinary Shares
at a premium of £0·1 per share; these issues were subscribed
and paid up in full, formation expenses amounting to £1 300.

You are required to record the above in the books of Bleak
House, Ltd., and to give the commencing Balance Sheet of the
new company.

Solution to Example No. 2

BOOKS OF BLEAK HOUSE, LTD.

B. BLEAK AND A. HOUSE—VENDORS

DR.		£	£		CR.		£	£
19x0 July 1	Sundry Creditors		8 440-00	19x0 July 1	Sundry Assets:			
	Bankers		18 600-00		Cash		120-00	
	Balance c/d		94 000-00		Sundry Debtors		20 780-00	
					Stock-in-Trade		42 140-00	
					Fixed Assets		58 000-00	121 040-00
			£121 040-00					£121 040-00
July 1	B. Bleak:			July 1	Balance, b/d			94 000-00
	5% Preference Shares	20 000-00			Goodwill			12 000-00
	Cash	55 800-00	75 800-00					
	H. House:							
	Ordinary Shares	27 000-00						
	Cash	3 200-00	30 200-00					
			£106 000-00					£106 000-00

GOODWILL

DR.		£	CR.
19x0 July 1	B. Bleak and H. House	£12 000-00	

5% PREFERENCE SHARES

Dr.			Cr.
			£
	19x0 July 1	B. Bleak	20 000·00
		Applications and Allotments	30 000·00
			£50 000·00

ORDINARY SHARES

Dr.			Cr.
			£
	19x0 July 1	H. House	27 000·00
		Applications and Allotments	60 000·00
			£87 000·00

APPLICATIONS AND ALLOTMENTS

Dr.		Ordinary £	Preference £		Cr.	Ordinary £	Preference £
19x0 July 1	Share Capital A/cs	60 000·00	30 000·00	19x0 July 1	Cash	66 000·00	30 000·00
	Share Premium A/c	6 000·00	—				
		£66 000·00	£30 000·00			£66 000·00	£30 000·00

SHARE PREMIUM ACCOUNT

Dr.					Cr.
			19x0 July 1	By Applications and Allotments	£ £6 000·00

CASH BOOK

Dr.		£	£		Cr.	£
19x0 July 1	B. Bleak and H. House		120·00	19x0 July 1	B. Bleak and H. House	18 600·00
	Applications and Allotments:			1	B. Bleak	55 800·00
	Ordinary Shares	66 000·00		1	H. House	3 200·00
	Preference Shares	30 000·00	96 000·00	1	Formation Expenses	1 300·00
				1	Balance c/d	17 220·00
			£96 120·00			£96 120·00

BLEAK HOUSE, LTD.
Balance Sheet at July 1, 19x0

	Authorised	Issued and Fully paid	£		Fixed Assets, at cost	£	£
Share Capital	£	£			Plant and Machinery		58 000·00
5% Preference Shares of £1·00	50 000·00	50 000·00					
Ordinary Shares of £1·00	100 000·00	87 000·00			Current Assets		
	£150 000·00		137 000·00		Stock	42 140·00	
					Debtors	20 780·00	
Capital Reserve					Cash	17 220·00	80 140·00
Share premiums account			6 000·00				
					Intangible Assets		
Share Capital and Reserve			143 000·00		Goodwill	12 000·00	
					Formation Expenses	1 300·00	13 300·00
Current Liability							
Creditors			8 440,00				
			£151 440·00				£151 440·00

Note : in future years comparative figures will also be shown.

Note to Student.

	B. Bleak	H. House
	£	£
Prior to sale the partners' Capitals are	74 000·00	29 000·00
They share profits and losses as 3 is to 2.		
They *lose* £9,000·00 on revaluation of Goodwill, etc.	5 400·00	3 600·00
	68 600·00	25 400·00
The net worth of their business is thus reduced to £94 000·00.		
But the Purchase Price is £106 000·00, a *profit* of	7 200·00	4 800·00
	£75 800·00	£30 200·00

FURTHER EXERCISES

1. A.B. & Co., Ltd., has an authorised Capital of £8 000, divided into 8 000 Ordinary Shares of £1 each. On December 31, 19x3, 6 000 shares had been issued and fully paid, and there were also balances on the books of the Company in respect of the following:

	£
Sales	10 350·00
Purchases	4 128·00
Wages	3 084·00
Stock (January 1, 19x3)	746·00
Salaries	525·00
Rent	135·00
Rates	48·00
Insurance	29·00
Repairs	37·00
Debenture Interest	75·00
Bank Charges	14·00
Travelling Expenses	197·00
Sundries	188·00
Goodwill, at cost	3 000·00
Patents, at cost	2 506·00
Plant and Machinery, at cost	1 240·00
Experimental Account (Asset)	1 777·00

	£
Trade Debtors	2 316·00
Trade Creditors	846·00
Bank Overdraft	187·00
5% Debenture	2 000·00
Preliminary Expenses	142·00
Profit and Loss Account (Liability) at January 1, 19x3	804·00

Stock, as taken on December 31, 19x3, amounted to £911, but includes an item of £65 for catalogues, the invoice for which has not yet been passed through the books.

The charges for Carriage Inwards, amounting to £102, have been debited to Sundries Account.

You are requested to prepare a Trading and Profit and Loss Account for the year ended December 31, 19x3, providing 5% depreciation on Plant and Machinery, and £84 for Bad Debts. It is also required to provide 2½% for discounts to be allowed to Debtors, ignoring any provision of a similar kind for Creditors.

2. Tompkins, the accountant of Gloria Tubes, Ltd., submits to you the following Revenue Account of the Company for the year ended February 28, 19x5.

DR.				CR.
		£		£
Wages		8 200·00	Balance of Profit, March 1,	
Purchases		12 500·00	19x4	1 250·00
Salaries		3 468·00	Stock, February 28, 19x5	2 350·00
Commission		2 803·00	Rates, Prepaid	21·00
Rates		105·00	Sales	27 550·00
Carriage Inwards		180·00	Discounts Received	125·00
Repairs and Maintenance		217·00		
Stock, March 1, 19x4		2 120·00		
Depreciation—	£			
Plant, 10%	110·00			
Fixtures, 5%	45·00			
Lorries, 20%	80·00			
		235·00		
Directors' Fees		105·00		
Packing and Carriage		486·00		
Insurance		37·00		
Debenture Interest		60·00		
Bank Interest		22·00		
Sundry Expenses		308·00		
Profit		450·00		
		£31 296·00		£31 296·00

The authorised capital of the Company is £5 000, in shares of
£1 each. Of these, 4 951 have been issued as fully paid to the
vendor, who is the managing director, and his wife.

A 6% Debenture for £1 000 is outstanding in favour of the
managing director's wife.

£1 452 is owing to suppliers, and £2 500 by customers, in
respect of which latter 2% is to be provided. At February 28,
19x5, the Company had £817 in the Bank, while at March 1,
19x4, the book values and original cost of the Fixed Assets
were:

	£	£
Plant	1 100·00	1 500·00
Fixtures	900·00	1 200·00
Lorries	400·00	1 000·00

Prepare in proper form Trading and Profit and Loss Account
for the year ended February 28, 19x5, and a Balance Sheet at
that date.

3. The authorised capital of the Waterloo Engineering Co.,
Ltd., is £80 000 in £1 shares. The Trial Balance opposite was
extracted from the Company's books as on March 31, 19x4.

You are required to prepare the Manufacturing Account, Profit
and Loss Account and Balance Sheet of the Company after
taking into consideration the following matters:

(a) The item 'Delivery Expenses' includes £175 in respect of the
    subsequent trading period.

(b) Wages £515 and Directors' Fees £100 are outstanding.

(c) No provision has been made for the half-year's Debenture
    Interest due on March 31, 19x4.

(d) The Machinery and Plant is to be depreciated at the rate of
    10% on the original cost of £36 450 and the Motor Lorries are
    to be written down to £3 000 being half of their original cost.

(e) The Bank Pass Book shows on March 31, 19x4, a credit of
    £15 for Interest on Deposit, but this item has not been
    entered in the Company's books.

(f) The General Reserve is to be increased by £2 000.

(g) The Stock held on March 31, 19x4, was valued at £8 765.

(h) Ignore income tax.

	Dr. £	Cr. £
Issued Capital (60 000 shares)		60 000·00
Sales		138 980·00
Land and Buildings	30 000·00	
Machinery and Plant	29 530·00	
Sundry Debtors and Creditors	30 059·00	8 131·00
Purchases	46 150·00	
Interim Dividend	3 000·00	
Delivery Expenses	3 910·00	
Stock, March 31, 19x3	5 782·00	
Discounts	1 537·00	729·00
Returns Inwards	1 110·00	
Salaries	2 697·00	
Travellers' Commission and Expenses	3 740·00	
Profit and Loss Account, March 31, 19x3		2 530·00
Motor Lorries	3 987·00	
5% Debentures		20 000·00
Rent and Rates (Factory £1 650, Office £224)	1 874·00	
Wages	61 846·00	
General Expenses	892·00	
Factory Power and Light	2 839·00	
Debenture Interest	500·00	
General Reserve		6 000·00
Repairs to Machinery	1 421·00	
Directors' Fees	300·00	
Bank Deposit	3 500·00	
Bank Current Account	1 696·00	
	£236 370·00	£236 370·00

CHAPTER XIX
VALUE ADDED TAX

Question
What is VAT?

Answer
Many countries have introduced a tax calculated as a percentage of the sales of the business. In Britain this is known as the Value Added Tax (VAT) and the appropriate percentage (currently 8%, originally 10%) on the value of sales has to be accounted for to the Customs and Excise. As allowance is given for VAT paid on purchases, a business in effect pays over the VAT on the value added by the business and recovers it from the customer. The balance of VAT charged to customers over the VAT suffered on purchases must be handed over to the Commissioners of Customs and Excise. On the other hand, if the tax suffered by him exceeds that which he has charged, repayment is due. Only registered traders are affected by this tax. Any trader may register. He is not forced to register unless his turnover exceeds £5000 per annum. A person not registered cannot charge VAT nor can he recover VAT suffered on his purchases.

Question
What extra records does the business have to keep?

Answer
The business with proper records will require very little extra; another column in the Purchase and Sales Day Books and an additional nominal ledger account being all that is necessary. Using the examples from pages 16 and 17, both day books would require an extra column to record the VAT. On the purchase from R. Ridgewell, which totalled £275·80, there would be VAT at 8%; this is £22·06 and would be added to the invoice to give a new total of £297·86. Similarly with the invoice from B. Davis VAT of £85·20 and a new total of £1 150·28 and from General Supplies £8 making £108. These will be recorded in the Purchase

Day Book and the VAT analysed into the additional column that has been added.

Exactly the same procedure takes place with the Sales. The VAT must be added to each invoice. This will increase each one by 8%, e.g. invoice no. 4 to W. Humphrey for £306·00 will now have £24·48 added and the new invoice total will be £330·48 and similarly for the other sales.

Question

What happens now that VAT has been recorded on the invoices and in the Day Books?

Answer

The nominal ledger account is written up and the balance will be the amount that is due to be paid to the Customs and Excise. Occasionally more may have been paid with purchases than has been charged on sales and a claim can be made for repayment.

NOMINAL LEDGER ACCOUNT
VAT

Dr.							Cr.
Date	Details	Fo.	Amount	Date	Details	Fo.	Amount
19x1 Mar. 31	Total for month	1	£ 115·26	19x1 Mar. 31	Total for month	2	£ 116·90

Question

This seems to be a very simple procedure. Why has all the publicity been necessary?

Answer

The book-keeping is straightforward. The difficulties arise because certain goods and services are exempt, others are zero rated.

Exemption. Exemption for a transaction means that no liability to account for tax to the tax authorities arises when the transaction is performed. Equally, the trader undertaking the exempt transaction is given no credit by the tax authorities for any tax invoiced to him by his suppliers, or paid at importation, in respect of the goods and services he uses for his exempt business. The operation of the credit mechanism throughout a chain of transactions is thereby interrupted.

D. MORRIS

Fo. 1

PURCHASE DAY BOOK

MARCH, 19x1

Date	Supplier	Description	In-voice No.	Details	Total	VAT	Cloth	Blankets	Shawls	Sundries	Special Items
				£	£	£	£	£	£	£	£
19x1 Mar. 12	R. Ridgwell	50 pairs Blankets at £3·50 pair 3 dozen Woollen Shawls at £2·80 each	— 1	175·00 100·80				175·00	100·80		
		VAT, 8%		275·80 22·06	297·86	22·06					
20	B. Davis, Ely	500 yards Black Cloth at £0·50 per yard 400 Shawls at 12·00 each Remnants	2	250·00 800·00 15·00			250·00		800·00	15·00	
		VAT, 8%		1 065·00 85·20	1 065·00 1 150·20	85·20					
29	General Supplies Ltd., London	Showcases and Fittings VAT, 8%	3	100·00 8·00	108·00	8·00					100·00
					£1 556·06	£115·26	£250·00	£175·00	£900·80	£15·00	£100·00

D. MORRIS SALES DAY BOOK Fo. 2

MARCH, 19x1

Date	Customer	Description	In-voice No.	Details	Total	VAT	Cloth	Velvet	Sundries
				£	£	£	£	£	£
19x1 Mar. 10	W. Humphrey Lincoln	200 yards Black Cloth at £1·00 per yard 100 yards best Brown Cloth at £1·40 per yard		200·00 140·00					
		Less 10% Trade Discount	4	340·00 34·00					
		Add VAT, 8%		306·00 24·48	330·48	24·48	306·00		
18	S. Boham, Coventry	100 yards Velvet at £1·50 per yard Less 5% Trade Discount		150·00 7·50					
		300 yards Black Cloth at £1·00 per yard Trimmings	5	142·50 300·00 15·00					
		Add VAT, 8%		457·50 36·60	494·10	36·60	300·00	142·50	15·00
24	T. Butterworth, Norwich	300 yards Velvet at £1·75 per yard Less 5% Trade Discount		525·00 26·25					
		150 yards best Brown Cloth at £1·40 per yard Less 10% Trade Discount		498·75 210·00 21·00					
		Assorted Buttons	6	189·00 10·00	697·75				
		Add VAT, 8%		697·75 55·82	753·57	55·82	189·00	498·75	10·00
					£1 578·15	£116·90	£795·00	£641·25	£25·00

Zero-rating. Zero-rating a transaction means that it is brought within the scope of the tax, but the rate applied to output is zero. If the person carrying out the transaction is a taxable person he is accountable in the usual way; but the result is that his outputs carry no tax because a zero rate is applied to them, while he is allowed credit for or repayment of tax on his inputs. Exports will be relieved from tax by means of this technique.

There are different rates for different products, and the local officer of the Customs and Excise should be consulted for the precise details applicable to a particular enterprise.

ANSWERS

49	3	Debit.
		Debit.
		Credit.
		Debit, if allowed: Credit, if received.
		Credit.
50	5 (b)	£101·23.
	(c)	Brown in indebted.
	6	Balance £1 002·52.
	7 (b)	Credit Bank. Debit Bank charges.
	(c)	Credit Motor Vans £25·00.
		Debit Loss on Sale A/c £25·00.
51	8 (a)	Plant A/c. Debit.
	(b)	Robinson's personal A/c. Credit.
		Cash £170·00 and Discount allowed £2·60.
	(c)	Fire Loss A/c. Credit.
	(d)	Motor Van A/c. Credit.
	(e)	Fitter's personal A/c. Debit.
		Cash £250·00 and Discount received £10·75.
68	4 (a)	Credit landlord.
		Debit rent.
		Debit cash.
		Debit landlord.
	(b)	Credit cash.
		Debit rent.
69	5	Dr. Bals. Cash £63·50.
		Bank £94·85.
		Discount. Dr. £1·00. Cr. £2·35.
	6	Dr. Bals. Cash £35·00. Bank £612·00.
		Discount. Dr. £6·75. Cr. £2·00.
70	7	Cheque payment £354·90.
	8	Cash Dr. balance £8·75.
		Bank Cr. balance £11·75.

71   9 (*a*)   Dr. side. Personal.
                        Impersonal.
                        Private.
            Cr. side Impersonal.
                        Personal.
                        Personal.
                        Impersonal.

         10   Dr. Bal. Cash £115·20.
                     Cr. Bal. Bank £267·15.
                     Discount. Dr. £1·25. Cr. £2·50.

80   2   Favourable Bal. £65·82.
         (*b*)   Unfavourable Bal. £233·96.
         3   Favourable Bal. £80·39.

82   9   Pass book. £914·87.

110 1   Capital £6 350·00. Dr. Cash £147·00.
                                         Cr. Bank £932·00.
                     T.B. Totals £10 475·00.

         2   Capital £5 000·00. Dr. Cash £50·00.
                                         Dr. Bank £1 690·40.
                                         Cr. Discount £41·25.
                     T.B. Totals £5 911·40.

111 3   Capital £1 750·00. Dr. Cash £60·00.
                                         Dr. Bank £1 310·50.
                                         Cr. Discount £2·50.
                                         Dr. Discount £2·00.
                     T.B. Totals £2 887·50.

112 4   Capital £4 310·80. Dr. Cash £50·00.
                                         Dr. Bank £117·95.
                                         Cr. Discount £19·50.
                                         Dr. Discount £1·75.
                     T.B. Totals £5 466·90.

         5   Capital £578·00. Dr. Cash £12·70.
                                         Cr. Bank £145·05.
                                         Dr. Discount £5·75.
                     T.B. Totals £977·90.

113 6   Capital £1 000·00. Dr. Cash £18·50.
                                         Dr. Bank £1 299·00.
                                         Dr. Discount £2·45.
                                         Cr. Discount £2·25.
                     T.B. Totals £1 730·50.

114	7	Capital £1 184·85. Dr. Cash £12·00.
		Dr. Bank £46·76.
		Cr. Discount £11·16.
		T.B. Totals £1 367·56.
115	8	Capital £1 650·00. Dr. Cash £20·00.
		Dr. Bank 1 265·98.
		Dr. Discount £0·92, Cr. £9·85.
		T.B. Totals £2 026·80.
116	9	Capital £10 759·00. Dr. Cash £42·00.
		Dr. Bank £440·17.
		Dr. Discount £4·35, Cr. £5·52.
		T.B. Totals £11 101·52.
125	3	Short Credit £103·20.
	7 (*b*)	T.B. Totals £4 247·00.
126	8 (*a*)	Short Dr. £12·25.
	(*b*)	Short Dr. £5·35.
	(*c*)	None.
	(*d*)	Short Dr. £0·50.
	(*e*)	Short Cr. £4·00.
127	9 (*c*)	T.B. Totals £46 147·24.
	10	T.B. Totals £39 546·00.
128	11	T.B. Totals £5 952·00.
129	12	Original Balance short Dr. £122·25.
142	6 (*b*)	Closing stock £320·00.
	7	Claim £3 703·00.
142	8 (*b*)	£10·00.
143	9	Net Profit. Dept. A £72·00.
		B £710·00.
		C £226·00.
		Dr. P/L A/c £8·00 Bal.
151	1 (*a*)	Short Dr. £100·00: None: Short Debit £30·00.
	(*b*)	Debtors understated £100·00: Fixtures understated £12·00: Profit understated £42·00: Bank balance understated £30·00.
	3	Pass Book Bal. £36·00 overdrawn.
	4	Bal. Sheet Totals £3 350·00.
152	6	T.B. Totals £2 717·00.
		Gross Profit £13·00. Net Loss £100·00.
		Bal. Sheet Totals £2 184·00.

152	7	Capital £23 264·00. Net Profit £1 994·00. Bal. Sheet Totals £24 054·00.
153	8	Gross Profit £8 700·00. Net Profit £5 250·00. Bal. Sheet Totals £12 750·00.
154	9	Gross Profit £1 155·00. Net Profit £1 100·00. Bal. Sheet Totals £58 200·00.
155	11	Gross Profit £10 250·00 (33⅓%). Net Profit £1 000·00 (3¼%). Bal. Sheet Totals £13 269·00.
156	12	Gross Profit £4 349·00. Net Profit £2 586·00. Bal. Sheet Totals £8 205·00.
157	13	£986·00 less £20·00 depreciation: £966·00.
	14	Profit £125·00. Bal. Sheet Totals £3 499·00.
158	15	Gross Profit £1 261·00. Net Profit £426·00. Bal. Sheet Totals £4 018·00.
166	3	Profits 19x2 £2 517·00. 19x3 £2 638·00.
	4	P/L Debit £2 941·00.
167	5	P/L Debit £214·50.
	6	P/L Debit £67·75.
	7	Bad Debts £14·09. Reserve £19·84.
168	9	P/L Dr. 19x4 £1 551·40. 　　　　　　19x5 £1 734·38. Omission overstates 19x4 Profits and understates Liabilities £41·18.
	10	P/L Dr. Rent £360·00. Rates £153·36.
	11	P/L Dr. Rates £180·00. Wages £7 134·00. Stationery, etc. £747·00. Bad Debts and Reserve £409·00. Discounts £107·54.
169	12	P/L Dr. £90·00.
	13	P/L Dr. £248·00 Prepayments, etc. £17·00. Accrued expenses £12·00.
	14	Profit £3 627·00. Bal. Sheet Totals £5 663·00.
178	4	P/L Dr. 19x2　£12·00. 　　　　　　19x3　£11·00.

178   19x4 £11·00.
                19x5 £103·00.
                19x6 £88·00.

5   P/L Dr. £1 500·00 p.a.

6   Depreciation £3 432·00 (calculating depreciation for a half-year where appropriate).
        Profit on sale £9·00.

7   Depreciation (nearest £) £2 602·00.
        Loss on sale £214·00.

8   Depreciation £500·00 p.a.
        Interest 19x5 £165·00.
                 19x6 £110·00.
                 19x7 £55·00.

179 9   Depreciation (opening Bals.): 19x4 £120·00.
                                          19x5 £133·00.

10   Gross Profit £5 545·00. Net Profit £900·00.
        12½% on Capital.
        Bal. Sheet Totals £7 836·50.

189 4   Interest on Loan £150·00.
        Profit Shares £1 175·00.

190 5 (a) Interest on Loan £50·00.
        Profit Shares £2 475·00.

   (b) Salary £1 500·00.
        Interest on Loan £50·00.
        Profit Shares £2 225·00.

   6 (a) A. £2 437·50. B. £812·50.
   (b) A. £2 587·50. B. £862·50.

191 7   X. £3 376·00. Y. £2 532·00. Z. £2 000·00.

   8 (a) A. £3 800·00. B. £1 800·00.
   (b) A. £1 900·00. B. £1 700·00.

   9   Profit Shares:
        Bright £1 080·00. Smart £720·00.

10   A. Profit £370·00. Interest £145·00.
        B. Salary £85·00. Profit £370·00.
                          Interest £95·00.
        C. Profit £80·00. Interest £25·00.

192 11   Gross Profit £5 000·00. Net Profit £2 845·00.
        Bal. Sheet Totals £12 445·00.

12   Gross Profit £4 800·00. Net Profit £3 250·00.
        Bal. Sheet Totals £4 282·00.

194 13   Gross Profit £4 099·62.
        Net Profit (before Interest) £608·36.

194   Plant A/c £5 950·00. Insurance A/c £99·75.
               Bad Debts Reserve £281·00.
               Commission A/c £398·91.

        14   Manufacturing A/c £39 561·00.
               Gross Profit £4 265·00.
               Net Profit (before Interest) £2 189·00.
               Bal. Sheet Totals £21 029·00.

222   1   Gross Profit £3 136·00. Net Profit £1 763·20.
               Bal. Sheet Totals £11 690·20.

223   2   Gross Profit £6 900·00. Net Loss £850·00.
               Bal. Sheet Totals £7 803·00.

224   3   Gross Profit.
               (Manufacturing A/c) £22 787·00.
               Net Profit £8 319·00.
               Bal. Sheet Totals £103 095·00.

EXAMINATION PAPERS

THE ROYAL SOCIETY OF ARTS
SINGLE-SUBJECT EXAMINATIONS

BOOK-KEEPING
STAGE I (Elementary)

March, 1975

[TWO HOURS ALLOWED]

ALL *questions in section A and* TWO *questions in Section B are to be attempted.*

SECTION A

ALL questions are to be attempted.

1 Show the entries to be made in the appropriate book of original entry in respect of the following credit transactions and then post the real and personal account items only to the ledgers.

Invoices received

January 2, 1975   A. Brown & Co. Ltd., goods for resale £54 (including VAT of £4)

January 4, 1975   Office Machines Ltd.—New filing cabinets for the office £108 (including VAT £8)

Invoice sent out for goods sold:

January 3, 1975   B. Taylor   £162 (including VAT £12)

2 A set of accounts was prepared for the year ended December 31, 1974 and the following errors were subsequently discovered:

   (a) Stock at December 31, 1974, was found to be under-valued by £50.

   (b) The purchase of a second-hand typewriter £25 had been included under the heading of repairs and renewals. Depreciation of Office Equipment had been provided at 10% and should be adjusted after the correction of the error.

(c) During the year the owner had taken goods from stock for his private use £60 (cost) but no entry had been made in the books to record this transaction.

Prepare journal entries to correct these errors or omissions and state the effect that the correction of each error or omission would have on the gross profit, net profit and balance sheet, naming the items affected on the balance sheet.

3   Angus Brown is a retail trader. From the following information prepare a Trading & Profit and Loss Account for the year ended December 31, 1974, and a Balance Sheet on that date.

Trial Balance—December 31, 1974.

	£	£
Capital January 1, 1974		6 400
Land & Buildings	5 000	
Motor Vehicles (cost £1 200)	600	
Drawings	1 400	
Stock	910	
Bank overdraft		96
Sales		14 260
Purchases	11 100	
Motor Expenses	310	
Sundry Expenses	106	
Wages	1 560	
Debtors	820	
Creditors		1 210
Rates & Insurance	160	
	£21 966	£21 966

The following should be taken into consideration:

(a) Stock at December 31, 1974, £1 820.
(b) A provision for doubtful debts of 5% on the debtors at December 31, 1974, is to be created.
(c) Depreciation is to be provided on motor vehicles at 20% on cost.
(d) Rates prepaid at December 31, 1974, £12.

(e) Motor expenses bill for December £26 is owing at December 31, 1974.

(f) Sundry expenses includes £15 for a private telephone bill of Angus Brown.

(g) A cheque for £250 was paid to a creditor on December 31, 1974, but had not been entered in the books at the time of extracting the trial balance.

4   Explain the term 'depreciation'. Name and describe briefly two methods of providing for depreciation of fixed assets.

Section B

Answer TWO *questions from this Section.*

5   *Either*

(i) The account of John Williams in the books of Fred Norman for the month of January 1975 was as follows:

1975		£	1975		£
Jan 1	Balance b/f	120	Jan 10	Cheque	117
				Discount	3
14	Goods	142			
			18	Returns	14
			20	Bought Ledger Contra	30
			31	Balance c/d	98
		£262			£262

1975
Feb 1 Balance b/d   98

(a) In which ledger would you expect the above account to appear?

(b) State the meaning of each entry in the account.

(c) Where would you expect the balance of £98 to be shown in the final accounts for the year ended January 31, 1975?

or

(ii) The ledger card of B. Parkes in the books of R. Foster for February 1975 was as follows:

	B. Parkes		
1975	Dr	Cr	Balance
Feb 3 Goods		460	460
6 Returns	40		420
20 Cheque	200		220
Discount	10		210

(a) State the meaning of each entry in the debit and credit columns, naming the book of original entry from which the item is posted.

(b) What does the balance of £210 represent?

6 You are employed as a book-keeper by G. Jones, a trader. State briefly what use you would make of the following documents in relation to your book-keeping records.

(a) A bank statement.

(b) A credit note received to correct an overcharge on an invoice.

(c) A paying-in slip.

(d) Petty cash voucher.

7 A grocer pays his employees 70p per hour for a 40-hour week, and time and a half for any hours in excess of 40 in any one week.

Prepare from the information given below the pay slip to be handed to John Brown for the week ended December 14, 1974.

Hours worked in the week 50

P.A.Y.E. £7.

National Insurance (Employees contribution) 75p.

Graduated Pension Contribution (Employee) £1·70.

THE ROYAL SOCIETY OF ARTS
SINGLE-SUBJECT EXAMINATIONS

BOOK-KEEPING
STAGE I (Elementary)

May, 1975

[TWO HOURS ALLOWED]

ALL *questions in Section A and* TWO *questions in Section B
are to be attempted.*

SECTION A

ALL *questions are to be attempted.*

1 The following figures are taken from a metal merchant's
books as at December 31, 1974:

	Tonnes	£
Stock of copper in warehouse		
January 1, 1974	500	350 000
Purchases for the year	10 825	7 361 000
Sales for the year	9 525	6 857 000

There were no weight gains or losses during the year.

The market price of copper on December 31, 1974, was
£650 per ton.

You are required:

(*a*) To calculate the tonnage and value of the stock at December 31, 1974;

(*b*) To prepare the Trading Account for the year ended
December 31, 1974.

2 From the following trial balance and the notes appended
below, prepare the Profit and Loss Account for the year ended
December 31, 1974, and a Balance Sheet as at that date.

Trial Balance of A. M. Dealer December 31, 1974

	£	£
Capital		66 365
Cash at Bank—Deposit A/c	50 000	
Cash at Bank—Current A/c	14 622	
Cash in Hand	374	
Debtors	30 003	
Creditors		34 681
Drawings	10 000	
Investments	5 000	
Office Furniture and Fittings	10 100	
Office Machines	4 000	
Motor Car	1 600	
Commission Received		53 740
Consultation Fees		1 250
Interest		2 476
Rent and Rates	5 240	
Salaries and National Insurance	21 478	
Travel and Entertaining	2 472	
Advertising	728	
Insurance	224	
Trade Subscriptions	1 280	
Telephone and Cables	1 284	
Sundry Expenses	107	
	£158 512	£158 512

Notes:

(*a*) No Trading A/c is required.

(*b*) Depreciate Office Furniture and Fittings and Office Machines by 10%. Depreciate Motor Car by 20%.

(*c*) Insurance paid in advance £34.

(*d*) Rates paid in advance £80.

(*e*) Advertising expenses accrued £72.

3 On April 1, 1972, Smallpiece Manufacturing Company purchased machinery at a cost of £50 000. It was decided to write off 10% of the cost of the machinery each year including a full 10% in the year of purchase.

On January 1, 1974, the Company purchased additional machinery for £12 000, including installation.

On September 1, 1974, the Company sold a machine for £7 500 which had been installed on April 1, 1972, at a cost of £10 000.

The Company closes its books on March 31, in each year.

Show the Machinery Account for the period from April 1, 1972, to March 31, 1975.

4 The following personal account appeared in S. Engineer's ledger on January 1, 1975.

L. Beech—a credit balance of £160. During January 1975 the following transactions took place relating to this account:

Jan 9 Bought goods from L. Beech for £60 less 20% trade discount.

Jan 11 Paid L. Beech by cheque the amount standing to the credit of his account on January 1 less 2½% cash discount.

Jan 18 Returned damaged goods purchased from L. Beech on January 9 at the catalogue price of £10.

(a) Make the necessary entries in the personal account of L. Beech and balance the account at January 31, 1974.

(b) Name the book of original entry in which each of these transactions would appear.

SECTION B

TWO, *and only* TWO, *of the questions are to be attempted.*

5 Draw up a petty Cash Voucher to cover expenditure for travelling expenses of £1·20.

6 Explain briefly what you understand by the following:

(a) A Post-dated cheque.

(b) Bearer cheque.

(c) Dishonoured cheque.

7 What is the difference between:

(a) A Deposit Account and a Current Account.

(b) Trade Discount and Cash Discount.

THE ROYAL SOCIETY OF ARTS
SINGLE-SUBJECT EXAMINATIONS

BOOK-KEEPING
STAGE I (Elementary)

June, 1975

[TWO HOURS ALLOWED]

ALL *questions in Section A and* TWO *questions in Section B are to be attempted.*

SECTION A

ALL *questions in this Section are to be attempted.*

1 You are keeping the books of W. Wright a wholesaler. Wellmaker is a supplier of goods. On May 1, 1975, Wellmaker is owed £200. The day books show the following transactions took place during the month of May 1975.

Date	Book	Page	Amount £
5 May 1975	Purchases	7	300
7 May 1975	Returns	3	10
9 May 1975	Cash		
	Bank column	9	285
	Discount		15
16 May 1975	Purchase	19	170
22 May 1975	Purchase	30	150
27 May 1975	Returns	4	15

(a) Write up Wellmaker's account in W. Wright's ledger.
(b) What is the purpose of the folio column?
(c) In which of W. Wright's ledgers should this account appear?
(d) Is the final balance on the account a debit or credit balance? (16 marks)

2 On June 1, 1974, J. Brown started business as a jobbing gardener with a capital of £2 000 in cash. A trial balance extracted from his records on May 31, 1975 shows the following:

	£	£
Purchases of seeds, plants, etc.	700	
new motor van	1 100	
mowing machine	70	
cultivator	250	
Motor van expenses	300	
Rent of garage	200	
Paid to wife for clerical work	500	
Insurance	200	
Private expenses paid from bank	1 500	
Cash in hand and bank	180	
Cash received from customers		3 000
Capital		2 000
	5 000	5 000

J. Brown expects the van to last for five years, the mowing machine for two, and the cultivator for ten. He agrees to write off depreciation using the straight-line method.

£50 rent is outstanding.

Prepare:

(a) An account to show J. Brown his profit or loss for the year ended May 31, 1975.

(b) A Balance Sheet as at May 31, 1975.

(c) A rent account as it would appear in J. Brown's ledger.

(d) The capital account as it would appear in the ledger

(25 marks)

3 N. Ramrod keeps cash and bank records. At the close of business on May 29, 1975, he reached the bottom of a page and carried forward the following:

	Discount £	Cash £	Bank £	
Total B/F	27·40	114·10	214·30	Debit side
Total B/F	40·10	74·50	210·00	Credit side

The following sums were received on May 30, 1975:

Cheque from J. Cuthbertson for £120 in settlement of an account for £125.

Cash from N. Green £40.

Cheque from Brian Way for £75 in settlement of an account for £76·50.

The following payments were made on May 30, 1975:

Cheque to Morris Brown for £140·40.

Cheque to local council in payment of rates for the half year £150·40.

N. Ramrod cashed a cheque for private drawings £50, and took from the office cash for the same purpose.

Write up N. Ramrod's cash and bank records and balance them at close of business on May 30, 1975.

Note: The business will be closed on May 31, 1975.

(13 marks)

4 From the following information set out B. Dickson's Balance Sheet as at May 31, 1975. Your Balance Sheet should clearly show the totals of the following:

Fixed assets, current assets, current liabilities.

	£	£
Capital June 1, 1974		10 000
Motor Vans at cost	4 000	
Provision for depreciation		1 500
Fixtures and fittings at cost	1 500	
Provision for depreciation		1 250
Stock	4 000	
Debtors	950	
Balance in bank	1 200	
Cash in hand	70	
Trade creditors		450
Sundry unpaid expenses		140
Rates in advance	150	
Drawings (cash)	1 400	
Stock taken by B. Dickson	700	
Net profit for year		630
	13 970	13 970

(22 marks)

Section B

Answer TWO questions from this section.

5 On May 31, 1975 J. Robert's cash book shows the balance in bank to be £375·48.

A bank statement written up to May 31, 1975, shows the following items which have not been entered in the cash book:

(*a*) A sum of £150 received from R. Black by credit transfer.

(*b*) An insurance premium of £50 paid by standing order.

When the bank statement is checked against the cash book the following are discovered:

(*c*) Cheques paid to creditors not yet presented for payment total £250.

(*d*) Cheques totalling £200 had been received by J. Roberts, entered into the cash book, but not yet paid into the bank.

You are required to:

1 Bring the cash book up to date, showing the actual balance which will be available in the bank.

2. Prepare a bank reconciliation statement showing the balance appearing on the bank statement.   (10 marks)

6 Rule up a petty cash book with columns for postages, stationery, and sundries. On June 2, 1975, the imprest had been restored to £25. During the following week transactions listed below took place:

		£
June 2, 1975	Stamps	2·50
	Envelopes	1·40
June 3, 1975	Errand boy's fare	75
	Soap	70
	Parcel post	1·40
June 4, 1975	Carbon papers	1·50
	Stamps	1·47
June 5, 1975	Letter paper	3·41

Balance the petty cash book on June 5, 1975, and obtain a refund from the main cashier.

7 (*a*) Make a list of the deductions which an employer is required by law to make from his employees' wages.

(*b*) Write down *three* deductions which an employer will make at the employees' request.

(*c*) What is the importance of an employee's code number?

(10 marks)

THE ROYAL SOCIETY OF ARTS
SINGLE-SUBJECT EXAMINATIONS

BOOK-KEEPING
STAGE I (Elementary)

November, 1975

[TWO HOURS ALLOWED]

Answer ALL *the questions in Section A and any* TWO *of the questions in Section B.*

SECTION A

ALL questions in this section are to be attempted.

1 On October 31, 1975, the Cash Book of N. Orange showed a balance at bank of £570. An examination of his records located the following errors:

   (1) Orange paid to R. Jones £175 by cheque on October 15. This cheque was entered in the Cash Book as £195.

   (2) Bank charges not recorded in the Cash Book amounted to £25.

   (3) A cheque dated October 19, value £150, payable to T. Jack was not paid by the Bank until November 5.

   (4) Orange on October 23 received from W. Green a cheque, value £125. This cheque was dishonoured on October 29. No entry for the dishonour has been made in the Cash Book.

   (5) On October 31 a cheque, value £200, received from F. Brown was banked; however, the bank statement was not credited until November 1.

   You are required to:

   (1) Make the necessary entries in the Cash Book in order to show the revised Cash Book balance at October 31, 1975.

   (2) Prepare a statement reconciling the corrected Cash Book balance with the Bank Statement at October 31, 1975.

(3) State the balance at Bank at October 31, 1975, as shown
by the bank Statements.

2 It is normal for a business, which receives a large number of
purchase invoices, to use a purchase invoice checking procedure before any entries are made in the books.

   You are required to list the points you would check on each
invoice.

3 On August 31, 1974, the sundry debtors of Henry Higgins
stood at £10 000 and the balance on the Provision for Bad
Debts Account at that date was £200. Of the debtors it was
considered that £500 were irrecoverable and should be written
off. It was decided that the Provision for Bad Debts should
be made equal to 5% of the outstanding accounts.

   At August 31, 1975, the debtors balances had fallen to
£8 000 of which £100 were considered to be irrecoverable and
should be written off. The Provision for Bad Debts was to be
at the same rate as in 1974.

   You are required to:

   (1) Show the Bad Debts Account at August 31, 1974 and 1975;

   (2) Show the Provision for Bad Debts Account at August 31,
   1974 and 1975;

   (3) Show the relevant figures, in the Balance Sheets for the
   two years 1974 and 1975.

4 B. C. Lever buys large machine tools at a cost of £1 000 each
and he sells them at £1 500 each. His administration costs
amount to a constant annual total of £800. Mr. Lever has
decided that he requires a minimum net profit of £3 200.

   You are required to:

   (1) Calculate the number of machines Mr. Lever must sell in
   order to achieve a net profit of £3 200.

   (2) Calculate the sales value of the total number of machines
   sold in (1).

   (3) Explain what is meant by the term 'Rate of Stock Turnover'.

Section B

Only two *of the following questions are to be attempted.*

5 It is essential that both accounting staff and the public understand the modern terminology used in the presentation of accounts.

You are therefore required to choose four of the terms listed below and briefly describe their meanings.

(1) Costs of goods sold
(2) Net worth
(3) Working capital
(4) First in, first out (F.I.F.O.)
(5) Capital expenditure
(6) Revenue expenditure

6 The following Balance Sheet was prepared by L. B. Jay on November 1, 1975.

L. B. Jay

Balance Sheet as at November 1, 1975

	£			£
Capital	18 000	Fixed Assets		
		Land and Buildings (net)		10 500
		Motor Vehicles (net)		3 000
				13 500
Current Liabilities		Current Assets		
Creditors	2 550	Stock	4 000	
		Debtors	2 000	
		Cash at Bank	1 000	
		Cash in Hand	50	7 050
	20 550			20 550

L. B. Jay later found that the Balance Sheet was not correct due to errors and omissions subsequently located and now listed hereunder.

    (1) Stock had been over valued by £300.

    (2) A motor vehicle had been completely destroyed in a road crash on November 1, 1975, value (net) £800. (Note ignore insurance.)

    (3) Included in creditors was a Bad Debt Provision of £450.

    (4) Depreciation on land and buildings of 10% on the net balances had been omitted.

You are required to:

    (1) Produce an amended Balance Sheet for Mr. Jay as at November 1, 1975, showing clearly how you calculated Mr. Jay's revised capital.

    (2) Calculate Mr. Jay's working capital from the revised Balance Sheet.

7 N. Lirn closed his Books of Account on October 31, 1975, and prepared a trial balance at that date. He subsequently located the following discrepancies.

    (1) N. Lirn received a letter from R. Fir stating that Fir would not allow Lirn to take the £20 cash discount which Lirn had deducted from his last payment.

    (2) N. Lirn had erroneously charged £200 to furniture and fittings instead of wages.

    (3) Depreciation not deducted from plant and machinery, 10% on net book value. (Plant cost £8 000, depreciation to October 31, 1974 £3 000.)

    (4) Credit note £100 for short delivery of oil from Lubricants Ltd. Not wishing to reopen his books of prime entry he decided to pass all of the adjustments through his General Journal.

You are required to:

Make the necessary adjusting journal entries with suitable narration explaining each entry.

INDEX

ACCOUNT, Appropriation, 141
  ,,   Current, 131
  ,,   Drawings, 131
  ,,   Final, 133
  ,,   Impersonal, 29
  ,,   Ledger, 25, 197
  ,,   Personal, 25
  ,,   Profit and Loss, 138, 200
  ,,   Revenue, 133
  ,,   Trading, 134, 198
Accounts, Company, 213, 214
Adjustments, 160
Agreement, Bank, 73
Articles of Association, 210, 211
  ,,   of Partnership, 182
Asset, 8
  ,,   Current, 8, 52
  ,,   Fixed, 8, 172
  ,,   Intangible, 184
  ,,   Liquid, 54
  ,,   Tangible, 184
Auditor, 214
Authorised Capital, 211

Bad Debts, 161
  ,,   ,,   Reserve or Provision, 162

Balance Sheet, 144, 201
Balance, Trial, 109, 118
Bank Commission, 76
  ,,   Interest, 76
  ,,   Pass Book, 73
  ,,   Reconciliation, 74
Book-keeping, 1
'Break-up' Values, 171

Capital, 7, 8, 9
  ,,   Interest on, 183
  ,,   Partners', 183
  ,,   Purchases, 32
  ,,   Sales, 37
  ,,   Working, 52
Cash, 52
  ,,   Book, 12, 62
  ,,   Discount, 57, 58
  ,,   Journal, 12
  ,,   Paid Journal, 58
  ,,   Petty, 84
  ,,   Received Journal, 55
Commission, Bank, 76
Compensating Error, 119
Credit, 26
  ,,   Note, 15, 20, 27
Cumulative Preference Shares, 212
Current Account, 131
  ,,   Assets, 8, 52

Debentures, 213
Debit, 27

Debit and Credit Journal, 90, 140

Debit Note, 19, 20

Debtors, 6

Deed of Partnership, 182

Depreciation, 171

Diminishing Balance Method, 175

Discount, Allowed, 65, 66
,,   Cash, 53
,,   Received, 65
,,   Trade, 14, 53

Dividends, 210

Double Entry, 2–5

Drawings Account, 131
,,   Partnership, 183

Error, Compensating, 119
,,   of Omission, 118
,,   of Principle, 119

Final Accounts, 133

First Entry, 5

Fixed Asset, 8, 52
,,   Instalment Method, 173

Four-Column Trial Balance, 123

'Going Concern' Values, 171

Goodwill, 184

Gross Profit, 134, 135, 199

Impersonal Accounts, 29, 33
,,   Ledger, 33, 38

Imprest System, 87

Intangible Asset, 184

Interest, Bank, 76
,,   on Capital, 183

Journal, 11
,,   Cash, 12
,,   Cash Paid, 58
,,   Cash Received, 55
,,   Debit and Credit, 90, 140
,,   Purchase, 12
,,   Purchase Returns, 18
,,   Sales, 12
,,   Sales Returns, 18

Ledger, 1, 25
,,   Accounts, 25
,,   Impersonal, 33
,,   Nominal (see Impersonal)
,,   Private, 34
,,   Purchase, 33
,,   Sales, 35, 44

Liability, 9

Limited Companies, 209
,,   Liability, 209

Liquid Asset, 54

Lodgment, Bank, 73

Loss, 133

Manufactured Goods, 6

Memorandum of Association, 210, 211

Merchanted Goods, 6

Narration, 90

Net Profit, 201

Nominal Capital, 211
,,   Ledger (see Impersonal)

Omission, Error of, 118
Ordinary Shares, 212

Partnership, 181
    ,,   Act, 182
    ,,   at Will, 182
    ,,   Capital, 183
    ,,   Deed, 182
    ,,   Drawings, 183
Pass Book, Bank, 73
Personal Accounts, 25
Petty Cash, 84
Postage Book, 88
Preference Shares, 212
Prime Entry, 5
Principle, Error of, 119
Private Companies, 209
    ,,   Ledger, 34
Profit, 130
    ,,   Gross, 134, 135, 200
Profit and Loss Account, 138, 200
Public Companies, 209
Purchase, Capital, 32
    ,,   Invoice, 24
    ,,   Journal, 12
    ,,   Ledger, 33
    ,,   Returns Journal, 18, 27, 42

Receiver for Debenture-holders, 213
Reconciliation, Bank, 73
Redeemable Preference Shares, 212
Reducing Instalment Method, 173, 175

Register of Charges, 214
    ,,   of Members, 214
Registered Capital, 211
Reserve for Bad Debts, 161
Revenue Account, 133

Sales, 34
    ,,   Capital, 37
    ,,   Journal, 12
    ,,   Ledger, 35, 44
    ,,   Returns Journal, 18 19
Shares, 210, 212
Sole Trader, 181
Special Resolution, 211
Stamp Book, 88
Statutory Books, 213
Stock-in-Trade, 6, 132, 135
Straight Line Method, 173
Subsidiary Books, 4

Table A, 211
Tangible Asset, 184
Trade Discount, 14, 53
Trading Account, 134, 198
Trial Balance, 109, 118
    ,,   ,,   Four Column, 123

Value Added Tax (VAT), 226 ff
Values, 'Break Up', 171
    ,,   'Going Concern', 171
Voting Rights, 212

Will, Partnership at, 182
Working Capital, 52

TEACH YOURSELF BOOKS

COMMERCIAL ARITHMETIC

J. H. Harvey

This book caters for the growing number of people whose work requires a knowledge of commercial arithmetic by providing simple and lucid explanations of the basic principles of the subject which the reader can apply to problems he encounters.

The text, which covers the elementary examination syllabuses of the Royal Society of Arts, the London Chamber of Commerce and similar bodies, is fully up-to-date.

'This book covers fully all the usual aspects of arithmetic with some excellent chapters at the end on Foreign Exchange, Rates and Taxes, Bills of Exchange etc . . . The student who conscientiously works through the well-chosen examples cannot fail to get a good grounding in the subject'   *Scottish Educational Journal*

UNITED KINGDOM	95p
AUSTRALIA	$3.05*
NEW ZEALAND	$3.05
CANADA	$3.25

ISBN 0 340 21845 2   *recommended but not obligatory

TEACH YOURSELF BOOKS

COMMERCE

R. Warson

This book has been written to describe and examine the nature and purpose of commercial activites. A general survey of the structure of the modern mixed economy is followed by a detailed analysis of the functions and inter-relationships of commercial institutions in both the public and the private sectors. The author describes commercial methods, retail and wholesale, and the role of banks and finance in commerce. Many other aspects of commerce are also covered in this book, including transport, insurance and trading overseas, while an important section describes the actual procedures involved in commercial transactions, such as bills of sale.

A readable and comprehensive text for students of Commerce at R.S.A., O.N.C./O.N.D. and G.C.E. Ordinary level and for students of economics and business studies, or for anyone involved in commerce seeking a wider picture.

UNITED KINGDOM		60p
AUSTRALIA		$1.95*
NEW ZEALAND		$2.05
CANADA		$1.95
ISBN 0 340 05914 1	*recommended but not obligatory	

TEACH YOURSELF BOOKS

COMPUTER SCIENCE STUDIES

ELECTRONIC COMPUTERS

F.L. Westwater

Computers and computer technology are increasingly becoming part of our everyday lives. If there has been any technological revolution in the past few years, it has been in this field.

This book explains with the help of illustrations, the use, principles and functions of digital computers. It is designed as a basic introduction to the complex subject of electronic computers and as such it will be of interest to those readers embarking on a career in computers, as well as to readers who come into contact with computers, either in business or through their many applications in everyday life, and who feel they want to learn more about them.

Fully revised and updated, by an expert in the computer field, this book will be of interest to the specialist and interested layman alike.

UNITED KINGDOM	95p
AUSTRALIA	$3.05*
NEW ZEALAND	$3.20
CANADA	$3.50

ISBN 0 340 21435 X

*recommended but not obligatory

TEACH YOURSELF BOOKS

ORGANISATION AND METHODS

R. G. Breadmore

Organisation and methods (O&M) can be defined as the systematic application of common sense to business problems. O&M techniques enable work to be simplified and more efficiently organised, and thus work time to be better allocated.

This book explains what O&M is, what it sets out to do and why, and illustrates how it can be applied in practice to most common business functions. It is based upon extensive practical experience and gives a down-to-earth, step-by-step guide to enable anyone concerned with office routines to apply the techniques to their work.

UNITED KINGDOM	£1.25	
AUSTRALIA	$3.95*	
NEW ZEALAND	$4.15	
CANADA	$4.50	

ISBN 0 340 20767 1   *recommended but not obligatory

TEACH YOURSELF BOOKS

BUSINESS & MANAGEMENT STUDIES

OFFICE MANAGEMENT

P. W. Betts

The role of the office manager has completely changed in recent years, but the critical part he plays in determining the success of a concern still remains often unrecognised.

The on-going business is dependent upon successful administrative operations at all organisation levels. Hence the generation of more and more paperwork and the ever increasing demand for administrative staff, but more paper and staff are not necessarily the answer. Increased administrative expertise is essential and the author examines here the information and techniques that are needed by the departmental office manager to be successful, and introduce the overall situation in administrative management — all of which is often not appreciated by students studying this subject or by executives who determine organisation structure.

An invaluable text for students of management studies and in particular for students of the Diploma in Administrative Management, the Certificate in Office Supervision and of the Final Examinations of the Institute of Chartered Secretaries and Administrators, the Institute of Cost and Management Accountants and the Association of Certified Accountants.

UNITED KINGDOM		95p
AUSTRALIA		$2.75*
NEW ZEALAND		$2.75
CANADA		$3.75

ISBN 0 340 19496 0   *recommended but not obligatory

TEACH YOURSELF BOOKS

OFFICE PRACTICE

J. Shaw

Anyone involved in any capacity in office work will find this book an invaluable source of practical information on how to increase their efficiency and effectiveness.

Every aspect of routine office operations is covered, from the elementary, such as using the telephone and receiving visitors, to the more complex understandings of export documentation and cash transactions. Useful background information to business – the Stock Exchange, banking and insurance – is also included.

The author is a leading expert on office administration and a member of the Institute of Office Management.

UNITED KINGDOM	90p
AUSTRALIA	$2.90*
NEW ZEALAND	$2.90
CANADA	$3.50

ISBN 0 340 12450 4   *recommended but not obligatory

TEACH YOURSELF BOOKS